Percy Hetherington Fitzgerald

The Lives of the Sheridans

With Engravings on Steel by Stodart and Every

Percy Hetherington Fitzgerald

The Lives of the Sheridans
With Engravings on Steel by Stodart and Every

ISBN/EAN: 9783744666107

Printed in Europe, USA, Canada, Australia, Japan

Cover: Foto ©Thomas Meinert / pixelio.de

More available books at **www.hansebooks.com**

THE
LIVES OF THE SHERIDANS.

BY

PERCY FITZGERALD,

AUTHOR OF
'THE ROMANCE OF THE STAGE,' ETC.

IN TWO VOLUMES.
VOL. I.

WITH ENGRAVINGS ON STEEL BY STODART AND EVERY.

LONDON:
RICHARD BENTLEY AND SON,
Publishers in Ordinary to Her Majesty the Queen.
1886.

PREFACE.

MORE than fifty years have elapsed since the appearance of the last editions of Mr. Moore's 'Life of Sheridan.' During the interval a vast number of political memoirs have been issued, of the highest importance, and illustrating in the fullest way the political incidents of the period. In Moore's day the system of publishing confidential papers, diaries, etc., was not in fashion, and his well-finished 'Life,' graceful as it is, like all his work, is meagre, and often wholly silent on some of the most interesting and critical passages in Sheridan's story. The materials are so abundant that it has been a matter of difficulty to keep within reasonable measure ; but I have tried to select only what seemed strictly relevant for the illustration of Sheridan's life and character.

This difficulty was particularly felt in dealing with his political life—the familiar and oft-told tale, known to all who have followed the careers of Pitt, Burke, and Fox. But I think it must be admitted that the share of Sheridan in these events was much less important than is popularly supposed. Though an active politician, he never was a leader. He seems to have had little power to influence; and he was himself but an uncertain and capricious follower. Though he twice held an office, he never was a Minister of the Crown. Certain high authorities have gone so far as to hold that he was 'no statesman at all;' and it will be seen that his political efforts, whether exerted in debate or in formal orations, never—except in the Hastings impeachment—appear to have influenced friends or opponents.

It will no doubt be thought that the view taken here is prejudiced, and that it is but fair to the memory of so eminent a man that a veil should be drawn over blemishes and failings. This is only due to the memory of men like Nelson or Fox, whose manly heroism and single-hearted devotion to their country blind us to other defects. It will be seen by the following account that Sheridan could exhibit no such self-sacrifice where the interests of his friends or country were involved, but, on the contrary, made these secondary to his pleasures. Any lofty idealization such as Moore's, the picture of a statesman, high-souled and loving his country, but frustrated, and soured by ill-fortune and the neglect of friends, is wholly false.

Taking, however, a lower standard, and following

him as a jovial, good-natured, pleasure-loving being, ready with sallies of wit, full of ingenious resource, and always amusing, even in his evasions and devices, we shall find much to admire. He, like Foote, seems to have been ' incompressible,' ever buoyant and irresistible. The marvellous feats he executed on the smallest resources ; the securing the direction of a great theatre, the retaining it for nearly thirty years, in defiance of debt and creditors ; his versatility in disposing of claimants ; his readiness in retort and banter ; his amusing power of illustration ; his delight in secret intrigue—all these go to make up a character of curious and original interest ; and it is surely better to set it out strictly as it is and as the facts warrant, than, out of complaisance ' to the great departed,' to varnish over and add a colouring that is not in the original. Such a character might have delighted Elia, who, indeed, alludes to it occasionally with much relish. In primary points there was much akin to the nature of another manager, Elliston, who combined high sentimental propriety with much laxity of practice.

I have been fortunate enough to discover many new particulars about Sheridan, and have also given the true version of many transactions hitherto accepted in an incorrect shape. Much information will be found here relative to the friends and connections of Sheridan, the interesting family of the Linleys, and others. About his great dramas, too, I have gathered some facts that are new. The facsimiles of the bills and the pleasing portraits will, it is hoped, add to the attraction of the work.

In conclusion, I have to thank many friends for assistance; notably Sir Percy and Lady Shelley, for a large number of letters from Mrs. Norton which they have allowed me to use. Another friend of that gifted lady has placed at my disposal a very full and confidential correspondence from which I have made selections, I trust discreetly. I have also to thank the Ulster King-at-Arms for his aid in the preparation of the pedigree. And I would venture to ask the reader, before he begins the perusal of these volumes, to glance at the astonishing gathering of clever and celebrated persons there displayed, all connected with a single family. His curiosity will be stimulated : and further, he may be inclined to be indulgent, considering the difficulties of the task undertaken.

ATHENÆUM CLUB,
        September, 1886.

CONTENTS OF VOL. I.

LIST OF ILLUSTRATIONS TO VOL. I.

(ON STEEL).

THE SHERIDAN FAMIL

Rev. Denis
P.P., Kildr

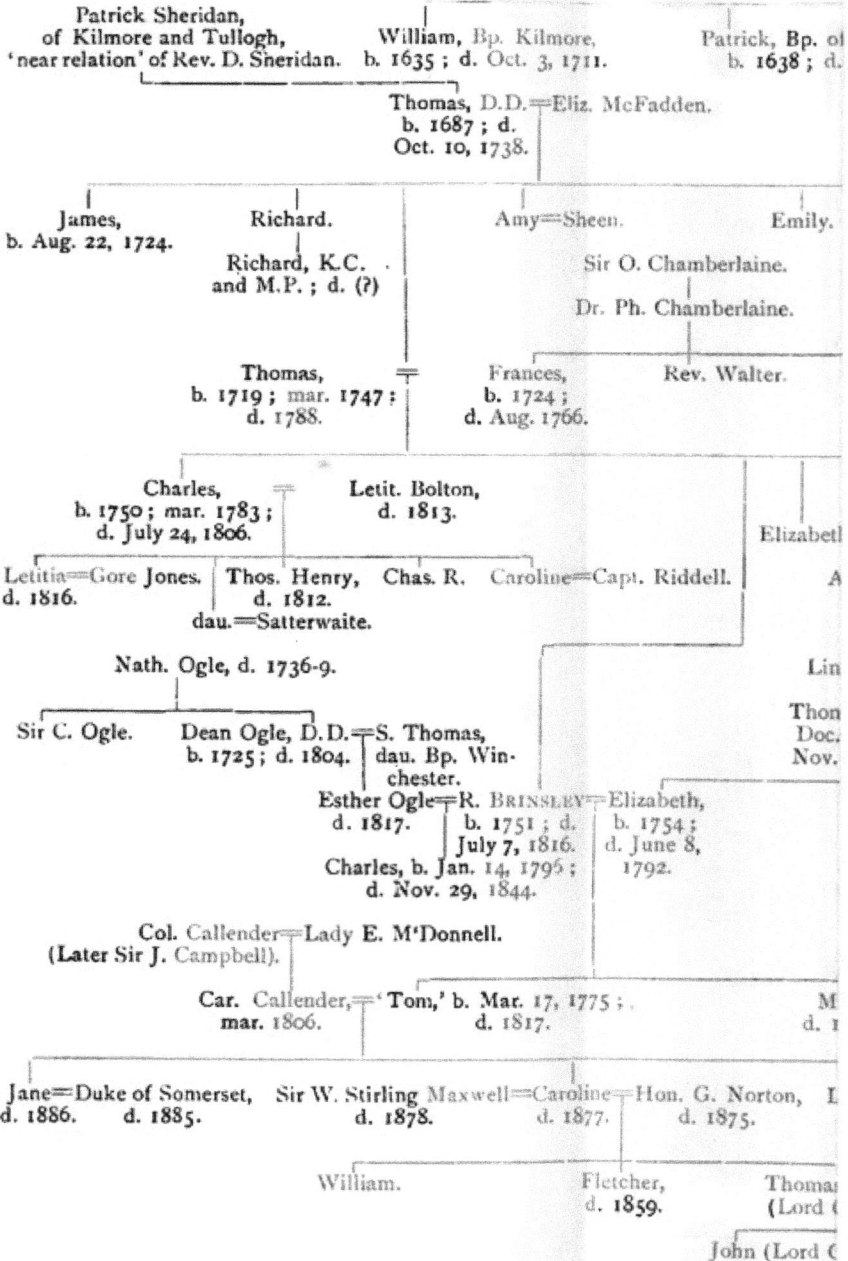

Patrick Sheridan,
of Kilmore and Tullogh,
'near relation' of Rev. D. Sheridan.

William, Bp. Kilmore,
b. 1635 ; d. Oct. 3, 1711.

Patrick, Bp. of
b. 1638 ; d.

Thomas, D.D.=Eliz. McFadden.
b. 1687 ; d.
Oct. 10, 1738.

James,
b. Aug. 22, 1724.

Richard.

Amy=Sheen.

Emily.

Richard, K.C.
and M.P. ; d. (?)

Sir O. Chamberlaine.

Dr. Ph. Chamberlaine.

Thomas,
b. 1719 ; mar. 1747 ;
d. 1788.

Frances,
b. 1724 ;
d. Aug. 1766.

Rev. Walter.

Charles,
b. 1750 ; mar. 1783 ;
d. July 24, 1806.

Letit. Bolton,
d. 1813.

Elizabeth

Letitia=Gore Jones.
d. 1816.

Thos. Henry,
d. 1812.

Chas. R.

Caroline=Capt. Riddell.

A

dau.=Satterwaite.

Nath. Ogle, d. 1736-9.

Lin

Sir C. Ogle.

Dean Ogle, D.D.=S. Thomas,
b. 1725 ; d. 1804. dau. Bp. Winchester.

Thon
Doc.
Nov.

Esther Ogle=R. BRINSLEY=Elizabeth,
d. 1817.   b. 1751 ; d.   b. 1754 ;
July 7, 1816. d. June 8,
Charles, b. Jan. 14, 1796 ;   1792.
d. Nov. 29, 1844.

Col. Callender=Lady E. M'Donnell.
(Later Sir J. Campbell).

Car. Callender,='Tom,' b. Mar. 17, 1775 ;
mar. 1806.   d. 1817.

M
d. 1

Jane=Duke of Somerset,
d. 1886.   d. 1885.

Sir W. Stirling Maxwell=Caroline=Hon. G. Norton,
d. 1878.   d. 1877.   d. 1875.

L

William.

Fletcher,
d. 1859.

Thoma
(Lord

John (Lord

'idan═Foster.
rton.

yne,   Thomas, F.T.C.D.═nat. dau. of King James II.   James,
2.   b. 1641.   b. 1649.

     Sir Thomas.   A daughter═Col. Guillaume.

Hester═J. Knowles.   Eliz.   Meliora.   Anne.

═(?)

J. Sheridan Knowles,
b. May 12, 1784 ; d. Dec. 1, **1862.**

Richard.   Anne═Rev. Fish,
                           d. 1760.

W. Le Fanu═H. de Pugillant.   Sackville.   **Dean** Dobbin, F.T.C.D.

I. Le Fanu.   Rev. Peter.   Joseph═Alicia, b. 1753 ; **d. 1817.**

                         Dean Le Fanu═Lucretia.

                       George Bennett, K.C.

d. 1797.   William.   Joseph Sheridan═Bennett.   Jane═Rev. Delves Broughton.

Linley═Mrs. Linley,   Rhoda Broughton.
s, d.   d. Jan., 1820,
1795.   aged 92.

Rev. Oziah,   Thomas,   William,   Samuel.   Dau.═C. Ward.
d. Mar., 1831.   d. 1778.   d. 1835.

                                 Tickell (Addison's).

                                 Tickell.

               Maria═R. Tickell═Leigh.
               J. R. Roebuck, grandson.

           Son,
           1777 (?).

Giffard═Helen═Lord Dufferin.   **Frank,**   Brinsley═Miss **Grant.**   Thomas,   Charles,
      d. 1867.   **d. 1843.**   d. 1826.   d. 1847.
        Earl of Dufferin.

insley═Maria Federigo.
tley).

dev)   Carlotta.

THE SHERIDANS.

CHAPTER I

DR. SHERIDAN—1687-1738.

THE family of the Sheridans, whose history is to be presented in these volumes, is remarkable as offering an almost unbroken line of conspicuous persons, stretching over a period of two hundred years. The roll commences with two brothers who were Bishops of Cloyne and Kilmore respectively; a third brother being a political writer of some merit, whose work has lately been reprinted.* We next come to the Bishops' grand-nephew, the well-known Dr. Thomas Sheridan, Swift's friend; then to his son Thomas, the actor; next to the more famous Richard Brinsley, his son; then to his son 'Tom Sheridan,' who achieved a social

---

* Dr. Watkins states that Thomas claimed only a sort of connection with the Bishops; but it is stated in his 'Case' that he was their brother.

reputation.   The present generation is familiar with 'Tom's' children, the three beautiful and clever sisters, Mrs. Norton, Lady Dufferin (afterwards Lady Gifford), and the Duchess of Somerset—the famous Queen of Beauty at the Eglinton Tournament. Lady Dufferin's son —author, statesman, diplomatist, and now Viceroy of India—needs no panegyric. Even in the collateral lines the same cleverness seems to have been transmitted. Richard's brother Charles was distinguished in a small way as a writer, became Irish Secretary, and, when very young, made some mark in diplomacy. A son of Tom Sheridan's, Charles, also enjoyed a reputation among his friends for particular gifts of pleasantry ; while a grandson of Sheridan's sister, Joseph Sheridan Le Fanu, was distinguished as a writer of many successful novels, in which he revived, with singular effect, the lurid vein of Mrs. Radcliffe ; his surviving brother being also remarkable for humour and powers of entertainment. A sister of Richard Brinsley wrote novels. His mother, though not of the line, wrote one of the most successful novels of her time, and also a comedy full of vivacity and character, which has much of her son's spirit and humour.

Mrs. Oliphant, in her late account of Sheridan, has ventured a speculation as to the influence of the mixture of the English with the Irish blood, and asks if that singular compound of brilliancy, mercurial temper, carelessness, and solid and enduring work be not owing to this conjunction ? There can be no doubt that such natures as Goldsmith's and Sheridan's are neither purely English nor Irish. They are ' uniques ;' and owe their charm to this commixture of races. Many Irishmen could be named with much of the wit and humour of this great pair, yet lacking their finish, elegant touch, and true sentiment : while in England there have been many with the same finish and sentiment as Goldsmith, yet without his humour and vivacity. Mrs. Oliphant seems to extend the results of this mixing of race to most of the conspicuous instances of Irish genius, and certainly many persons of celebrity that country has produced have sprung from well-known families of English origin who have intermarried with the Irish. Such were the Wellesleys, Castlereaghs, Butlers, Wolseleys, Grattans, Parnells, with many more.*

---

* This interesting question will bear fruitful investigation. Mr. Francis Galton, who is a competent authority in such matters, has written to me as follows, holding out a hope that he will take up the subject :

' I have a strong opinion, which I believe I have somewhere published, that a strain of Irish or of French blood greatly improves the ordinary English breed. This opinion is based on a large number of well-known cases of its prolonged influence and success, but I have not as yet made a really trustworthy investigation by comparing the number with that of the cases of failure. The inquiry is difficult, and though I have often desired to make it, I have thus far abstained from doing so, because I was unable to

Steele's character offers the most curious parallel to that of Sheridan. He, too, was a dramatist, a manager, and a politician; a wit also, and, if not an orator, could make speeches. He was a spendthrift, ever in difficulties, fond of the bottle, a loving but neglectful husband, exactly as was Sheridan. Steele's father was English, his mother Irish, and he was born and bred in Ireland. So here again we have the same result following the same conditions. Even Congreve had the same intermixture in his blood. It may, indeed, be stated here that the Irish contribution to the ranks of the English dramatists is extraordinary, comprising O'Keefe, Farquhar, Goldsmith, Macklin, Steele, Kane O'Hara, Southerne; while in the roll of actors and actresses we find the names of Wilks, Doggett, Delane, Quin, Ryan, Mossop, Barry, Thomas Sheridan, Macklin, Macready, G. V. Brooke, Farren, Cooke, Moody, Mrs. Clive, Woffington, Miss Bellamy, Miss Farren, Mrs. Glover, Miss Jordan, and Miss O'Neil.

Returning now to our history, it may be said

---

find sufficiently large groups, selected without bias, between which a comparison might justly be made.'

In further illustration of what Mr. Galton says as to the mingling of French and English blood, it may be noted that Garrick's father was the son of a French refugee. To this he certainly owed his exceptional disposition or curious combination of gifts—great vivacity, wit, 'cleverness,' and histrionic power, with strong sagacity and good sense; and generosity, with a sort of Scotch thrift.

that the earliest conspicuous members of this family are the two Bishops, already mentioned, of Kilmore and of Cloyne.* A third brother, Thomas, seems to have been a man of some literary and oratorical power; but, like the Bishop, became obnoxious to the ruling powers. Suspected of being concerned in the 'Popish Plots,' and denounced by Tongue and others, he was thrown into prison by

---

* My friend Mr. J. Ribton Garstin, F.S.A., has communicated to me the following particulars with regard to one of these prelates :

'William Sheridan, M.A. (afterwards D.D.), probably the same who had been a Prebendary of St. Patrick's, Dublin, is said to have been son of the Rev. Denis Sheridan, who possessed property in County Cavan, of which he was "dispossessed" in the troubled times, and was elder brother of Patrick Sheridan, who became Bishop of Cloyne. He was godson of Bishop Bedell, who bequeathed him forty shillings to buy a mourning ring. He was appointed chaplain to the Duke of Ormonde (Lord Lieutenant), and in 1667 became Rector of Athenry, County Galway. He was presented to the Deanery of Down, 25th August, 1669, and in 168½ was advanced to the Bishopric of Kilmore with Ardagh, and consecrated in Christ Church, Dublin, 19th February. He thus succeeded Bedell after two Bishops had intervened— Maxwell and [an ancestor of mine] Francis Marsh, afterwards Archbishop, who on his seal put, as his style, instead of "permissione divina," "favore regio." Bishop Sheridan was deprived, 1691 or 1692, for refusing to take the oaths to King William and Queen Mary. I met with the entry of his interment at Fulham, Middlesex (Hammersmith side), and noted it : "Dr. William Sheridan, buried 3rd October, 1711." He published some discourses and sermons between 1665 and 1706; one on the death of Sir M. Eustace, Chancellor of Ireland, to whom he had been chaplain. See Ware's "Hist.," i. 243-4; Cotton's "Fasti Ecc. Hib.," iii. 167; Lysons' "Environs of London," 2nd ed., ii. 270.'

order of Parliament, but, by favour of the Speaker,
was allowed to plead his cause before the House of
Commons. This he did with a certain native
eloquence, though his case seems to have been
rather a feeble one. He, at least, produced no
effect, and might have languished in prison, until he
bethought him of taking the bold step of applying
for a Habeas Corpus. He found a courageous judge,
Sir Richard Weston, who was not afraid of en-
countering the power of the House of Commons,
and who, after many difficulties, caused the writ to
be served on the Serjeant-at-arms. The difficulty
was, however, surmounted by the unexpected pro-
rogation of the House, and to which Mr. Sheridan
owed his release.

In his pleading before the House, we find some
biographical details. He told them : ' I was born a
gentleman, of one of the ancientest families, and
related to many considerable in Ireland. In one
county there is a castle and a large demesne ; in
another a greater tract of land for several miles
together, yet known by our name. . . . My grandfather was the last that enjoyed it ; and my father,
left an orphan, soon found himself dispossessed. . . .
My mother, a gentlewoman of England of good
fortune, a Foster.'

Here, again, we find the infusion of the English
strain of blood ; and it is curious that, in almost
every generation, each Sheridan should have allied

himself with a lady of another nation. It is characteristic that when he was restored to his country, his taste for sporting and generous liberality to his neighbours speedily impoverished him, so that he could not afford to send his son to the University.

But the most curious incident in the family history is that the most remote known ancestor of Richard Brinsley should have been an Irish Catholic priest, the Rev. Denis Sheridan, having a parish at Kildrunferton, in the diocese of Kilmore. This person conformed to the Established Church, under the influence of Bishop Bedell, who afterwards promoted his interests.

Through this favour he was appointed Rector of Drongland and Lara, in Kilmore, about the year 1645; and marrying in due course, became the father of the two Bishops.*

* My friend Sir Bernard Burke, Ulster, has supplied me with the following additional particulars concerning the two Bishops :

'William Sheridan was born at Togher, 1635; became Dean of Down; consecrated Bishop of Kilmore and Ardagh in Ch. Ch. Cathedral, Dublin, 19th February, 1682; deprived of his Sees for refusing to take the oath of allegiance to William and Mary; died 3rd October, 1711. Patrick Sheridan, D.D., was born near Enniskillen, in 1638; entered Trin. Coll., Dublin, 15th May, 1652, aged 15; Fellow Trin. Coll., 1660; Senior Fellow, 1665; Dean of Connor, 1667; Archdeacon of Dromore, 1667 to 1682; Bishop of Cloyne, 1679; died 22nd November, 1682. He is stated to be "buried in the College Library," an odd place of interment. Thomas Sheridan, the third brother, was born 1641; stated to have been knighted, and to have been Secretary to James II. James Sheridan was born near Trim, Co. Meath, 1649; entered Trin. Coll., Dublin, 1665.'

The dramatic interest of the line, however, begins with Swift's friend, Dr. Thomas Sheridan— pleasant, careless, eccentric, ever the butt of fortune, whose life would be an entertaining one in itself. He was a strange, mercurial person, fond of pleasure and joviality, but constantly struggling with debt—the victim of perpetual failure. He had an extraordinary gift for occasional poetry, and he and his friend Swift almost daily exchanged verses of an amusingly personal character, full of a broad coarse humour and vivacity. These fill nearly a volume, and at least betoken a serious waste of time. Like his son, he was devoted to education as a study, and Swift held that he was ' the best schoolmaster in the kingdom ;' yet he was also the most unsuccessful in his profession.

Dr. Sheridan lived in a quaint old house in Capel Street—No. 27—of some architectural pretensions, and known as the former ' King James's Mint,' a picture of which is given in one of " Sam " Whyte's books. His wife was Miss Elizabeth Macfadden, from the north of Ireland—not ' Macpherson, a Scotch lady,' as she is set down in various accounts, though probably of Scotch descent. In this ' Mint House ' were born no less than seven children : three sons, James (the eldest, who died August 22, 1724), Thomas, and Richard ; and four daughters, Elizabeth, Amee (afterwards Mrs. Sheen), Emily, who died early, and Hester (later Mrs.

Knowles, a schoolmistress). Of these, save of Thomas and Elizabeth, we know little.*

The Doctor held a good Church living in the south of Ireland, given him by Lord Carteret. 'A friend of the Doctor's,' says Swift, 'prevailed on him to grant it' (this friend was Swift himself), 'and it was worth £150 a year. He changed it very soon for that of Dunboyne.' Swift goodnaturedly suppresses the extraordinary indiscretion or careless-ness of his friend by which he lost this living, and also the chaplaincy to the Viceroy. When he went to Cork to be inducted, he agreed to preach for Archdeacon Russell, and forgetting that it was the anniversary of the accession of the House of Hanover, chose for his text, 'Sufficient for the day is the evil thereof.' An enemy of his hurried with this news to Court, and though Swift exerted himself, the luckless preacher was dismissed. It was really a pure accident. In Swift's happy phrase, 'He shot

---

* Miss Elizabeth Sheridan believed firmly in the family 'Banshee,' declaring that on the eve of the death of Mr. Thomas Sheridan in France, his spirit was heard wailing under the windows of Quilca. She was, her grand-niece tells us, distinguished in her youth as a beauty at the Castle of Dublin, and nine years older than Mr. Sheridan. 'She had a lively and agreeable recollec-tion of the days of Swift and Stella, and often mentioned, from memory, many circumstances connected with that extraordinary pair.' Mr. Sheen was an Englishman, who came over with one of the Lord Lieutenants, and had a place in 'the Castle.' Mrs. Knowles 'presided over an eminent boarding-school for young ladies in York Street.'

his fortune dead, by chance medley.' The Archdeacon kindly gave him another living of the same
value, but 'by the knavery of the farmers' he never
got £80 a year. He then exchanged this for a
school at Cavan, worth £80 a year, and here he
might have lived well; 'but the air,' says his friend,
'was too moist and unwholesome, *and he could not
bear the company of some persons* in that neighbourhood.' Before his death, however, the unwearied
Swift had obtained for him an offer of the Royal
School at Armagh, with a view to taking him away
from Dublin, where the temptation to expense was
overpowering. But he was persuaded by designing
friends to refuse; or, probably, like his grandson,
was too much attached to the pleasures of the town.
'These very people actually set up a school in opposition to him. Upon this he sold the school for about
£400, spent the money, grew into disease, and died.'

Two letters, selected from hundreds, will give a
good idea of his disposition. In January, 1736, he
wrote to Swift :

'DEAR SIR,

'I received your letter of reproaches with
pleasure, and as I know you hate excuses I shall
make none. Whoever informed you that I was not
in my school at the right time appointed has not
done me justice. As for my quondam friends as
you call them, *quon dam* them all! It is the most

decent way I can curse them ; for they lulled me to sleep till they stole my school into the hands of a blockhead, and have driven me towards the end of my life into a disagreeable solitude, where I have the misery to reflect upon my folly in making such a perfidious choice.'

And again in February he wrote :

' My school only supplies me with present food, without which I cannot live. This year has been to me like steering through the Cyclades in a storm without a rudder ; and as you are out of danger, to feel the like suffering *I pray God you may never feel a dun* to the end of your life, for it is too shocking to the honest heart.'

He had a little place at Quilca, which passed to his son Richard, and which he once or twice lent to his great friend for a time. The latter, in his most sardonic humour, never tired of ridiculing the dilapidation and miserable condition of this tenement.* It was the fitting sequel to this lifelong

* As in these rather offensive lines :

'TO QUILCA, 1725.

' Let me thy properties explain :
   A rotten cabin dropping rain,
   Chimneys with scorn rejecting smoke ;
   Stools, tables, chairs, and bedsteads broke.
   Here elements have lost their uses,
   Air ripens not, nor earth produces.

buffoonery that when he grew old the Doctor was
treated with unkindness and brutality by his friend,
being *chassé'd* from his house after a severe illness.

> In vain we make poor Sheelah toil,
> Fire will not roast, nor water boil.
> Through all the valleys, hills, and plains,
> The goddess Want in triumph reigns,
> And the chief officers of State,
> Sloth, dirt, and thrift, around her wait.'

The Dean never had patience with the Irish failing of pretence
and making a show, which he always ridiculed mercilessly.   As
again, in prose, on the same subject :

'THE BLUNDERS, DEFICIENCIES, DISTRESSES, AND MISFORTUNES
OF QUILCA.   APRIL, 1724.

' But one lock and a half in the whole house.

' The key of the garden-door lost.

' The empty bottles all uncleanable.

' One hinge of the street-door broke off, and the people forced
to go out and come in at the back-door.

' The Dean's bed threatening every night to fall under him.
The little table loose and broken in the joints.

' A messenger sent a mile to borrow an old broken tin dish.

' Bottles stopped with bits of wood and tow, instead of corks.

' Not one utensil for the fire, except an old pair of tongs, which
travels through the house, and is likewise employed to take the
meat out of the pot.

' The spit broken with probing in the bogs for timber, and tears
the meat to pieces.

' *April* 28. This morning the great fore-door quite open, dancing
backward and forward with all its weight upon the lower hinge,
which must have been broken if the Dean had not accidentally
come and released it.

' A great hole in the floor of the ladies' chamber, every woman
hazarding a broken leg.'

There is a character of him written by Swift, and reflecting the cynical temper of that extraordinary man. When his weary life ended, his friend wrote of him : ' Doctor Thomas Sheridan died at Rath. farnham the 10th October, 1738, at three of the clock in the afternoon : his diseases were a dropsy and an asthma. He was doubtless the best instructor of youth in the three kingdoms, and perhaps in Europe, and as great a master of the Greek and Latin languages. He had a very fruitful invention and a talent for poetry. His English verses were full of wit and human nature, but neither his prose nor verse sufficiently correct ; however, he would readily submit to any friend who had a true taste in prose or verse. He has left behind him a very great collection, in several volumes, of stories—humorous, witty, wise, or some way useful—gathered from a vast number of Greek, Roman, Italian, Spanish, French, and English writers. But among them there were many not worth regard. He was, as is frequently the case in men of wit and learning, what the French call " a dupe," and in a very high degree. The greatest dunce of a tradesman could impose upon him, for he was altogether ignorant in worldly management.' He then describes how well he judged of a boy's physiognomy, and never turned out wrong in his prognostications. He goes on to say he was very indiscreet, notably in marrying very young, whence proceeded all the miseries of his life. Mrs. Le Fanu tells us that he received an income of £500 with his lady, Miss Macfadden ; but the Dean says that ' the portion he got proved to be just the reverse of £500, for he was poorer by a thousand, so many incumbrances of a mother-in-law and poor relations, whom he was forced to support for many years. Instead of breeding up his daughters to housewifery and plain clothes,' goes on the pitiless Dean, ' he got them at a great expense to be clad like ladies who had plentiful fortunes ; made them learn to sing and dance, gave them rich silks and other fopperies ; and his two eldest were married without his consent to *young lads who had nothing to settle on them.*'*

---

* Lord Cork was as unflattering : 'He was slovenly, indigent, cheerful. He knew books much better than men, and he knew the value of money least of all. In this situation, and with this disposition, Swift fastened upon him, as upon a prey with which he intended to regale himself when his appetite should prompt him. This ill-starred, good-natured, improvident man retired to Dublin, unhinged from all Court favour ; but he still remained a punster, a quibbler, a fiddler, and a wit. Not a day passed without a rebus, an anagram, or a madrigal. His pen and his fiddlestick were in continual motion, and yet to little or no purpose, if we may give credit to the following verses, which shall serve as the conclusion of his poetical character :

' " With music and poetry equally bless'd,
    A bard thus Apollo most humbly address'd :
    Great Author of poetry, music, and light,
    Instructed by thee, I both fiddle and write ;
    Yet unheeded I scrape, or I scribble all day—
    My tunes are neglected, my verse flung away." '

This, with some unimportant changes, might serve for his grandson. The Dean also wrote a specially ill-natured epitaph on his friend :

> ' Beneath this marble stone here lies
> Poor Tom, more merry much than wise ;
> Who only liv'd for two great ends,
> To spend his cash, and lose his friends ;
> His darling wife of him bereft,
> Is only griev'd—there's nothing left.'

CHAPTER II.

THE death of the jovial Doctor left his large family in serious straits. This care seemed to devolve on the son, THOMAS SHERIDAN, a youth of much promise. There can be no doubt that under a less erratic parent he would have turned out a remarkable character. But every child of the race seemed to suffer from lack of discipline and training. The Doctor himself, the Doctor's son, the actor's son, the dramatist's son, all grew up wild. The young fellow's career opened in the most promising way, only to be checked and thwarted by the difficulties of the family, and the careless joviality of his father. As a youth he made the most brilliant use of the opportunities offered to him. Dean Swift, who was his godfather, tells us of him : ' The early part of his education he received from his father, who afterwards sent him to Westminster School, at a time when he could very ill afford it. He was there immediately taken notice of upon examination ; and, although a mere stranger, was by pure merit elected a King's scholar.

But their maintenance sometimes falling short, the Doctor was so poor that he could not add fourteen pounds to enable his son to finish the year ; which if he had done, he would have been removed to a higher class, and in another year would have been sped off (as the phrase is) to a fellowship in Oxford or Cambridge.' Being thus recalled to Dublin, he was sent to the university there, and was chosen of the foundation ; soon after obtained an exhibition, and in 1738 proposed to stand for a fellowship. He likewise took his degree of M.A.

This was all creditable and most promising, and it seems certain that he would have made a distinguished figure at the English universities. Johnson's opinion that he was ' naturally dull ' must be limited to his temper and conversation, though the Doctor, we are told, found great pleasure in his company. The constant struggling with a succession of trials, that began early, must have a souring effect on the character.

Left with the burden of a family upon him, when a mere student, he seems to have early thought of the stage as a profession. When at Trinity College he had made acquaintance with Mr. Garrick, in 1742, about whom the whole town had gone ' horn mad.' Not unnaturally, he was filled with an eagerness to go on the stage, and shortly made his *début* with much success. The fashion was set at that time of young men of birth taking to the profession, and it was known that Mr. Garrick was the son of an officer. It was curious that, like him, Sheridan should have begun with Richard. 'On the twenty-ninth of January, 1742-3, the part of Richard was attempted by a young gentleman at Smock Alley Theatre. This attempt succeeded beyond the most sanguine expectations of the friends of our young candidate for fame, and equalled any first essay ever remembered by the oldest performers on the Irish stage.'[*]

The young man had extraordinary success in Dublin, but already his rather arbitrary or combative temper began to show itself. This is generally evidenced by various public controversies with his brethren of the stage. Thus in 1743 we find him engaged in a quarrel with that strange eccentric, Theo Cibber, who had come to Dublin under one Phillips, a sort of travelling manager. This person, like many a wandering manager of our time, had left his company, the musicians, etc., all unpaid, with the result of disorder and mutiny. 'Theo,' always insubordinate, seems to have been a ringleader. An angry jealousy already existed between him and Sheridan, but one night matters came to a crisis. The orchestra struck. Sheridan, who was to play, came rushing from his dressing-room in a tempest of fury, saying that his 'robe had been stolen, and that he could not "go on" without it.' In vain it was urged upon him that another dress would be provided. As he

[*] Hitchcock: 'History of the Irish Stage.'

grotesquely explained to the town, the character
was one for which he was personally very unfit,
'and in which nothing could have made my appearance supportable but a large robe to cover my
defects, and give a gravity and dignity to my person
which I wanted.'

He insisted that the audience should be dismissed.
Theo naturally thought this selfish and arrogant.
Sheridan relates the discreditable scene that followed:
'On that night I found Mr. Cibber's behaviour, which
before was very complaisant, and rather meanly
subservient, suddenly changed. When I said what
a despicable figure I would make, he said, " D—n
me if I care what you do! the play shall not stand
still for you!" and immediately ran to the front
to draw up the curtain. When I heard his voice
I was stunned at the insolence of the fellow. The
terror I was under lest the curtain be drawn up
before there was time to make an apology made me
rush precipitately on to the stage, like a madman.
Mr. Cibber came on after me and offered to read the
part of Cato.'

The College authorities, provost, and scholars
were all drawn into this unseemly scuffle. About
the same time he had another dispute with one Lee,
manager at the theatre at Edinburgh, who appealed
to the public in a letter headed 'A man of honour,
but not a man of his word.'

Mr. Garrick, in a very cordial way, had offered

him his interest and aid in London—a promise which he fulfilled to the letter. Mr. Sheridan's head was a little turned by his great success in his native city, and his letter in answer to his new friend's offer is full of a rather amusing conceit.

'Sir,' he wrote in April, 1743, 'I am almost ashamed to acknowledge that it is more than a fortnight since I was favoured with the receipt of your obliging letter, and delayed so long to answer it; but, I believe, I shall stand readily excused with you, when I assure you, that in that fortnight I had three new characters to study, as well as to play— Othello being one of them. I thank you for your kind invitation to me, to pass the summer with you at Walton, though I could wish you had not mentioned it, for it has given me no small concern that the posture of my affairs will not permit me to enjoy that happiness. It is not improbable but that I may see London about the middle of May, though, if I do, I shall not stay above three weeks there; I intend it only as a jaunt of pleasure, and the hope of seeing you is not, I assure you, my least inducement. I have not as yet fixed any scheme for the next winter, but I have been offered such advantageous terms for the next winter as will, I believe, detain me here till January at least. As to your proposal of our playing together, I am afraid I have too many powerful reasons against it; a well-cut pebble may pass for a diamond till a fine brilliant is placed near it, and puts it out of countenance. (A bold metaphor that ; or, as Bayes says, " Egad, that's one of my bold strokes.") Besides, *we should clash so much in regard to characters, that I am afraid it is impossible we can be in the same house.* Richard, Hamlet, and Lear, as they are your favourite characters, are mine also ; and though you were so condescending as to say I might appear in any part of yours, yet I question whether the town would bear to see a worse performer in one of your characters in the same house with you, though they might endure him in another. I have a scheme to propose to you, which at first view may seem a little extraordinary to you, but if rightly considered, must turn to both our advantages : if you could be brought to divide your immortality with me, we might, like Castor and Pollux, appear always in different hemispheres (now I think on't, I don't know whether the old simile of the two buckets would not do as well, but that is beneath the dignity of a tragedian) : in plain English, what think you of dividing the kingdoms between us—to play one winter in London, and another in Dublin ? But more of this when I have the pleasure of meeting you. Pray remember my best respects to Mrs. Woffington : I should own myself unpardonable in not having wrote to her, were it in my power ; but I have been already sufficiently punished in the loss of so agreeable a correspondence, for, I assure you, I have a long time envied her pretty Chronon that pleasure.'

This ambitious scheme was not encouraged ; but it brought the result that Sheridan was engaged at Drury Lane in October, 1744, and made his *début* the night after Garrick. He appeared in all the leading parts, even in those which belonged to Garrick—Hamlet, Richard—and gained in favour with the town.

But soon a party was formed who affected to think that the Irish actor was kept back by Garrick's jealousy. Hence arose sensitiveness and soreness which bred a coolness, then a quarrel. Before this crisis, Sheridan had a house at Kingston, where he lived in jovial fashion enough, seeing his friends Mrs. Woffington, Miss Bellamy, Garrick himself, ' M. Sullivan, Fellow of T. C. D.,' and others. Here they got up theatricals, and had much amusement and jollity.

Soon he was fired with ambition to become a manager, and undertook the government of Smock Alley Theatre—an ungrateful task considering the shocking state of disorder into which it had fallen. The 'committee of noblemen and gentlemen' who directed it, thirty-five in number, begged of him to undertake the direction. What its barbarous state was may be conceived from the account given by Sheridan himself in his 'Case :'

' The Playhouse was looked upon as a common, and the actors as *feræ naturæ*. To such an absurd height had popular prejudice arisen, that the owners were considered as having no property there but what might be destroyed at the will and pleasure of the people . . . It was not uncommon to see about twenty persons in the pit, not a creature in the boxes, and more than a hundred people on the stage, who mixed with the actors in such a way as to be scarce distinguished from them. The upper gallery, indeed, as everyone could get admission to it for twopence, was generally crowded, and the time constantly passed in squabbles and battles between the footmen and the mob. Every stripling could bully his way behind the scenes. The galleries would call for any tune they pleased. If it was not played they threw glass bottles and stones.'

He determined to 'reform it altogether,' though the opportunity had not yet come—a resolution creditable to so young a man. As a first step he made proposals to Garrick, then at Bath, to come over and play for him. These were in a singular if not hostile tone : he told him 'he might depend on receiving every advantage and encouragement he could in reason look for, but must expect nothing from his friendship.' Garrick naturally thought it 'the oddest letter he had ever received.' The success of this second engagement is well known ; but it unfortunately developed a new hostility between the pair. There were thin houses on Mr. Sheridan's nights.

After Garrick's departure, Sheridan's bold attempts

at reform led to the riot of 1747, which ended in the wrecking of the theatre and, later, to his exile. A young fellow had clambered on to the stage and made his way to Miss Bellamy's room, whence he was expelled by order of the manager, who behaved with great spirit and independence. At a trial for rioting, during which he was called upon the table, a very learned counsellor, on the side of the prisoner, got up, and said he 'wanted to see a curiosity. I have often seen,' continued he, 'a gentleman soldier, and a gentleman sailor; but I have never seen a gentleman player.' Mr. Sheridan (who was well dressed) bowed modestly, and said, 'Sir, I hope you see one now.' This was considered an admirable retort, and Mr. Sheridan obtained further popularity by begging off the culprit and becoming his bail. But now as to a very romantic incident.

During these disorders the manager had noticed in the papers some complimentary verses, and was piqued into endeavouring to discover the author.*

---

* They were entitled 'The Owls—A Fable—Addressed to Mr. Sheridan, on his late Affair in the Theatre;' and began:

> 'Envy will Merit still pursue,
>   As shade succeeds to light;
> And though a shade obstructs the view,
>   It proves the substance right.

> 'If Worth appears, and gets its due
>   (But oh, how rare that gain!),
> The satyrs and the mimic crew
>   Shall grin behind the scene,' etc., etc.

On making inquiries he found that the flattering lines were the work of a young lady of the city named Chamberlaine. He forthwith got introduced to her through the aid of his sister, Mrs. Sheen, and 'was so captivated by her conversation, that a lively and reciprocal attachment was the result of this first meeting,' and they were married by her brother, the Rev. Walter Chamberlaine, in the year 1747, Miss Chamberlaine having just completed her twenty-second year.

Miss Frances Elizabeth Chamberlaine was the daughter of one of the numerous clergymen who 'came over' and secured excellent preferment in Ireland. Her grandfather was Sir Oliver Chamberlayne, or Chamberlaine, and his son Archdeacon of the picturesque Glendalough, and rector of St. Nicholas Without, a Dublin parish. He was a much-admired preacher. 'He was, at the same time,' we are told by Mrs. Le Fanu, 'a great humourist, the strongest proof of which is, that he was with difficulty prevailed on to allow his daughter to learn to read ; and to write, he affirmed to be perfectly superfluous in the education of a female.' She, however, was secretly instructed by her brothers in writing, in defiance of this singular prohibition, and also in Latin. Another brother taught her botany, so the designs of the so-called 'humourist' were thus frustrated. She was, in truth, an extremely bright, clever young woman, with marked literary talent, which she displayed so early as the age of fifteen, having then written a novel, ' Eugenia and Adelaide.' Her granddaughter tells us that ' Mrs. Sheridan, though not strictly handsome, had a countenance extremely interesting. Her eyes were remarkably fine and very dark, corresponding with the colour of her hair, which was black. Her figure would have been good, but for an accident that happened when she was an infant, by which she contracted a lameness that prevented her from going any distance without support. The fairness and beauty of her bust, neck, and arms were allowed to have seldom been rivalled.'*

Her father having sunk into a state of imbecility or dotage, his daughter was glad to seize the opportunity of visiting the theatre, and, as we have seen, became quite captivated by Mr. Sheridan. This destined mother of a wit belonged herself to a mercurial family, her two brothers being fellows of infinite jest. The eldest, Richard, who was a surgeon, presided at the Grecian, where he delighted the young Templars ; but his fame rests on a well-known pun, and one of merit. He had presented his cousin, Sam Whyte, who was opening his school, with a chest of tea, on which was the

* Long after, going up from Windsor in a public coach, Mrs. Sheridan, who, like most ladies of that period, took snuff, drew off her glove to take a pinch. A fellow-passenger, smiling, observed, 'There are few ladies, madam, who would have concealed such a hand and arm so long !'

inscription, *Tu doces!* ('Thou teachest'). The family took pride in this quip, and when Mr. Disraeli, senior, quoted Mr. Erskine as its author, vindicated their kinsman's claim.

After the marriage Mr. Sheridan 'launched out' in the true family style—purchased the family property at Quilca from his elder brother, and divided his time between it and Dublin. Mrs. Sheridan 'passed here some of the happiest hours of her life,' we are told in her 'Life,' which has been written by her granddaughter, Mrs. Le Fanu, of Dublin; and her husband contributed to the general enjoyment by various sportive exercises and jests which show that he was of humorous turn.*

It was in the month of October, 1751 (the exact date has not been preserved), that RICHARD BRINSLEY BUTLER SHERIDAN was born in the house, No. 12, Dorset Street, Dublin, now a very decayed and obscure quarter of the town.† It has been often

---

* As when some of his antiquarian guests having insisted that the old Irish system of cooking was far superior to the modern—particularly dwelling on an old dish known as 'swilled mutton'—he invited his friends to partake of a specially prepared *menu*. The floor was strewn with rushes, and the 'swilled mutton' duly served—a sheep roasted whole, with a lamb put inside. There was also a goose stuffed with a whole duck. These, however, in spite of loud praises to save consistency, were found far too rich for the stomachs of the party ; but they ate on. Presently was introduced a magnificent modern banquet—' venison and turbot from Dublin,' etc.—and the host heartily enjoyed the disappointment and anger of the sated antiquarians.

† The date is unknown, but the baptism was probably a few

repeated that Richard was born at Quilca, in Cavan.
The actor and his wife had seven children in all,
Charles Francis being the eldest. Then came
Thomas, born in 1747, but who died in a few
months; Richard Brinsley Butler; Sackville; Alicia,
born in January, 1753; and Anne Elizabeth.*

On this event Mr. Sheridan seems to have broken
out into a course of hospitable extravagance.
He filled his house at Quilca with guests. He
gathered all the Sheens and Knowles' under his
roof-tree. Further, 'Mrs. Sheridan enjoyed the
friendship of Mrs. Montgomery, mother of the three
celebrated beauties, the Hon. Mrs. Beresford, Mrs.
Gardiner, and Ann, Lady Townshend.'

Sheridan, it seems, was an ardent Tory, and at the
Beefsteak Club took the side of the Court party.
It was truly unfortunate that he did not show
more discretion, as his reforms were beginning to
bear fruit. Dress, 'mounting,' scenery, order, regu-

---

days after birth. Extract from the register of St. Mary's Parish,
Dublin: 'Charles Francis, son of Thomas and Frances Sheridan,
baptized July 23, 1750. Richard Brinsley, son of Mr. and Mrs.
Sheridan, baptized November 4, 1751.' The house was built by
Mr. Thomas Sheridan, to gratify his wife, whose uncle, Captain
Whyte, lived in the same street.

* Nearly all these names were selected in compliment to influential friends: Charles Francis being called after his godfather,
father of the first Lord Mountjoy; Alicia, after 'the Hon. Alicia
Caulfield,' sister of the Earl of Charlemont; and Sackville, after
the Duke of Dorset, then Lord Lieutenant.

larity, and decorum, we are told, now distinguished the Irish stage. 'The theatre was the fashionable resort of all ranks. . Crowded every night with the first characters in the kingdom, it was in reality a source of entertainment and instruction. Its professors were held in the highest estimation.' Unfortunately the manager's perverseness, which was part of his character, destroyed all these fair hopes in a night.

The well-known Peg Woffington was playing at the theatre, and seems to have exercised much influence over Sheridan, who made her president of the Dublin Beefsteak Club, and caused some gossip by bringing her down to Quilca, where, it turned out, she had conformed to the Established Church. This actress was, indeed, to be mainly accountable for the serious troubles which were now at hand. A play full of dangerous political allusions, viz., 'Mahomet,' was performed on Saturday, February 2, 1754; and when Mr. Digges repeated these lines :

> ' If, ye Powers divine !
> Ye mark the movements of this nether world,
> And bring them to account ! crush, crush those vipers,
> Who, singled out by the community
> To guard their rights, shall for a grasp of ore,
> Or *paltry office*—sell them to the foe '—

the pit clamoured for an encore, on which the actor repeated the whole speech, amid much riot. It was extraordinary that at the request of some patrons Sheridan should have 'put the play up' again, and run the risk of another disturbance. The rash venture was fixed for March 2.

The reasons he afterwards assigned appear totally insufficient; they were, 'that he had consulted some of the coolest of his friends, who told him they could see no reason why he should lose all the advantage of the time and labour which it cost him and the company to prepare this play, because about twenty persons in a former audience had stamped the name of a party play on it; that he received many messages that the play was desired, and unless performed would be insisted on;' and on the Friday morning before, he sent a general summons to the company to meet him in the green-room, where, being all assembled, he read them a lecture, which has been preserved.*

The actor asked for specific instructions in case he was again 'encored,' when Mr. Sheridan oddly said that 'he would leave him to act as he thought proper.' As may be conceived, when the actor came to the contested passage, 'Encore' was loudly called out. The audience required the manager to appear, but he disdained to do so, and went home. The handsome Woffington, who appealed to them, was not

---

* It is given at length in Hitchcock's 'History of the Irish Stage,' p. 231.

listened to. A frightful riot followed, in which the house was deliberately sacked, the boxes torn to pieces, etc., and finally it was attempted to set the theatre on fire. This catastrophe may be said to have ruined the manager. The state of hostility to him was such that he could not venture to appear or even open his theatre, and accordingly he retired from the management. 'The grave and judicious, nay even the courtiers, agreed he should have stroked the growling lion, and not have gored him.'*

During these exciting scenes at the theatre a servant had rushed home to Mrs. Sheridan, then near her confinement, with news that 'the theatre was all in flames, and the manager in danger.' The poor lady showed the greatest courage ; but the child born soon after did not live more than three months.

The unfortunate manager, thus ruined, his theatre torn to pieces, had no resource but to leave the country. The Duke of Dorset, indeed, offered him 'in the handsomest terms' a pension of £300 for what he had suffered in the cause of order and authority. This he respectfully declined, 'alleging that such a favour from Government would confirm

---

* The 'family' version of the affair, however, was that Mr. Sheridan was altogether in the right : that he had *forbidden* Digges to repeat the obnoxious passage, but had given him a discretion in the matter ; and that the actor had conceived a grudge for some fancied affront.

all the unjust reports to his disadvantage, and cut
him off from all future hopes of the patronage of the
public.'*

---

* Boswell, it will be seen later, confounded this offer of a pension
with the one of £200, given him on the ground of literary merit.

CHAPTER III.

DRIVEN from the stage, now on the verge of ruin,
Thomas Sheridan had to repair to England to teach
elocution. He left his children behind, excepting
Charles, the eldest and favourite son. Richard and
his sister Alicia were for a time placed at Quilca, in
charge of William Sheridan. Sam Whyte, the
Captain's son, cousin to Mrs. Sheridan, was now
opening a school in Grafton Street, and his friendly
relative enlisted the aid of her friends and connections,
persuading them to send their children to the new
establishment. After a short time her own two children were brought up to Dublin, and Alicia, the granddaughter, relates how they were placed in Dorset
Street, under the care of Mrs. Knowles, who with
her husband resided there. Thence they attended
Whyte's school; but as Dorset Street and Grafton
Street were at the extremities of the town, they
were soon placed as regular boarders with Whyte.*

* Mr. Moore, many years later, was at this very school, where
he took part in theatricals, and was noticed by the Le Fanus, who

Richard was now seven years old. His thoughtful, affectionate mother wrote concerning her children to her cousin Whyte on November 11th, 1758:

'DEAR SAM,—I should indeed have fixed them with you entirely as boarders on my leaving Ireland; but as I expected to have returned long before this time, I thought that for so short a space, and especially as the exercise of walking in summer might be of use to them, that they could not be the worse for spending their evenings at home. Though I have an entire reliance as well on your care as that of Mrs. Whyte, yet I should not choose, at this distance from myself, to have the children deprived of the servant they have been so long used to. I know it would be a great hardship on the poor younger one in particular to lose nurse, who has always hitherto been their attendant. They must

---

had married into the Sheridan family. 'Among the most intimate friends of my schoolmaster,' says Moore, in his fragment of autobiography, 'were the Rev. Joseph Le Fanu and his wife—she was the sister of Richard Brinsley Sheridan. This lady, who had a good deal of the talent of her family, with a large alloy of affectation, was, like the rest of the world at that time, strongly smitten with the love of acting; and in some private theatricals held at the house of a Lady Borrowes, in Dublin, had played the part of Jane Shore with considerable success.'—('Memoirs,' vol. i., p. 10.) When Moore first went to London, he seems to have known Mr. Thomas Sheridan, and describes how difficult it was to get him to give a dinner.

necessarily have somebody to dress them, wash for them, and mend their clothes; and if nurse can be made any otherwise useful in the family, I dare say she will be very willing to do her best. If you want a bed or beds on the occasion, you may be supplied from the Blind Quay.'

Mr. Sheridan had gone to Oxford, where he proposed to give a course of lectures, being in sore straits for money. In his wife's letters we can read 'between the lines,' as it were, and see how the anxious lady was striving to reassure the schoolmaster as to payment of his account.

'How are my dear little ones?' she asks. 'Do they often talk of me? Keep me alive in their remembrances. I have all a mother's anxiety about them, and long to have them over with me; but I believe we shall not send for them till the end of June. I mention this as a matter of business, as I know your number is limited. If you will send your amount for the children by nurse, I hope Mr. Sheridan will discharge it by the first opportunity. But as to the bad debt, I can say nothing. That is a more serious object, and I fear we must trespass on your friendship to wait some time longer till our affairs come about, and we can get a better hold in the world.'

So it was to be even from the beginning, and little Brinsley was to be nursed in the doctrines of debt and excuses. There is a pleasant and irresistible simplicity in this amiable lady's apologies.

By September 12th the children had joined their parents at Windsor.

'DEAR SAM,' she wrote—'My children are, thank God, arrived safe and well. They did not come down to me here till last Thursday; they stayed a week in London, nurse being willing to wait for their baggage, which 'twas proper she should see safely lodged before she left town. I can't say they do their preceptor as much credit as George Cunningham does, for their progress has been rather small for eighteen months; but, mistake me not, I don't say this, as is too much the absurd custom of parents, by way of throwing a reflection on the teacher; my children's backwardness I impute to themselves; owing to their natural slowness, their illness and long and frequent absences.* I gave Mr. Sheridan your account, and he desires me to tell you the instant it is in his power he will discharge as much of it as he can. I believe you are not a stranger to the bad situation of our affairs in Ireland; he is here working his way through difficulties; meantime, as all our resources from your side are cut off, we are obliged

---

* This must be the foundation of the story that Richard was pronounced by parent and master '*a most impenetrable dunce!*' and which Whyte corroborates. See 'Memoirs of Thomas Moore,' vol. i., pp. 6, 7.

to be œconomists, till our affairs are settled upon a better footing, which we hope next winter will effect. I assure you, Sam, Mr. Sheridan laments the not having it in his power,' etc., etc.

In December she wrote : ' The two boys are getting on in their learning, and I endeavour to assist them, particularly in the English branches, as well as I can. I should often be at a loss what to do with my time in this unsociable place, if I had not the children, with whom I find sufficient employment.'

They were now settled in London, where the agreeable lady, whom Dr. Parr was later to declare ' quite celestial,' soon made hosts of friends, among whom were Dr. Young, Dr. Johnson, Mr. Wedderburn (afterwards Lord Loughborough), Lord Shelburne, Mrs. Cholmondeley, and Samuel Richardson. The latter encouraged her in the literary attempt which she was now making.*

* A lamented and ever brilliant member of this family, the late J. Sheridan Le Fanu, the novelist, who for many years was the writer's intimate friend, possessed a number of Sheridan portraits, which were hung round his dining-room. They were singularly interesting from the Sheridan cast of face, strictly preserved in all, not without a certain air of clever pedantry. Here was Thomas Sheridan, the father, in a skull-cap, sitting in a chair, and composed to a rather theatrical attitude; with his wife, from whom the Sheridans inherited the large and long, pale face. What struck one most, in the portraits of other ladies of the family, was the expression of

Mr. Sheridan had entered into an engagement with his late stage-manager, Victor, to take over the wrecked theatre for two years, on the term of a fixed sum—£5 for every acting night, and a loan of £2,000 on a mortgage of the properties, wardrobe, etc. This put him in a comfortable position, though it proved to be a disastrous bargain for the new lessees.

One would have thought that the manager would have had a sufficiently painful experience of the Irish stage and of Irish audiences; but he still hankered after the old flesh-pots. The deputies he had left behind him were not flourishing; and one, Sowden, anxious to be out of the concern, advertised in the papers for a purchaser for his share of the mortgage—£2,000 advanced to Sheridan. This kindled the latter at once. He seems to have shared in that wonderful art of 'money-raising' which his son possessed so transcendently, and found a gentleman in London to advance him this money. He then entered into an agreement with Victor to come over and perform.

But what might have been anticipated was now to occur. His reappearance amounted to a challenge

---

the mouth, which was like Goldsmith's, a little coarse and large, but full of intelligence. There was also a remarkable pastel drawing of Swift, which had been given to Sheridan by the great writer himself.

to the 'rowdy' spirit of the place, and it was insisted
that he must first apologize for his behaviour on
the occasion when his theatre was wrecked. This
was insisted on, and on the opening night, as he did
not appear, a party was sent to demand the reason.
The poor player had to make a promise, and on the
night he appeared had to pass through this humiliating ordeal : 'When the curtain drew up, he advanced
to the centre of the stage with a paper in his hand.
*Tears gushed from the eyes of several of his male
auditors.* After his apology was over, and, his
pardon having been signed by the loudest acclamation, he had begun to retire ; he advanced again,
and with broken, faltering accents, spoke as follows :
" Your goodness to me at this important crisis has so
deeply affected me, that I want powers to express
myself ; my future actions shall show my gratitude."
He appeared a few nights after in the character of
Hamlet to a crowded audience, and received the
utmost applause.'

It must be confessed this was a painful and
undignified spectacle—a player apologizing for what
was no offence. But ill-luck now began to pursue
him. News arrived that Barry, another excitable
and reckless nature, after declining engagements
from Sheridan, was about to build a new rival
theatre in Dublin. Negotiation was attempted to
make him give up this insane scheme, as the town
was 'over-theatred,' but ineffectually. Sheridan

then made engagements with Foote and King at extravagant salaries, involving himself more and more. Among other ventures he brought out Home's 'Douglas,' then in great vogue, and which he admired so much that he wrote to the author promising him the third night's receipts as a present. On the first and second nights there were crammed houses. But by the third it had become known in Dublin that the author had been censured, as a clergyman, for writing for the stage. Instantly the house was deserted. Mr. Sheridan, in a sort of embarrassment, did not know how to act to the author, though it might be thought his course was simple enough to a man of business. A medal was ordered, worth about twenty guineas, and bearing an inscription, with a laurel-wreath, etc., to this effect :

'Thomas Sheridan, Manager of the Theatre Royal, Smock Alley, Dublin, presents this small token of his gratitude to the Author of "Douglas," for his having enriched the Stage with a Perfect Tragedy.'

'Soon after I carried it,' says Whyte, 'with me to London, and through the favour of Lord Macartney, it was delivered to the Minister, Lord Bute, for his countryman the author of "Douglas." But even this also he was near being deprived of ; for on the road, a few miles from London, I was stopped by highway-men, and preserved the well-meant offering by the sacrifice of my purse, at the imminent peril of my life.'*

With Foote had come over that odd amusing mimic of a mimic, Tate Wilkinson, then a poor unfriended waif and stray of the stage, but rich in impudence and a certain talent. He had been engaged as a humble assistant in Foote's 'Monopolylogues,' a kind of puppet for the master to exhibit his pranks upon. Being allowed one night to exhibit a little mimicry of actors while the principal was resting, the impudent fellow so delighted the audience that they insisted on his going on ; and with inconceivable audacity he proceeded to take off Foote himself ! No situation in comedy could be more diverting or more awkward for the

* All this bears out Boswell's criticism of the actor's having ' a Quixotic mind.' Johnson, meeting him afterwards in a coffee-house at Oxford, called out to him roughly, ' Mr. Sheridan, Mr. Sheridan ! how came you to give a gold medal to Home for writing a foolish play ?' 'This, you see, was wanton and insolent ; but I *meant* to be wanton and insolent. A medal has no value but as a stamp of merit. And was Sheridan to assume to himself the right of giving that stamp ? If Sheridan was magnificent enough to bestow a gold medal as an honorary reward of dramatic excellence, he should have requested one of the Universities to choose the person on whom it should be conferred. Sheridan has no right to give a stamp of merit : it was counterfeiting Apollo's coin.' Johnson was certainly in the right. Surely an explanation of the cause of failure, with a remittance even of the value of the medal, would have been more suitable. But the dignity of '*conferring* a medal' would have been lost.

chief performer. The audience roared with delight.
Foote was furious, yet dared not check him.

Wilkinson also describes a characteristic scene with
Sheridan, when he had to wait on him to fix his
benefit night. Sheridan suggested to him that they
should share the profits, and that to increase the
attraction he should mimic the Dublin actors, the
London ones whom he took off not being very
familiar to the audience. ' I observed to him that I
had not had leisure to have paid a sufficient attention to that company as objects for imitation ; it
could not be the work of a week, or a month ;
besides, were I capable, if I should take that freedom, they would most likely not only insult me, but
make it a plea to refuse acting for my benefit. Mr.
Sheridan persisted angrily. I then intimated that if
I complied, I hoped he would not have any objection to my using his name, and that I did not do it
of my own accord, but had his express command for
that purpose. Mr. Sheridan seemed much vexed ;
said that what he had asked me to do was to get
me applause, and to serve *me*—not *himself.* He
wished it to come before the audience as a sudden
surprise, and as my own voluntary act, and after
that had been done, he would have taken care to
have had it so called for by the audience, as to
prevent a possibility of the performers' anger being
of weight sufficient to prevent its repetition ; and
the more it vexed the actors and actresses, the

greater relish it would give the audience ; that I believe was too true.

'However, I continued my objection; but at last (like a fool in the knowledge of mankind and the human heart) a lucky bright thought, as I judged it, occurred to me ; and I said, " My good Mr. Sheridan, I have hit upon the very thing to establish myself as a favourite with you and the town." He seemed all impatience to know what it could be. " My dear sir, a thought has just entered my pate, which I think will draw money, and be of infinite service to myself." " What is it ? what is it ?" says Sheridan, with the utmost eagerness. " Why, sir," says I, "your rank in the theatre, and a gentleman so well known in Dublin, on and off the stage, must naturally occasion any striking imitation of yourself to have a wonderful effect."

' Hogarth's pencil could not testify more astonishment—he turned pale and red alternately—his lips quivered. I instantaneously perceived I was in the wrong box ; it was some time before he could speak. He took a candle from off the table, and showing me the room door—when at last his words found utterance—said he never was so insulted. *What! to be taken off by a buffoon upon his own stage !* and he then very politely desired me to walk downstairs. Mr. Sheridan held the candle for me only till I got to the first landing, and then hastily removed it, grumbling and squeaking to himself, and leaving me to feel my way in the dark, down a pair and a half of steep stairs, and to guess my road in hopes of finding the street door.

'Mr. Sheridan's voice was deep, and as oppositely sharp; and I should not have disliked then to have put in practice what I proposed, had he given leave, for I was really perfect and ready.

'After that fracas he neither permitted me to play, nor spoke to me during my stay in Ireland.'

This Wilkinson's nature was so full of suspicious corners, that almost every transaction he records is coloured; but there is, no doubt, a basis of truth in this lively little scene.

In the meanwhile the unfortunate Sheridan made desperate attempts to crush his rivals, petitioning Parliament against the new enterprise, which he declared was 'dangerous to public morals.' His pleasing wife had her share of trials also. As she wrote to Richardson:

'As for my own little family, the joy of seeing them again has been embittered by the illness of my two youngest children: they have both had fevers, and are but now recovering. Our present abode we find, on many accounts, so inconvenient, and in an air so very confined, that we have been looking out for a little retreat where the children and I may breathe more freely, and Mr. Sheridan be more master of his time; such a portion of it, I

mean, as he is not unavoidably obliged to pass in
Dublin. We have at last fixed on a little place in
the neighbourhood of the Dean of Down's villa, to
which I believe we shall remove next week ; and
here Mr. Sheridan hopes to find time himself to tell
you how much he esteems, how much he honours
you. Meanwhile, he commissions me to say thus
much for him.'

Among other schemes, he was now busy with a
grand educational one—' The Hibernian Academy,'
a sort of Lyceum—on which he expended great
labour, and of which he was to be principal. But in
his absence it was whispered about that an actor was
an unsuitable person to be at the head of such an
institution ; and by an intrigue he was thrust out.
Never was there such a tide of ill-luck ! All the
' ass-load' of worries, as Sterne says, seemed to be
piled on his back. Sam Whyte was to have been
one of the masters, but he had already set up a
school of his own.

The rival theatre in Crow Street was being
pushed on, and Sheridan's actors and actresses were
drawn away from him. Everything promised
disaster. The competition, indeed, now to be entered on was to prove one of the most disastrous in
theatrical annals. It brought ruin to all concerned.
The joint managers, Barry and Woodward, ever
secure of handsome salaries and favouring audiences,

were to lose every shilling of their savings, beside being sunk in debt and embarrassment. Sheridan was to share the same fate. All who were embarked with them, and who followed them, suffered. As a last desperate resource, Sheridan had rushed to London to engage performers from Sadler's Wells, and had gone to vast expense preparing a pantomime. With this view he had secured his old enemy, Theo Cibber, and a number of funambulists, with dancers, dresses, and scenery, to say nothing of Madox, the famous 'wire-dancer,' and the 'man who played on twelve bells fastened to his head, hands, etc.,' all of which were put on board a vessel. Poor Victor, the deputy manager, had been left behind to carry on the struggle until all should be retrieved by this grand coup. The vessel was cast away, and all on board lost !

Mr. Sheridan on this disaster did not come over to the relief of his theatre. He was, indeed, at this moment sorely pressed by his personal embarrassments in London.

In the summer of 1761, he found his way to Edinburgh on an elocutionary tour, where he delivered lectures 'On the English Language and Public Speaking' to large audiences. There he became acquainted with the genial and appreciative Boswell, to whom he was never weary of expatiating on the great Dr. Johnson, who, he said, often stayed with him till three and four o'clock in the morning; and he held out to the young Scot the hope of an introduction to the great Cham of literature.

On his return home he removed to Windsor, where he sent for his children, and fixed himself. He was now giving lessons to Mr. Wedderburn, and other Scots with the broadest accents, which he undertook to remove by his system. He also turned his thoughts to his profession, and having signified his desire to appear at Drury Lane, the good-natured Garrick at once agreed to bring him out—this, too, in spite of the old coolness and jealousy. His proposals were of the most modest kind. Anything that suited the theatre, he said, would suit him. If he was wanted to play but now and again, that would fall in very well with his plans. Remuneration was no object. All this should be borne in mind when he later became discontented and made bitter complaints.

Garrick agreed with him cordially, and gave him a fourth share of the profits. 'King John' was 'put up,' in which Garrick was to play the King, and Sheridan Falconbridge ; but Davies says, 'Garrick secretly determined to the contrary,' and later took Falconbridge for himself. When the play was performed, he adds that Garrick was much nettled; for the King was more pleased with Sheridan, and did not care for his rendering of the Bastard. When this was reported to the manager by 'some d——d good-natured friend,' he is said to have at once withdrawn

the play.   This has been a subject of controversy;
but his wife, who must have known the truth, tells
the story of what really occurred.   The truth is,
the play was performed several times, and had to
give place to a new piece, the 'Earl of Essex,' in
which Sheridan himself was to play.

In March, 1761, a novel on which Mrs. Sheridan
had long been engaged was published, and had
extraordinary success.   This was the well-known
'Sidney Biddulph,' which, like so many of the stories
which delighted that generation, is almost forgotten,
and is now difficult to read.   The aim in such productions appears to have been to give a literal copy
of the ordinary prosaic course of life : a literalness
which is opposed to all canons of art.   But we who
find it 'stupid,' find it yet harder to conceive the
popularity it attained, for it was translated into
many languages.   The author, though her name
was not on the title, was well known, and enjoyed
all the sweets of reputation.   Indeed, being full of
esprit and lively remark, and at the same time good-
natured, she became one of those characters whom all
admired and were glad to be with, and her pleasant
and witty talk suggested to many the idea that 'she
ought to write a comedy.'   It may be said that
there is no direct connection between these gifts : a
witty conversationalist has often proved but a bad
dramatist.   Goldsmith did not particularly shine in
talk.   But good spirits, wit and vivacity furnish an

admirable fund for both conversation and composition, especially when the speaker or writer adds
the charm of being natural and unaffected.

Mrs. Sheridan, at all events, took the advice of
her friends, and succeeded beyond her hopes. Her
comedy, ' The Discovery,' is written in a spirited
vein, and the characters are all marked, distinct,
and little exaggerated. It is impossible to read it
without interest and amusement, or the feeling that
its author must have been a woman of superior and
even masculine ability. Sir Anthony Branville, the
pedantic lover, with his reservations and parentheses,
is original, and worked out with due variety and
spirit. The Flutters, a young and newly married
pair, always quarrelling, are pleasantly conceived ;
and the whole eminently deserved the success it
enjoyed.

It is likely enough that Lord Medway may have
suggested Joseph Surface to the author's son. This
loose nobleman engages to Sir Harry that he will
soothe Lady Flutter, and make up matters between
them. But he uses this opportunity to press his
own suit, with artful and ingenious arguments.
Garrick, when he heard that Mrs. Sheridan had
written a comedy, begged eagerly to see it. She
read it to him herself, and he immediately took a
fancy to the character of Sir Anthony. This was a
remarkable advantage, for, as she wrote to a friend,
' Most of us poor authors find a difficulty in getting

our pieces on the stage, and perhaps are obliged to dangle after managers a season or two : I, on the contrary, was *solicited* to give *mine*, as soon as it was seen.'*

Mr. Sheridan acted the part of Lord Medway in his wife's piece. O'Brien and Miss Pope were the Flutters. Thus it was brought out with every advantage. Yet 'the family' *would* have it that Mr. Garrick was still consumed with a mean jealousy of Mr. Sheridan.

The clever authoress had not courage to attend the theatre on the night of the performance, which was February 5th, 1763. While she was waiting for news, the vivacious Mrs. Cholmondeley—Peg Woffington's sister—burst in with a large party to tell of its perfect triumph, and called for supper. She and Mr. Forbes had gone up to the middle gallery to lead the applause among the foot-men.

Here was a gleam of prosperity. 'Mr. Sheridan,' his wife wrote, 'stands here in high reputation, with a prospect of being every day more and more esteemed. The late King's death, which shut up the theatres for a time, together with the necessity the managers were under of bringing

* Garrick was ever hearty and genuine in his admiration of this piece, which he assured a publisher was 'one of the best comedies he ever read, and that he could not do better than lay out his money in so valuable a purchase.'

on the stage five new pieces (farces and comedies), has prevented him appearing so often as it was expected. He is now preparing for another course of practical lectures, which he intends to read and then to publish.' Nor did he lack a patron.

Mr. Sheridan, in 1762, had been adroit enough to draw Lord Bute's attention, by addressing his ' dissertation' to that influential Minister. ' It has been as well received by him,' wrote his fond wife, 'as we could possibly wish, and even beyond the expectation of our friends. He expressed himself highly pleased with the design, and sent Mr. Sheridan word it should receive all countenance and encouragement. Lord Bute is a man of his word, and everybody knows his great influence, so that the affair now seems likely to become of great importance.'*

' Sam Whyte,' however, had not yet been paid his money, and the tranquil simplicity of Mrs.

---

* Certainly his lectures were being attended with extraordinary success, ' his auditory seldom consisting of less than five hundred people, and this is the utmost the hall will contain ; many have been disappointed for want of room, and he is strenuously solicited to repeat the course again immediately in the same place.' And from another account we learn that ' Mr. Sheridan admitted in print that to three courses he had upwards of fifteen hundred subscribers at a guinea each, besides occasional auditors, and the benefit arising to him afterwards from the publication of the lectures (price half a guinea in boards), which had a rapid sale ; so that his emolument on the whole must have been considerable indeed.'

Sheridan once more supplies a happy touch, in the difficult art of dealing with a creditor. ' Mr. Sheridan is much obliged to you for *the great delicacy* with which you make your application, in giving it the air rather of requesting a favour than making a just demand. Few people, Sam, can *think*, much less act, generously, or even genteelly. He will not fail to send you the sum mentioned in about a month's time at farthest.'

But when the time named came round, she had to make fresh excuses. It is characteristic that Mr. Sheridan should have left this duty altogether to her. Everything, it seems, had gone wrong. His Scotch expedition had fallen through. However, in November, 1762, she was enabled to write of two satisfactory items of news—the production of her comedy and the pension. Mr. Sheridan was busy on his Dictionary, and the pension, she says, was an encouragement to his undertaking, and this without solicitation, which ' makes it the more valuable.'*

* It is to Sam that she sends a pleasing, touching ' Ode to Patience,' which sets out her own trials, and is not without merit, as the following stanzas from it show :

> ' Thro' all the various turns of fate,
> Ordain'd me in each several state
> 　　My wayward lot has known,
> What taught me silently to bear,
> To curb the sigh, to check the tear,
> 　　When sorrow weigh'd me down?

Among those who cheered this little circle was
Dr. Johnson, who came frequently, sat long, and not
uncommonly uttered a rough thing. As when Mrs.
Sheridan was telling him that she allowed her little
girl to read such works only as ' The Rambler,' and
others of the same improving cast, he burst out with
' *Then you are a fool, madam !* Turn your daughter
loose into your library ; if she is well inclined, she

' 'Twas Patience. . . Temperate Goddess, stay !
  For still thy dictates I obey,
     Nor yield to Passion's power ;
  Tho' by injurious foes borne down,
  My fame, my toil, my hopes o'erthrown,
     In one ill-fated hour.

' 'Twas Patience ! . . Goddess ever calm !
  Oh ! pour into my breast thy balm,
     That antidote to pain ;
  Which flowing from thy nectar'd urn,
  By Chymistry divine can turn
     Our losses into gain.

' When sick and languishing in bed,
  Sleep from my restless couch had fled
     (Sleep, which even pain beguiles),
  What taught me calmly to sustain
  A feverish being rack'd with pain,
     And dress'd my looks in smiles ?

' 'Twas Patience ! . . Heaven-descended maid !
  Implor'd, flew swiftly to my aid,
     And lent her fostering breast ;
  Watch'd my sad hours with parent care,
  Repell'd the approaches of despair,
     And sooth'd my soul to rest.'

will choose only nutritious food ; if otherwise, all your precautions will avail nothing to prevent her following the natural bent of her inclinations.'

It is admitted that to Sheridan's influence with Wedderburn, Johnson was indebted for his pension of £300 a year. As Lord Loughborough said, 'Sheridan rang the bell.'* This was a weighty obligation, which should not have been forgotten. Yet with all this intimacy, a breach was now to occur in their friendship.

'When I returned to London in the end of 1762,' says Boswell, 'to my surprise and regret I found an irreconcilable difference had taken place between Johnson and Sheridan. A pension of £200 a year had been given to Sheridan. Johnson, who, as has been already mentioned, thought slightingly of Sheridan's art, upon hearing that he was also pensioned, exclaimed, " What ! have they given *him* a pension ? Then it is time for me to give up mine." '

Johnson, indeed, always declared that he added to his unkind speech, 'that he was glad Sheridan had got the pension, for he was a very good man.'

---

* Sheridan, it seems, had 'taught pronunciation' to Mr. A. Wedderburn, whose sister was married to Sir H. Erskine, an intimate of Lord Bute's. Mr. Sheridan, however, who seems to have been extremely sensitive and touchy, afterwards complained loudly of the ingratitude of this Mr. Wedderburn, whom he did much service to at this time of his life.

The worthy Boswell often tried to reconcile them, and was rejoiced one morning in 1783—alas! the enmity had gone on for twenty years !—to extract from Johnson, ' Tell Mr. Sheridan I shall be glad to see him, and shake hands with him.' On Boswell adding, naturally enough, ' that it was wonderful resentment should be kept up so long,' Johnson explained, with his usual acuteness, that it was not resentment so much as ' partly *falling out of the habit*, partly disgust, as one has at a drug that has made him sick. Besides, he knows that I laugh at his oratory.'

About a year later Boswell got his friend Dilly to invite Johnson, himself, and ' old Mr. Sheridan,' as ' It was very earnest to have him and Johnson brought together again by chance.' But his benevolent intentions were frustrated. Mr. Sheridan arrived early, and hearing that Johnson was expected, departed. Who can hesitate, after this, to take Johnson's side in this unlucky quarrel, or to form an unfavourable judgment of a nature that could nourish for so many years such an unworthy hostility—all owing to one lightly uttered speech !

CHAPTER IV.

In May, 1764, we find Sheridan and his wife setting out for Edinburgh, full of hope and spirits. 'My dear Sam,' he wrote to Mr. Whyte, ' I know it will give you pleasure to hear that my friends have settled matters for me in such a way that I shall be no longer in apprehensions with regard to what my humane creditors may do. I am at present on a visit, for a few days, to a particular friend in Richmond, while Mrs. Sheridan is preparing for our expedition to Scotland, on which we shall set out in eight or ten days, so that you need not answer this, or write, till I shall have given you notice of where. One of my friends, a powerful one, has cut out an employment for me, which will place me in a conspicuous point of view, *beyond the reach of my enemies ;* and I have reason to believe that the thing will be done early.'

Alas ! creditors are always the debtor's enemies. Unfortunately, however, everything as usual turned out disagreeably. At Edinburgh he was seized with gout, and for three months could do nothing. It had, indeed, been 'a most unfortunate year.' However, his Grammar and Dictionary were nigh completed, and the sanguine author had 'great hopes' it was 'to be the foundation of his fortune, and that a large superstructure may be raised on it.' Further, 'When that is completed my friends have something in view for me, which will make me easy during my life; and probably enable me to provide well for my family.' *

With all these various aids and resources Sheridan ought to have been in comfortable circumstances. He had his pension, his salary as an actor,† his receipts from his lectures and private tuitions, and the handsome sum he had received for his interest in his theatre. But pressed with a load of debt, and no doubt living handsomely, excluded from his own country by fear of creditors, he determined now

* This may refer to the scholastic institute in Ireland, spoken of at page 45. Sheridan's various elocutionary works were highly successful, and his Dictionary, which sounded, as it were, ingenious 'notes' for the proper pronunciation, has passed through many editions. His lectures and schemes of education were all successful, and attracted attention. He also edited the works of Swift for the booksellers.

† Sheridan, as an actor, always 'drew' good houses. In 1758, the total receipts for twenty-one nights of his playing amounted to £1,631. This, had he and his son left 'management' alone, and held fast, the one to his acting, the other to his dramas, would have secured them ease and comfort. In 1776, for twenty-five nights, £2,955 was taken; in 1760, for fourteen nights, £1,669.

to repair to France, where living was cheaper—a
fresh expatriation.   It would seem, indeed, in Johnson's rude phrase, that 'England could well *want*
Sheridan.'   Accordingly, in September, 1764, he set
out, taking with him his wife, his two daughters,
and his eldest son Charles, Richard Brinsley being
left at Harrow.   They were persuaded by a casual
acquaintance, met with in Paris, to fix on Blois as a
residence.   A short time after his arrival he described his situation to his ' Dear Sam.'

' My friends were unanimously of opinion that it
was the best measure I could take, in order to have
leisure to finish my work, without which I could
have no further pretensions to any favours.   My
state of health, too, made it absolutely necessary that
I should remove into a better climate ; for, as my
disorder was gaining ground, I should not have been
able to do anything in England.   The air here is
inconceivably fine, and the alteration it has already
made in me makes me confidently hope for a perfect
cure.   Dick continues at Harrow.   The journey
was confoundedly expensive ; but the cheapness of
the place will make full amends.   I could support
my family here better upon a hundred pounds a year
than upon five in London.   As I can now bid
defiance to my merciless creditors, I shall be able to
make such terms with them before my return as will
make me easy for the rest of my life.'

An amusingly contradictory letter—the last portion giving the true reason of his retirement. But here the old spirit of expense and hospitality would assert itself, and he could not resist entertaining the various wandering young Englishmen of condition who came by. He was well received by some French families, and notably by a Colonel Montigny, a worthy French officer of some reputation ; and here, too, the clever and amiable Mrs. Sheridan gained many friends.

Mr. Sheridan, though far away from his native country, was now to experience a very flattering testimony of the respect with which he was regarded. Johnson told, in various companies, how 'his old friend, Mr. Sheridan, had been honoured with extraordinary attention in his own country, by having had an exception made in his favour in an Irish Act of Parliament concerning insolvent debtors. Thus to be singled out,' said he, 'by a Legislature as an object of public consideration and kindness, is a proof of no common merit.'*

---

* It seems that in 1766, when there was to be a general Act for the relief of such insolvent debtors as their creditors would allow to benefit by it, Whyte determined, unknown to Sheridan, to petition for him. He was a creditor himself, and other creditors were hostile. It required, therefore, some management, as enemies would interpose. Whyte, therefore, consulted with influential members of the House, and it was brought forward by Mr. Tottenham, of 'boots' celebrity, who, with many compliments, said ' it was quite unusual that a creditor should petition for his debtor.

Mr. Sheridan, on receiving the news, was greatly gratified, especially as he was in serious straits for money, and then gave Mr. Whyte an account of himself and his plans:

'And now, my dear Sam, I must tell you that without your father's assistance it will be impossible for me to reap the benefit of what you have done for me. From the perpetual fluctuation in the Ministry, the payments are no longer punctual at the Treasury. There is now due to me a year of my pension; and at the moment I am writing to you I am reduced to my last louis. I had relied upon receiving about fifty pounds from Sheen, for the books and a year's rent of a certain farm at Quilca. I had before applied to some friends in England, who had made large professions to me; but I find, by an obstinate silence on their part, that nothing is to be expected from them. But I must conjure you by all that is sacred in friendship to raise a hundred pounds for me, as speedily as you can, on the receipt of which I will immediately set out for England on my way to Dublin. Mrs. Sheridan and the children will continue in France till my affairs are settled; and after that you may rely upon

He moved that the petitioner be not put on his oath, but that his word should be taken.' Repeated testimonies of applause and congratulations on success followed this. Mr. Croker has quite mistaken this transaction in his notes to Boswell.

it that this is the first debt I shall think myself bound to discharge.'

He then gives an account of all his literary plans, the Grammar, Dictionary, etc.—he was, indeed, a very industrious writer—and continues :

'And after the most unprejudiced inquiries, I remained in the full conviction that it is from religion alone that we can hope for contentment in this life, or happiness in a future one : and the result of my self-examination was a determined resolution to make her sacred dictates the guide of all my future actions. Don't think, Sam, that either superstition or melancholy have had the least influence on this occasion, for I have not a grain of either in my composition ; it has been the effect of a long, cool, deliberate train of reflection.'

Mrs. Sheridan, in ill health, still toiled at her literary work, and had completed a new novel called ' Nourjahad,' which was to enjoy some popularity. Her new comedy was entitled a ' Trip to Bath.' This her gifted son must have seen, as there is a *Mrs. Surface* among the characters, a good deal of chatter about scandal, and the scene is laid at Bath.* Her strangely sensitive temperament, excited the more by the many shocks and anxieties she had

* The manuscript is in the British Museum, but, it must be said, is a rather jejune, thin production, all 'talk,' and with little

experienced, had been tried in an odd way, even on the journey from Paris.*

The hope of improved health from change of air proved to be delusive, and in 1766 Mr. Whyte received the following letter from Paris, dated October 13 :

'Often have I sat down to write to you an account of the most fatal event that could befall me in this life, and as often have thrown aside the pen. Oh, my dear Sam ! the most excellent of women is no more. Her apparent malady was an intermitting fever, attended with no one bad symptom, till the day before her death, when she was suddenly deprived of her senses, and all the fatal prognostics of a speedy dissolution appeared. She died the death of the righteous, without one pang, without a groan. The extraordinary circumstances attending her case made me resolve to have her opened, when it was found that the whole art of medicine could not have prolonged her days, as all the noble parts were attacked, and any one of four internal maladies must have proved mortal. If the news of this event has not yet reached Dublin, break it to my sister as

action or character. She sent it over to be submitted to Mr. Garrick, who did not relish it. She defended herself and her piece in a sprightly letter to Victor, which gives a good idea of a charming character.

* Mr. Sheridan had gone to look for lodgings, and lost his way, leaving her to the care of a valet picked up on the road.

gently as you can. I set out from this in a few days for St. Quentin, a town about half-way between this and Calais, where I purpose to leave my children, in the hands of Protestants, to whom they are strongly recommended. As soon as I have settled them, I shall set out for London, and thence proceed to Dublin as speedily as possible. I thank you for your last letter and the remittance, without which I should not have been able to have made this arrangement. Sam! you have lost a friend who valued you much. I have lost what the world cannot repair, a bosom friend, another self. My children have lost —oh, their loss is neither to be expressed nor repaired! But the will of God be done.'

There is feeling in this, and the apostrophes to ' Sam,' if a little grotesque, seem outbursts of genuine grief.

It seems that the prospect of her husband's approaching departure caused a struggle in Mrs. Sheridan's finely strung disposition between maintaining outward cheerfulness and indulging secret anxiety. On the eve of his departure she was seized with a sort of feverish attack; all through her illness she showed a surprising firmness and consideration for others. She died in August, 1766, and was buried at Blois. Altogether, a singularly interesting and remarkable woman, from whom it is clear her son inherited much of his gay temperament and talent. From her came also that peculiar restlessness which was a defect in his character. It is remarkable that the mother and the son's wife should have had much the same *cast* of temperament.

Mr. Sheridan's debts at this time amounted to about £7,000, the unfortunate result of trying to combine working as an actor with living like a gentleman of condition. In short, it seems probable that his son inherited his taste for extravagance from his sire—with, however, much development—just as he inherited so many talents from his mother. To Richard, also, seem to have been transmitted all the paternal arts and contrivances for fending off the pressure of debt.*

Sheridan, after the loss of his wife, came over to Dublin, arriving in October, 1766, and appearing at the theatre. He had resolved to acquit himself of all his obligations, and called a meeting of his creditors, which did not meet the approval of his old friend Sam Whyte, with whom he quarrelled. He made over his property at Quilca, and devoted it, so far as it went, to the discharge of his debts.

It is now time to return to his son Richard, whom we left at Harrow.

During the Sheridans' visit to Windsor they had

---

* In other directions we trace this lack of thrift. Mrs. Sheridan's only sister, Anne, was married to the Rev. T. Fish, Chaplain to the Blue Coat School, who, dying in 1760, 'left a young family totally unprovided for.'

made acquaintance with Dr. Sumner, who had taken a fancy to them ; and so intimate did the families become, that on his visits to town the Doctor always put up at their house. He was then head-master at Eton, but was presently transferred to Harrow School. This seems to have determined Mr. Sheridan to put his second son under Dr. Sumner's care, and accordingly in 1762, Richard, then eleven years old, was despatched to the school.* Charles, as the hope of the family, was reserved for Mr. Sheridan's own private instruction. Dr. Parr was then one of the under-masters, and from a letter of this enthusiastic and eccentric man, written to Moore, a good idea can be gathered of what the boy was like. He says of his pupil :

'He went through his lessons in Horace, and Virgil, and Homer well enough for a time. But, in the absence of the upper-master, Dr. Sumner, it once fell in my way to instruct the two upper forms, and upon calling up Dick Sheridan, I found him not only slovenly in construing, but unusually defective in his Greek grammar. Knowing him to be a clever fellow, I did not fail to probe and to tease him. I stated his case with great good-humour to the upper-master, who was one of the best-tempered men in the world ; and it was agreed between us that

* I have applied to the authorities of the school for exact dates of entry, etc., but am informed that no record remains of this period.

Richard should be called oftener and worked more
severely. The varlet was not suffered to stand up
in his place ; but was summoned to take his station
near the master's table, *where the voice of no prompter
could reach him ;* and in this defenceless condition
he was so harassed, that he at last gathered up some
grammatical rules and prepared himself for his lessons.
While this tormenting process was inflicted upon
him, I now and then upbraided him. But you will
take notice that he did not incur any corporal punishment for his idleness : *his industry was just sufficient
to protect him from disgrace.* All the while Sumner
and I saw in him vestiges of a superior intellect.
His eye, his countenance, his general manner, were
striking. His answers to any common question were
prompt and acute. We knew the esteem, and even
admiration, which, somehow or other, all his school-
fellows felt for him. He was mischievous enough,
but his pranks were accompanied by a sort of vivacity
and cheerfulness which delighted Sumner and myself.
I had *much talk with him about his apple-loft, for the
supply of which all the gardens in the neighbourhood
were taxed, and some of the lower boys were employed
to furnish it.* I threatened, but without asperity, to
trace the depredators, through his associates, up to
their leader. He with perfect good-humour set me
at defiance, and I never could bring the charge
home to him. All boys and all masters were pleased
with him. I often praised him as a lad of great

talents—often exhorted him to use them well ; but my exhortations were fruitless. He was removed from school too soon by his father. The father, you know, was a wrong-headed, whimsical man, and perhaps his scanty circumstances were one of the reasons which prevented him from sending Richard to the University. I ought to have told you that Richard, when a boy, was a great reader of English poetry ; but his exercises afforded no proof of his proficiency. In truth, he, as a boy, was quite careless about literary fame. He was well aware that we thought highly of him, and anxiously wished more to be done by him than he was disposed to do.

' I once or twice met his mother—she was quite celestial. One of Richard's sisters now and then visited Harrow, and well do I remember that, in the house where I lodged, she triumphantly repeated Dryden's "Ode upon St. Cecilia's Day," according to the instruction given to her by her father. Take a sample :

> ' " *None* but the brave,
> None but the *brave*,
> None *but* the brave deserves the fair."

' In the later periods of his life Richard did not cast behind him classical reading. He spoke copiously and powerfully about Cicero. He had read, and he had understood, the four orations of Demosthenes read and taught in our public schools. He was at home in Virgil and in Horace. I cannot

5—2

speak positively about Homer, but I am very sure
that he read the "Iliad" now and then ; *not* as a professed scholar would do, critically ; but with all the
strong sympathies of a poet reading a poet.* Richard
did not, and could not, forget what he once knew ;
but his path to knowledge was his own—his steps
were noiseless—his progress was scarcely felt by
himself—his movements were rapid but irregular.

'Let me assure you that Richard, when a boy,
was by no means vicious. The sources of his
infirmities were a scanty and precarious allowance
from the father.'

There are here, in the passages marked in italics,
some significant touches of character, to be found in
abundance in Sheridan's later life. Such as the
suspicions of being 'prompted' that attached to him,
when brought up for examination, and that of ' recruit-
ing his apple-store at the expense of others.'

His uncle Chamberlaine was deputed to look after
his wants as to money ; but as he was prudently
sparing in supplying him, the youth took his own
mode of rebuking this parsimony. Having on
Speech-day to deliver a Greek oration in the
character of a military chief, he ordered for himself
an English general's uniform, in which he spoke it,

---

* 'It was not one of the least of the triumphs of Sheridan's
talents,' adds Mr. Moore, 'to have been able to persuade so acute
a scholar as Dr. Parr, that the extent of his classical acquirements
was so great as is here represented.'

and which was duly charged to his uncle's account. At Harrow he made many friends, among whom were Sir W. Jones, Halhed, Grenville, and Horne. While here he is said to have furnished the first specimens of that ready wit for which he was famous later. A schoolfellow, the son of a doctor, having taunted him with his father's profession, Richard retorted, ' 'Tis true, my father lives by pleasing people; but yours lives by killing them.'

Here his father came to stay for a short time, waiting, something after the fashion of Mr. Micawber, till his creditors could be pacified.

On leaving Harrow, which Richard did when about seventeen years old, it was found impossible to send him to a university owing to the expense. Both sons, therefore, stayed with the father in a house in the King's Road, Chelsea. Their mother had just died, and their father, in sore pecuniary straits, had, as we have seen, gone over to Dublin upon a theatrical engagement. Here is Richard as he appeared in the eyes of a loving sister :

' He was handsome, and generally allowed to be so. His cheeks had the glow of health, his eyes— the finest in the world—the brilliancy of genius, and were as soft as a tender and affectionate heart could render them. The same playful fancy, the same sterling and innoxious wit, that was shown after- wards in his writings, cheered and delighted the family circle. I admired—I almost adored him.'

Angelo gave the lads lessons in fencing. A Mr. Reed taught them Latin and mathematics. Richard, however, was already showing that he had literary taste, and with a friend, had made some translations from the classics, which both were eager to publish. The father carried out a sort of patriarchal system of education, reading prayers every morning and expounding a portion of Scripture, after which a selection from some sterling author was read aloud with just and due elocution, which he seemed to think the only safeguard for society. The son must have profited—even *malgré* himself —by these wholesome exercises. He often looked fondly back to those days.

After his marriage his sister recalled his coming to see his father on business. 'Ah!' said he, 'I could fancy myself back among old times, seated with Charles and my sisters at this table, and my father looking round upon us, and giving his favourite toast—" Healths, hearts, and homes!" '

It must be said there was always this vein of tender retrospect, if not romance, in his heart, and it is often found in the case of men of pleasure, who are generally affectionate and sentimental.

Richard thus early became engrossed with literary schemes, and plans of a sober kind, which prove that under strict judicious direction and discipline he might have been fashioned into a serious character with a purpose in life. He had laboured with his friend Halhed at a translation of Aristænatus, which was published in 1771, and passed through several editions; with the same coadjutor he was planning a weekly journal, which never came to anything. But he had shown that he inherited his father's taste for the stage, and with his friend had written a burlesque on a subject which a 'fellow of infinite jest,' Mr. Burnand, in our day, has treated with pleasant wit, viz., 'Ixion.' This was really the first *ébauche* of 'The Critic,' or rather a new version of 'The Rehearsal.'*

* The original manuscript is in the British Museum. A specimen may be quoted. Some of the touches are as spirited as anything in 'The Critic:'

'SIMILE. Sir, you are very ignorant on the subject,—it is the method most in vogue.

'O'CUL. What! to make the music first, and then make the sense to it afterwards?

'SIMILE. Just so.

'MONOP. What Mr. Simile says is very true, gentlemen; and there is nothing surprising in it, if we consider now the general method of writing *plays* to *scenes*.

'O'CUL. Writing *plays* to *scenes* !—Oh, you are joking.

*   *   *   *   *   *

'MONOP. Come, gentlemen, resume your seats.

'SIMILE. Now for it. Draw up the curtain, and (*looking at his book*) enter Sir Richard Ixion,—but stay!—zounds, Sir Richard ought to overhear Jupiter and his wife quarrelling! But, never mind,—these accidents have spoiled the division of my piece.— So enter, Sir Richard, and look as cunning as if you had overheard them. Now for it, gentlemen,—you can't be too attentive.

This play was sent to the Haymarket, to **Foote**. It is curious, during this century and a portion of the next, that anyone with a fair amount of merit might be certain to have his play read, and possibly

---

'MACD. But pray, Mr. Simile, how did Ixion get into heaven?

'SIMILE. Why, sir, what's that to anybody? — perhaps by Salmoneus's Brazen Bridge, or the Giant's Mountain, or the Tower of Babel, or on Theobald's bull-dogs, or—who the devil cares how?—he is there, and that's enough.

*　　*　　*　　*　　*　　*

'SIMILE. Zounds, where's the ordnance? Have you forgot the pistol? (*to the Orchestra.*)

'ORCHESTRA (*to someone behind the scenes*). Tom, are not you prepared?

'TOM (*from behind the scenes*). Yes, sir; but I flashed in the pan a little out of time, and had I stayed to prime, I should have shot a bar too late.

'SIMILE. Oh then, Jupiter, begin the song again. We must not lose our ordnance.

'SIMILE. Well, how do you think we go on?

'O'CUL. With vast spirit,—the plot begins to thicken.

'SIMILE. Thicken! aye,—'twill be as thick as the calf of your leg presently. What, ho, Amphitryon! Amphitryon! Why, where the devil is he?

'*Enter* SERVANT.

'MONOP. Tom, where is Amphitryon?

'SIMILE. Zounds, he's not arrested, too, is he?

'SERV. No, sir, but there was but *one black eye* in the house, and he is waiting to get it from Jupiter.

'SIMILE. To get a black eye from Jupiter,—oh, this will never do. Why, when they meet, they ought to match like two beef-eaters.'

received.* Sheridan, his father, could of course have secured this *entrée* for his son's production ; but the thing was sent unknown to him, as he would have been indignant at his son having to do with the stage. The authors were unsuccessful, and the piece was not received.

But now Mr. Thomas Sheridan, perhaps finding London too expensive, determined to remove to Bath. He was already acquainted with the place, having, in one of his elocutionary tours, visited that surpassing and handsome city of crescents, circuses and parades, bringing with him his accomplished wife.

Now settled at Bath, ' metal more attractive ' was to engross this promising and impulsive youth ; and a critical and romantic episode was to end in an adventure that made him a reputation, and the hero of the hour.

* The voluminous and amusing Garrick correspondence shows this in a curious way. Strangers send him their dramas, which are read, rejected, and often accepted. Then comes in the true art of the manager, now forgotten, viz., of rewriting the play for the theatre. The correspondence with Colman, while the 'Clandestine Marriage' was being written, is in this view truly instructive, every scene and character being twisted and re-twisted, altered with a view to the audience, the players, the critics. The play was thus written *in* the theatre.

CHAPTER V.

THERE were then a few centres which obtained a
sort of reputation for social attractions, of which
the most leading were Bath, York, and Lichfield.
The diversions of Bath were akin to those of
some great foreign watering-place. That handsome city, with its fine situation, keen, reviving
air, salutary waters, its truly architectural and
imposing streets, to say nothing of its dramatic
nursery for the London stage, was at the height of
its prosperity during the last thirty years of last
century. Even now, though somewhat shorn of its
old glories, it has made an astonishing rally and
revival. It has a surprising attraction for the
stranger, and as he surveys Pulteney Street, and the
'Parade,' and the Pump-room, and the handsome,
old-fashioned Baths, he thinks of Smollett and
'Evelina' Burney, and even of more recent times,
when Dickens visited it and the 'M. C.' still
flourished.

When Mr. Sheridan and his family arrived in the pleasant city, there was living there a very remarkable and gifted family, that of Dr. Linley, an accomplished musician and teacher.

The organist of Bath Abbey, Chilcot, about the year 1735, had noted a little boy who showed extraordinary musical taste, and had taken him as his pupil. This young fellow came from Wells— and was afterwards to be well known as Doctor of Music. So promising was his talent, that he went to London, and was placed under the care of one Paradise, a well-known musician. After completing his education, he returned to Bath to 'set up' as a teacher. Here he successfully established himself, became well known as a local personage, and set on foot a series of fashionable concerts at the Assembly Rooms, which were well supported by persons of distinction. Such was Dr. Linley.

Of him his friend, the genial Dr. Burney, wrote : ' He loved music, was a studious man, equally versed in theory and practice. Having a large family, he pointed his studies to singing, and became the best master of his day. He was a masterly performer on the harpsichord, and a good composer.'

The sons were a strangely mixed compound of extraordinary musical gifts and eccentricity. One, Thomas, was a prodigy of precocious talent, a composer and violinist at an early age ; indeed one of the most promising young men of his day, and the idol of his sisters. *

Michael Kelly was introduced to Mozart at Vienna, and at supper found himself seated next the eminent composer, who, he says, 'conversed with me a good deal about Thomas Linley, the first Mrs. Sheridan's brother, with whom he was intimate at Florence, and spoke of him with great affection. He said that Linley was a true genius; and he felt that had he lived, he would have been one of the greatest ornaments of the musical world.'

This was high praise from such a man. To this youth a brother musician, Cooke, has paid a generous tribute in a detailed account of his musical life.†

* When Thomas Linley was a very little boy, he was already a proficient on the violin. A gentleman who had been complimenting the elder Mr. Linley upon the dawning talents of his charming daughters, observing little Tom, asked him, 'Are you, too, musical, my little man?' 'Oh yes, sir,' replied Tom Linley, with *naïveté;* 'we are all geniuses!'

† MS., British Museum. The account runs: 'He seems to have been a perfect musical prodigy. Born at Bath in May, 1756, he early showed such signs of musical taste that he was put to study under his father, who was a strict disciplinarian. When he was only seven years old, his father took him to Dr. Boyce, the organist and composer to the King, who was so pleased with his precocity that he agreed to instruct him for five years. At the end of that time he had written six violin solos, dated 1768. He was sent to Italy, studied under Nardini, and returned in 1773, when a work of his was performed at the Worcester Festival. He was, moreover, an eminent violin-player.' It is generally supposed that

The other brothers were of a convivial type, and distinguished for their liveliness and oddity. These were the oddly-named Oziah, and William. One of the sisters, Maria, afterwards married to Sheridan's friend Tickell, sang exquisitely.

But the cynosure of the family, and its chief attraction, was the captivating Elizabeth Linley, a young creature universally admired and loved, and clearly of a pattern not very common—interesting, lively, and sympathetic, light and airy, and it might seem to some frivolous, yet with an undercurrent of earnestness and tender devotion, which, when the occasion was supplied, made her capable of serious efforts ; a mixture of the tragic with pleasant comedy. Such was this charming being, who attracted all she met. She was born at No. 5, Pierrepont Street, Bath, in the year 1754. Humphry, the painter, we

---

Mr. Linley, senior, wrote all the songs in "The Duenna ;" but it seems he was assisted by his clever son. He contributed "Tell me, my lute ;" "Could I each fault remember ;" "Friendship is the bond of reason ;" "My mistress expects me ;" and "Turn thee round, I pray thee."

'He was an industrious composer, and wrote several cantatas for Drury Lane, sonatas, etc. A glee for five voices, "Hark, the birds' melodious strain," he wrote at the desire of his sister, Mrs. Sheridan, who usually sang the upper part. He continued to increase in science, at once the delight and comfort of his parents, and beloved by a most numerous host of acquaintances, when at length, on a fatal day of August, 1778, he was unfortunately drowned by the upsetting of a pleasure-boat at the Duke of Ancaster's, aged only twenty-two years and three months.'

are told, coming to Bath, in 1762, took lodgings with Linley, 'whose lovely daughter, Elizabeth, was then in her ninth year. She knew all the songs in " Thomas and Sally," " The Beggar's Opera," " The Chaplet," and " Love in a Village ;" and these she would sing so sweetly, that many a day, at the young painter's solicitation, she chanted them seated at the foot of his easel, looking up to him, unconscious of her heavenly features : with such looks as prevailed upon the motley visitors of Bath when she so gracefully held up her little basket with her father's benefit-tickets, at the door, as they passed in and out of the Pump-room.'

Nothing, indeed, so exhibits the spell and charm of this fascinating creature as the almost rapturous terms in which various friends and acquaintances speak of her. A bishop, Dr. O'Beirne, of Meath, declared, with unepiscopal rapture, she was ' the link between an angel and a woman.' It was impossible to do justice to her exquisite nature. Dr. Burney's tongue seems to grow wanton in praise. She sang in public so early as twelve years old. When she was singing at the oratorio, in 1773, she attracted universal admiration—even the sober monarch's. Walpole tells us, ' Miss Linley's beauty is in the superlative degree. The King admires and ogles her as much as he dares to do in so holy a place as an oratorio.' And when speaking of the loss of her gifted brother, Tom Linley, Dr. Burney says :

' This amiable and promising youth was drowned at an early age, to the great affliction of his family, particularly his matchless sister, Mrs. Sheridan, whom this calamity rendered miserable for a long time, during which her affection and grief were distilled in verses of a most sweet and affecting kind on the sorrowful event. The beauty, talent, and mental endowments of this St. Cecilia Rediviva will be remembered to the last hour of all who heard or even saw and conversed with her. The tone of her voice and expression, manner of singing, were as enchanting as her countenance and conversation. In her singing, with a mellifluous-toned voice, a perfect shake and intonation, she was possessed of the double power of delighting an audience equally in pathetic strains and songs of brilliant execution, which is allowed to very few singers. When she had seen the Agujari, the Danzi, she astonished all hearers by performing the " Bravura " air, extending the natural compass of her voice above the highest note of the harpsichord before additional keys were in fashion.'

Mr. Dibdin, a professional judge, declared that ' those who have never heard Mrs. Sheridan can be no more able to conceive the force and effect of her merit than I can be capable of describing it. I can easily make it understood that, if she was possessed of every perfection, and free from every fault as a singer, she must have been superior to every other ;

but this is theory : the practical part of the argument cannot be felt but by those who were fortunate
enough to hear her, who, if they have any recollection, and will take the trouble to repeat Milton's
passage, uttered by Comus immediately after he has
heard the lady sing "Sweet Echo," they will find
their sensations were at that time delighted equal to
that description, for indeed "she took the prisoned
soul and lapped it in elysium."'

When Mr. Wilkes was in Bath, in 1772, lodging
in the South Parade, he passed an evening with
Mr. Brereton's family and the Miss Linleys. 'The
eldest,' wrote this strange being, 'I think still
superior to all the handsome things I have heard of
her. She does not seem in the least spoiled by any
of the idle talk of our sex, and is the most modest,
pleasingly delicate flower I have seen for a great
while. The youngest, a mere coquette—no sentiment.'

Such was the verdict of this cool, experienced
judge of the sex. Indeed, we have only to look
at Gainsborough's and Sir Joshua's paintings, both
evidently stimulated by love of their subject—to
gather an idea of what her spell was. It seemed
to work by an irrepressible sweetness joined with
a gentle and amiable *espièglerie* — a charming
combination which some have at times encountered in 'life's dull round.' All the members of
this gifted family, 'a nest of nightingales,' were

destined to have a sad career. The young Thomas
Linley, we have already seen, was drowned; his
sister Maria, Mrs. Tickell, it used to be long repeated, died at her harpsichord—the fact being
that she died in her bed of a fever. 'But a
little before her death,' we are told, 'she raised
herself up, and with unexpected and momentary
animation sang a part of the anthem, "I know that
my Redeemer liveth." The pathetic and almost
superhuman sweetness of the notes breathed by the
young and lovely creature who was just departing,
gave an appearance of inspiration to this last effort
of a voice that had delighted every ear. The
attending physician was greatly overcome by the
scene, and could only exclaim, " She is an angel !" as
he left the room.' Her brother Samuel, a promising young officer of the Navy, was cut off also by
a fever. Mrs. Linley, the mother, had to become
wardrobe-keeper to Drury Lane. The unhappy
father was left alone, all his children being snatched
from him within the space of a few years; and,
reduced to ruin by his son-in-law, sank into imbecility.

Dr. Burney thought Mrs. Tickell little inferior
to her sister in talents and beauty. In the
pleasantly situated Dulwich Gallery, one of the
most interesting we have, hang many portraits
of the Linley family. There is one in the first
room—a full-length of these two engaging sisters,

by Gainsborough, painted in his most limpid style
—which has a perfect fascination for the visitor.
Two more elegant figures could not be conceived.
One sister is standing, the other sitting, and their
faces, though they can hardly be called beautiful,
have a thoughtful grace, a tranquil sweetness that
is indescribable. It is sad to think that these
two charming women were married to dissipated,
careless husbands, who brought on them many an
hour of anxiety, suffering, and sorrow.

Mr. Garrick had found his way to Bath about the
year 1770, and attracted like the rest, had thought
Elizabeth Linley would be a great addition to his
theatre. But her father declined his proposals on
the odd ground that he himself was entitled to
the full benefit of her talents. He refused to avail
himself of a 'middle-man.' Colman was anxious
that she should come to him at the Haymarket, but
his proposals were declined in the following highly
candid letter (unpublished), which throws light on
the character of our musical doctor.

'I think,' he wrote, 'as she has acquired a reputation, I ought to have the advantage of her first
performing in London myself; and as the public
rooms in London are open to me on the same terms
as to all the performers, there is a great probability
that I may get more than the sum Mr. Jones offers,
by my attempting a concert on my own account.

Were I properly settled in London, I think I could conduct the business of oratorios regularly; therefore I do not relish giving the prime of my daughter's performance to support the schemes of others. Still,' adds this wary negotiator, 'as you are so earnest, I would take two hundred guineas and a clear benefit, with choice of oratorios. In regard to her engaging as an actress, I shall never do that, *unless it were to ensure to myself and family a solid settlement* by being admitted to purchase a share in the patent on reasonable terms, or something adequate to this; either of which I perceive no probability of obtaining; and I shall never lay myself at the mercy of my children, especially when their power of being of service to me depends so entirely upon chance.'

This rather mercenary strain in the professor's character was now to tempt him to yield his cherished daughter to an ancient but wealthy admirer, Mr. Walter Long, of Wiltshire.* This sacrifice excited much discussion in a place like Bath, and the poor girl herself, being disinclined to it, made an appeal to her elderly lover, to which, so went the story, he very handsomely responded, and released her. Nay, he took the whole odium

---

* This gentleman's fortune, of nearly a quarter of a million, descended to a celebrated heiress, who was carried off by Mr. Wellesley Pole, the ' Long Pole Wellesley Long.'

upon himself, and was served with an action for
breach of promise by the greedy father, who proceeded to London to prosecute it.   The good-
natured Long, however, satisfied him with a sum
of £3,000 (or £1,000), which became a very suitable portion for the young heroine.*   Such is the
pretty tale told by Moore, and repeated by many
others.   But the truth appears to be that this Mr.
Long was a well-known and notorious miser, who
had treated the young lady infamously—so badly
that Foote, who used to frequent Bath, seized on
the incident, and fashioned it into one of his highly
personal plays, in which the miser was duly
gibbeted.   Garrick, as a friend of the family,
furnished a prologue to the 'Maid of Bath,' and it
seems probable, from a comparison of dates, that
his kind offer to the family to bring her out on his
stage was prompted by sympathy for her case.
Foote read the piece to Garrick and Cumberland on
the eve of its production ; while Garrick, in his
prologue, speaks of the

> 'Monster who had it in his power
> A young and tender virgin to devour.'

As we now read the play, we are surprised at the
personality in which Foote could indulge ; for here

---

* Sir N. Wraxall reports that the father claimed compensation for his child's engagements broken, or given up ; 'and,'
he adds, 'it was regularly submitted to arbitration, when £1,000
was given to *him* as compensation.'

we find 'Miss Linnet, the Maid of Bath' (Miss
Linley's pet name) ; Mrs. Linnet, her mother;
Flint, the miser, played with gusto by Foote himself ; the well-known 'Bear Inn,' with all sorts of
local allusions ; while Major Racket may have stood
for Captain Mathews. The Major asks after his
'little flame—la petite Rossignol—the lovely little
Linnet,' and is told that she is going to be buried
alive, to be married to that 'old fusty, shabby,
shuffling, money-loving, water-drinking, mirth-
marring, amorous old hunks.' Mrs. Linnet is represented as pressing her daughter to marry. She is
convinced there is some little low paltry passion that
lurks in her heart. 'Ten thousand a year! There's
not a lady in town would refuse him.' 'Not his
fortune,' says Miss Linnet. 'Well,' answers her
mother, 'who nowadays marries anything else?
Would you refuse an estate because it happens to be
a little encumbered ? You must consider the man
in this case a kind of mortgage.' (A passage which
Sheridan later stole for his 'Rivals,'—'You must
take the estate with the live-stock ;' while in the
'School for Scandal,' Lady Teazle makes nearly the
same point as to the disproportion of age.) Then
her mother reminds her that she has only a baby
face, and 'can bawl a few ballads,' and she was
bound, moreover, to support her family ; all which
agrees curiously with the characters of the Linleys,
Mrs. Linley being notorious for her miserly ways.

Flint then makes her a present of 'a small paper of tea' which he had in his pocket, and is exhibited in a most degrading light. The play further represents him as being alarmed by his friends as to the costly responsibilities of the step he was about to take, and he determines to 'get out' of the business, which he does by making some shameful proposals. He is threatened by the family with an action at law.

Mr. Forster says that it was this scathing attack that enforced from the unwilling Long the damages in question. The legend of the romantic elderly admirer so generously withdrawing and presenting his flame with a fortune, is therefore completely dissipated, and, it is to be hoped, will be no longer circulated.

Among the intimates of the music-master's family was Mr. Richard Tickell. This gentleman was the grandson of Thomas Tickell, Addison's friend, and resembled his ancestor in many points. He was a pleasant humourist, an agreeable writer, a jovial companion, and later held a public office. He belonged to an Irish family, and within living memory there was a gentleman of the family also well known in the sister country for his humour and pleasantry.

Richard Tickell, who lived at Beaulieu House, on Newbridge Hill, became an admirer of Miss Polly Linley, and later, her husband. He attained an

odd sort of notoriety for the invention of a patent
medicine, which he called ' *Ethereal anodyne spirit*,'
and which the eccentric Thicknesse used to puff
diligently in his books.* One of Tickell's daughters
became the mother of the well-known John Arthur
Roebuck.   And thus, as in Sheridan's case, we
have another illustration of cleverness transmitted
through several generations of a family.

With the ' Siren,' as Elizabeth Linley was called,
the two Sheridan brothers fell desperately in love,
as did their friend Halhed.   But they had a dangerous rival in a Captain Mathews, one of the visitors
at Bath, who seems to have been a practised
Lothario.   He was married, yet playing the bachelor
at a watering-place, as one of the brothers Linley
assured Moore some thirty or forty years later,
when the captain was still living, and residing at
Bath, a place that must have had disagreeable
associations for him.   None of Miss Linley's family
then suspected this disability, and no doubt they
thought Mathews a desirable suitor for the music-
master's daughter.

' Presuming,' says Mr. Moore severely, ' upon the
innocent familiarity which her youth and his own
station permitted between them, he had for some time

---

* I take these and some other particulars relating to Bath, from
some pleasant volumes written by Mr. Peach of that city—' Historic
Houses of Bath '—which invest that interesting and handsome city
with a new charm.

not only rendered her remarkable by his indiscreet
attentions in public, but had even persecuted her in
private with those unlawful addresses and proposals
which a timid female will sometimes rather endure
than encounter that share of the shame which may
be reflected upon herself by their disclosure. To
the threat of self-destruction, often tried with effect
in these cases, he is said to have added the still
more unmanly menace of ruining her reputation, if
he could not undermine her virtue.'

This was after the pattern of the fashionable rake
in the comedies. But the young heroine soon
showed her preference, to the despair of two of
her other admirers, Charles Sheridan and young
Halhed. The former was in such a state that, we
are told, ' he withdrew to a farmhouse,' some miles
from Bath, and did not further interfere. Halhed,
utterly hopeless, also resigned further attempts, in
these farewell lines :

> ' I yield you—what I cannot cease to love.
> Be thine the blissful lot, the nymph be thine :
> I yield my love,—sure, friendship may be mine.
> Yet must no thought of me torment thy breast ;
> Forget me, if my griefs disturb thy rest,
> Whilst still I'll pray that thou may'st never know
> The pangs of baffled love, or feel my woe.
> But sure to thee, dear, charming—fatal maid !
> (For me thou'st charm'd, *and me thou hast betray'd*),
> Forget the lover thou, as he the friend.'

This seems to hint that the lady was a coquette,
and that 'the friend' had not been strictly loyal.

All this was enough to make a heroine of the young songstress, who was more pursued than ever, turning the heads of the young men at Oxford before whom she sang, fascinating a public singer Norris, and Mr. Watts, a young gentleman of fortune.

But young Richard Sheridan had recommended himself the most, and by many devices had gained her heart. To him, as Mr. Moore has told us, she at length confided her distresses, and he, having consulted with his sister, and for the first time disclosed to her the state of his heart with respect to Miss Linley, lost no time in expostulating with Mathews upon the cruelty, libertinism, and fruitlessness of his pursuit.

Through this adventure, what strikes us is the rather crafty behaviour of the youngest lover; his brother Charles, his friend Halhed, and Mathews evidently thinking they had nothing to fear from him. Mathews he seems to have quite imposed on, and persuaded that he was his friend; all which is rather like the later Brinsley. The young Richard, while thus beguiling his friends, was prosecuting his suit with ardour, meeting his innamorata in a grotto 'in a retired part of Sidney Gardens.' He here once rather offended her by some 'grave' remonstrances on her encouragement of the captain, and later left on the seat of the grotto some extenuating lines :

'Uncouth is this moss-cover'd grotto of stone,
    And damp is the shade of this dew-dripping tree;
Yet I this rude grotto with rapture will own,
    And willow, thy damps are refreshing to me.

'For this is the grotto where Delia reclin'd,
    As late I in secret her confidence sought;
And this is the tree kept her safe from the wind,
    As blushing she heard the grave lesson I taught.

'Then tell me, thou grotto of moss-cover'd stone,
    And tell me, thou willow, with leaves dripping dew,
Did Delia seem vex'd when Horatio was gone?
    And did she confess her resentment to you?

'Methinks now, each bough, as you're waving it, tries
    To whisper a cause for the sorrow I feel:
To hint how she frown'd when I dar'd to advise;
    And sigh'd when she saw that I did it with zeal.

'True, true, silly leaves, so she did, I allow;
    She frown'd, but no rage in her looks did I see:
She frown'd, but reflection had clouded her brow:
    She sigh'd, but perhaps 'twas in pity for me.

'Then wave thy leaves brisker, thou willow of woe;
    I tell thee no rage in her looks could I see;
I cannot, I will not, believe it was so—
    She was not, she could not, be angry with me.

'For well did she know that my heart meant no wrong;
    It sunk at the thought but of giving her pain;
But trusted its task to a faltering tongue,
    Which err'd from the feelings it could not explain.'

The gossips of Bath were presently to be fluttered
by an episode of a highly sensational character,
and which attached a flavour of romance to the
story of the young man and his innamorata. This
was the well-known elopement to France—an epi-

sode treated by Mr. Moore in a highly poetical
fashion. He seems unconscious of many inconsistencies in his account. To escape from Mathews's
persecution, he tells us, Miss Linley resolved to fly,
and take refuge for ever in a French convent. So,
early in 1772, Mr. Sheridan, in concert with his
sisters, helped in planning the escape, persuading
them that he merely wished to act as travelling
companion, and receiving from Miss Linley a sum of
money for expenses. This was a highly original if
unromantic mode of contriving an elopement, and
shows thus early Sheridan's art in finding pecuniary
resources for what he had planned.

'On the evening appointed for their departure,'
says Mr. Moore, 'while Mr. Linley, his eldest son,
and Miss Maria Linley were engaged at a concert,
from which the young Cecilia herself had been, on
a plea of illness, excused, she was conveyed by
Sheridan in a sedan-chair from her father's house in
the Crescent to a post-chaise which waited for them
on the London Road, and in which she found a
woman whom her lover had hired, as a sort of
protecting Minerva, to accompany them in their
flight.'*

---

* We find it got into the papers at once. *London Chronicle* for
March 24, 1772 : ' Bath, March 23.—Wednesday, the eldest Miss
Linley, of this city, justly celebrated for her musical abilities, set
off with Mr. Sheridan, junior, on a matrimonial expedition to
Scotland.'

'When they reached London, with an adroitness *which was, at least, very dramatic,* he introduced her to an old friend of his family (Mr. Ewart, a respectable brandy merchant in the City), as a rich heiress who had consented to elope with him to the Continent; in consequence of which the old gentleman, with many commendations of his wisdom for having given up the imprudent pursuit of Miss Linley, not only accommodated the fugitives with a passage on board a ship which he had ready to sail from the port of London to Dunkirk, but gave them letters of recommendation to his correspondents.'*

This deception at starting, again, is a little out of keeping with the generous carelessness of a lover engaged in so romantic an expedition. It would

---

* When Lamb, as a child, was taken to his 'first play,' the orders were a present from 'F.,' his godfather, who 'kept the oil-shop, now Davies's, at the corner of Featherston Buildings in Holborn.' 'F. was a tall, grave person, lofty in speech, and had pretensions above his reach. He associated in those days with John Palmer, the comedian, whose gait and bearing he seemed to copy. It was to his house, in Holborn, that young Brinsley brought his first wife on her elopement with him from a boarding-school at Bath. My parents were present (over a quadrille-table) when he arrived in the evening with his harmonious charge.' This seems like one of Elia's pleasant mystifications, but he was enwrapping the truth in a quaint disguise of invented names, etc., as in the case of 'Barbara S.' Mr. Ewart was not a shopkeeper, but there can be little doubt that the scene in question occurred, for Lamb was acquainted with the Sheridans.

appear, also, that Sheridan obtained money from this friendly old gentleman.

The fugitives met with many adventures in their flight. They had hired a vessel, but were driven by stress of weather into Margate ; and the lady being ill they went ashore, the captain, whose name was Curley, engaging to wait till next morning. But they found he had sailed without them. The mercurial Sheridan, however, consoled himself by writing on the window-pane of an inn some lines, miscalled an epigram :

> ' The sea was once the Halcyon's nest ;
> The winds, the zephyrs playing round its breast ;
> Oh, why then now so faithless and unruly ?
> Alas, 'tis plain they're intimates of Curley.'*

---

* Mr. Moore, when relating his difficulties in extracting information from the rambling Tom Linley, would describe one scene connected with the elopement. The story found its way to the ' Steaks,' and is reported by Mr. Marsh, a member :

' " Now, then, let me have the epigram !" exclaimed the biographer, taking out his note-book. " I'll give it you presently, Mr. Moore ; but I must first mention the circumstance in which it originated, that you may enter completely into its spirit. Why, you must know, Mr. Moore, that Mr. Sheridan, just after his marriage, was determined to take a trip to the Continent with his wife, my sister. For this purpose, they took a small vessel at Harwich, which was bound to Rotterdam. It was the *Minerva*, Captain Brown—stop, stop ! it was the *Venus*, Captain Thompson—or, I think, it was the *Eliza*, Captain——" " It does not matter, Mr. Linley, what the ship was, or who commanded her. Pray, let's have the epigram." " You shall have it presently, Mr. Moore ; but I have not yet come to it. Well, sir, this Captain Brown of the *Minerva*, or Captain

On arriving in France, the popular version goes on, Mr. Sheridan represented to his companion, as delicately as he could, that her position was compromised, and that it could only be 'regulated' by a marriage. Miss Linley consented, and at a village not far from Calais they were married, about the end of March, 1772, 'by a clergyman well known for his services on such occasions.' They then proceeded to Lille, where he placed the lady in a convent. Sheridan used to relate to Mr. Rogers and others a humorous scene at the Lille theatre, where two French officers kept staring insolently at his beautiful companion. Sheridan, not knowing a word of French, was reduced to putting his arms akimbo and darting back looks of blustering defiance.

In the convent she remained till her father arrived, when, 'after a few words of private explanation

---

Thompson of the *Venus*, was a surly, ill-behaved fellow ; and used Mr. Sheridan and my sister very shamefully. They were detained by contrary winds, and there was not a morsel to eat or drink on board. So, sir, Sheridan was determined that the fellow should suffer for it ; so he wrote an epigram upon him, which is the severest thing I ever saw ; it did for him completely." "Ay," said Moore, who was beginning to be impatient; "now for the epigram." "To be sure," continued Linley ; " it was the happiest hit that ever was—it did not spare the fellow, I assure you." Here a pause ensued, during which the reciter was biting his lips in an apparent agony. "The epigram—the epigram, Mr. Moore—why—by G—, I have forgot the epigram !"'

from Sheridan, which had the effect of reconciling him to his daughter,' he naturally 'insisted on her returning with him immediately to England, in order to fulfil some engagements which he had entered into on her account ; and, a promise being given that as soon as these engagements were accomplished she should be allowed to resume her plan of retire-ment at Lille, the whole party set off amicably together for England. Sheridan returned to Bath, and settled down to his old pursuits.'

We find this story comfortably accepted, while her reputation was apparently not in the least affected by the compromising escapade.

Now the whole of the account seems incoherent, and in parts even incredible. Mr. Moore received the chief incidents and glosses from the surviving brother and sister of the heroine, over *forty years* after the transaction, when their affection was likely to impart as favourable and romantic a turn to it as possible, in view of publication. Some unfrocked priest might have been found to go through some sort of ceremony, probably some refugee parson at Calais. But Dr. Watkins heard that Sheridan failed in securing even this aid, and hence took her to the convent. It is clear she was a heroine, and sat for Lydia Languish. She was attended by a faithful abigail, and the whole was no doubt conducted with the maximum of romance and propriety. The father, glad to recover her, accepted her romantic tale, which the lover was to support at the point of the sword.*

Sheridan, however, took care to leave behind him letters which were shown about Bath, attributing the flight entirely to the lady's desire to escape the persecution of Mathews. As that gentleman put it, he 'attempted, in a letter left behind him for that purpose, to account for his scandalous method of running away from this place by insinuations derogatory to my character and that of a young lady, innocent as far as related to me or to my knowledge.' Yet having left this communication behind him, it is strange to find that he wrote from abroad to Mathews, 'which,' he says, 'I think was necessary and right;' adding, 'I hope he has acted the one proper part which was left to him to act.'

In his behaviour to his brother, there is also want of candour. Moore declares, though Charles had '*withdrawn to the farmhouse*,' that he was totally ignorant of his brother's attachment! In a guarded

---

* There appeared in the *Gentleman's Magazine* a long and detailed letter, supposed to be written to a friend by Miss Linley, and giving an account of all her adventures on this trip. Anyone who reads this carefully will see that it is one of those fictions which magazine-writers like Coombe were fond of concocting. Mr. Moore rightly rejects it—though the *Quarterly* accepted it—but Mrs. Oliphant in her late account of Sheridan has been taken in by this spurious narrative. It is altogether worthless, on the face of it.

letter which Richard wrote to him, we see a consciousness that he had not behaved candidly :

' All is well, I hope ; and I hope, too, that though you may have been ignorant for some time of our proceedings, *you* never could have been uneasy lest anything should tempt me to depart, even in a thought, from the honour and consistency which engaged me at first.'

This might mean that the brothers had entered into some understanding to take no advantage of each other in relation to their charmer. He also imposes on him the fiction that the sole object of the expedition had been to see her safely landed in the convent and to avoid Mathews. ' You will soon see me in England. Everything on our side has at last succeeded. Miss Linley is now fixed in a convent, where she has been entered some time. This has been a much more difficult point than you could have imagined, and we have, I find, been extremely fortunate. She has been ill, but is now recovered ; this, too, has delayed me.'* Yet we are told he had gone through a ceremony of marriage ! No wonder Charles felt that he had been duped, and in his meetings with Mathews, who was vowing vengeance, joined him in loud complaints of the behaviour of his brother.

* This placing the lady in a convent shows that no marriage had then taken place. This seemed the most proper course for the pair to take.

After they had been nearly five weeks away, Mathews inserted an advertisement in the *Bath Chronicle*, 'posting' Mr. Sheridan as 'a liar and a treacherous scoundrel;' on hearing of which proceeding Sheridan immediately set out for home, vowing that 'he *would never sleep in England*' till he had obtained satisfaction from Mathews, and actually *sitting up all night* on arriving at Canterbury to avoid breaking his vow. In the same spirit of absurdity, on reaching London at nine o'clock at night, he found out Mathews at his lodgings in Crutched Friars; after 'storming' which for some hours, he succeeded in gaining entrance at two o'clock in the morning. Mathews, according to Sheridan's story, behaved with timidity: 'Mr. M. had been previously down to the door, and told Mr. S. he should be admitted, and had retired to bed again. He dressed, complained of the cold, endeavoured to get heat into him, called Mr. S. his *dear friend*, and forced him to—*sit down*.' With some humour, Mathews had begged of Sheridan '*not to deprive himself of so much sleep.*' He added that he 'never meant to quarrel with him. He convinced him that his enmity ought to be directed solely against his brother and another gentleman at Bath.'

On this the pair parted harmoniously, it being agreed that amicable advertisements should be put in the Bath papers. Mr. Sheridan next hurried down to Bath to settle accounts with his brother.

The latter, however, denied all the charges that were made against him (whatever they were); though, as we have seen, he had been loud in Richard's condemnation, and so heated was the debate and recrimination between them that the ladies of the family feared that a fratricidal duel would take place. The heroine was thrown into hysterics and fainting-fits. The famous Dr. Priestley, then lodging in the house, happened to witness the scene. It ended by the brothers, instead of fighting each other, resolving to fight Mathews.*

* In illustration of what has been said, that the Brinsley of twenty was the same Brinsley of forty years later, the following story used to be related by Mr. Taylor, the journalist, who had it from Woodfall: 'A letter on this subject, containing severe reflections on Mr. Sheridan, appeared in the *Bath Chronicle*, or some other Bath journal. In consequence of this letter, Mr. Sheridan waited upon Mr. W. Woodfall, then the proprietor and conductor of the *Morning Chronicle*, of which he was the founder, and requested that Mr. Woodfall would copy the letter from the Bath paper into his own journal. Mr. Woodfall expressed his surprise that Mr. Sheridan should wish to give a wider circulation to so bitter an attack on him. "That is the very reason," said Mr. Sheridan, "for, as I can refute every part of that letter, I wish the attack and the answer to be spread over the kingdom, instead of being confined to a provincial paper." Mr. Sheridan added, that on the day after the letter appeared in the *Morning Chronicle* he would bring the refutation. Accordingly, the letter was published in the *Morning Chronicle*, but Mr. Sheridan, though applied to for the refutation, never wrote a syllable on the subject, and from mere negligence or contempt thus disseminated a calumny against himself. Mr. Woodfall said, that when people came to him with complaints against Mr. Sheridan for inattention, he used

Sheridan thereupon again posted up to town, and a challenge was sent to Mathews, who at once accepted it. They met in Hyde Park about six o'clock in the evening. Being interrupted, as seems natural, they adjourned to a tavern.* Sheridan says in a letter to a friend :

' Mr. Ewart took lights up in his hand, and almost immediately on our entering the room we engaged. I struck Mr. Mathews's point so much out of the line, that I stepped up and caught hold of his wrist, or the hilt of his sword, while the point of mine was at his breast. You ran in and caught hold of my arm, exclaiming, " *Don't kill him.*" I struggled to disengage my arm, and said his sword was in my power. Mr. Mathews called out twice or thrice, " *I beg my life.*" We were parted. You immediately said, " *There, he has begged his life, and now there is an end of it.*" Mathews then hinted that I was rather *obliged to your interposition* for the advantage ; you declared that " *before* you did so, both the swords were in Mr. Sheridan's power." Mr. Mathews still seemed resolved to give it another

to relate this anecdote to them, and ask how they could expect more attention from one who was so negligent in matters that so nearly affected his own reputation.'

* The scene of this strange encounter has been ascertained to be a house that stood at the west end of Henrietta Street, Covent Garden, at the corner of Bedford Street. Thirty years afterwards it was converted from a tavern into a china-shop.

turn, and observed that he *he had never quitted his sword.* Provoked at this, I then swore (with too much heat, perhaps) that he should either give up his sword and I would break it, or go to his guard again. He refused—but, on my persisting, either gave it into my hand, or flung it on the table, or the ground (*which*, I will not absolutely affirm). I broke it, and flung the hilt to the other end of the room. He exclaimed at this. I took a mourning sword from Mr. Ewart, and presenting him with mine, gave my honour that what had passed should never be mentioned by me, and he might now right himself again. He replied that he " *would never draw a sword against the man who had given him his life;*" but, on his still exclaiming against the indignity of breaking his sword (which he had brought upon himself), Mr. Ewart offered him the pistols, and some altercation passed between them. Mr. Mathews said that he *could never show his face if it were known how his sword was broke—that such a thing had never been done—that it cancelled all obligations*, etc. You seemed to think it was wrong, and we both proposed that if he never misrepresented the affair, it should not be mentioned by us. This was settled. After much altercation, and with much ill-grace, he gave the apology, which afterwards appeared. We parted, and I returned immediately to Bath. Mr. Mathews came down, and in two days I found the whole affair had been stated in a different light, and insinuations given out to the same purpose as in the paper, which has occasioned this trouble.'

Mathews's apology, however, was duly inserted in the Bath papers :

'Being convinced that the expressions I made use of to Mr. Sheridan's disadvantage were the effects of passion and misrepresentation, I retract what I have said to that gentleman's disadvantage, and particularly beg his pardon for my advertisement in the *Bath Chronicle.*—Thomas Mathews.'

This handsome *amende*, and the withdrawal of Mathews from the scene, ought to have set the matter at rest, and certainly Sheridan had nothing now to complain of. But it would seem that Sheridan still continued attacking Mathews for his behaviour, which was duly reported. Another account says that Mathews's friends now egged him on to try a fresh encounter, as he had been too submissive. The first seems the most probable, as Sheridan, having acted with some duplicity to Mathews, would be inclined to make him appear as odious as he could, which would moreover fortify the position of the young lady. The result was a *second* duel, which came off at Bath on July 4th. Sheridan was attended evidently by an Irish second —the model of Sir Lucius O'Trigger.

'Mr. Sheridan,' says Mathews's second, 'drew his

sword, and, in a vaunting manner, desired Mr.
Mathews to draw (their ground was very uneven,
and near the post-chaises). Mr. Mathews advanced
fast on Mr. Sheridan ; upon which he retreated, till
he very suddenly ran in upon Mr. Mathews, laying
himself exceedingly open, and endeavouring to get
hold of Mr. Mathews's sword. Mr. Mathews
received him on his point, and, I believe, disengaged his sword from Mr. Sheridan's body, and
gave him another wound.

'Mr. Mathews, I think, on finding his sword
broke, laid hold of Mr. Sheridan's sword-arm, and
tripped up his heels : they both fell ; Mr. Mathews
was uppermost, with the hilt of his sword in his
hand, having about six or seven inches of the blade
to it, with which I saw him give Mr. Sheridan, as I
imagined, a skin-wound or two in the neck—for it
could be no more, the remaining part of the sword
being broad and blunt ; he also beat him in the face
either with his fist or the hilt of his sword. Mr.
Sheridan's sword was bent, and he slipped his
hand up the small part of it, and gave Mr.
Mathews a slight wound in the left part of his
belly : I that instant turned again to Captain
Paumier, and proposed again our taking them up.
He in the same moment called out, "Oh ! he is
killed—he is killed !" I as quick as possible turned
again, and found Mr. Mathews had recovered the
point of his sword, that was before on the ground,

with which he had wounded Mr. Sheridan in the belly ; I saw him drawing the point out of the wound. By this time Mr. Sheridan's sword was broke, which he told us. Captain Paumier called out to him, " *My dear Sheridan, beg your life, and I will be yours for ever.*" I also desired him to ask his life : he replied, " No, by God, I won't!" I then told Captain Paumier it would not do to wait for those punctilios (or words to that effect), and desired he would assist me in taking them up. Mr. Mathews most readily acquiesced, first desiring me to see Mr. Sheridan was disarmed. I desired him to give me the tuck, which he readily did, as did Mr. Sheridan the broken part of his sword to Captain Paumier. Mr. Sheridan and Mr. Mathews both got up, the former was helped into one of the chaises, and drove off for Bath, and Mr. Mathews made the best of his way to London.'

It will be noticed that in this affair Sheridan seems to have conducted the conflict in a very disorderly fashion, quite unbecoming the honourable *duello*, in both instances rushing in on his enemy and with his hands dragging his sword from him. This seems a strange style of fighting, more after the fashion of ' Tiger ' Roche or ' Fighting Fitzgerald.' It was not surprising that charges of ' unfairness ' and other recriminations were bandied about, and a third duel was spoken of.

Sheridan, senior, had now arrived from Dublin,

warmly protesting he would take the information of the postboys and bring the matter to a trial. But though his son was seriously wounded he took up a haughty, injured bearing, and refused to forgive or even to see him. He forbade all intercourse with the Linley family, considering the music-master beneath the actor. The heroine was actually singing at Oxford when the news of the duel arrived; but it was carefully concealed from her, and a clergyman on the way back, 'taking her from her father's chaise into his, *employed the rest of the journey* in cautiously breaking to her the particulars of the alarming event. Notwithstanding this precaution, her feelings were so taken by surprise, that, in the distress of the moment, she let the secret of her heart escape, and passionately exclaimed, " My husband! my husband!"—demanding to see him, and insisting upon her right as his wife to be near him, and watch over him day and night.'*

The young man, who had received several wounds, but was not seriously injured, speedily recovered. He was sent away to some friends in Essex. He was even required by his father to take an oath that he never would marry Miss Linley, which promise he gave—Mr. Moore adds oddly, 'with the view, perhaps, of blinding his father's vigilance.'†

* This has been urged as proof of a ceremony; but it surely does not go that length.

† At this time he had made acquaintance at Bath with Mr.

Read by this light, the scenes between Sir Anthony and his son show how they have been drawn from life; and it will be remembered that Sir Anthony tries to extract such a promise from the Captain.

Charles Sheridan, more fortunate than his brother, though without his brilliant qualities, had now obtained the office of Secretary to the Embassy in Sweden, and was setting off. There is a characteristic touch in one of his letters at this time :

'I am exceedingly unhappy,' wrote Charles to Richard, 'at the situation I leave you in with respect to money matters, the more so as it is totally out of my power to be of any use to you. *Ewart was greatly vexed at the manner of your drawing for the last £20*—I own, I think with some reason. As to old Ewart, what you were talking about is absolutely impossible ; he is already surprised at Mr. Linley's long delay, and, indeed, I think the latter much to blame in this respect. I must therefore conclude with wishing you speedily restored to health, and that if I could make your purse as whole as that will shortly be, I hope, it would make me exceedingly happy.'

The allusion to 'old Ewart' seems to point to

Thomas Greville, who with his elder brother had come to receive instruction, and afterwards set off to Dublin. With this gentleman he maintained an intimate correspondence, which his biographer was eager to obtain ; but Mr. Greville was obstinate in his refusal to allow its publication.

the expenses incurred for Miss Linley. That young
lady was now to appear at the Lent oratorios in
Covent Garden, and was 'vastly followed,' which
excited the jealousy of her lover, and led to quarrels.
It seems that she was *volage* enough. We are told
of another incident in the Lydia Languish vein—
namely, that he often disguised himself as a hackney
coachman, and drove her home from the theatre.
This kept alive the feeling of romance in his heroine,
and shows how skilful was the young suitor in the
management of the female heart.

At last, however, the aspirations of the lovers
were to be no longer resisted, and, as is invariable in
such cases, all opposition gave way. On April 13th,
1773, they were married, with the consent of Dr.
Linley. But Sheridan's father, to whom he had
given so solemn an engagement, refused all consent
or forgiveness. The young couple repaired to a
small cottage at East Burnham, living on a portion
of Mr. Long's money, and were full of love and
devotion. Sheridan wrote verses to his wife, of
which the following are a specimen :

> 'Teach me, kind Hymen, teach—for thou
> Must be my only tutor now—
> Teach me some innocent employ,
> That shall the hateful thought destroy,
> That I this whole long night must pass
> In exile from my love's embrace.'

They found their way to London, and there
speedily made friends, having introductions to

Storace and others; and at last were finally
established in Orchard Street, Portman Square.
Dr. Linley furnished the house for them. His son-
in-law had been offered the post of director of the
oratorios, but declined it. 'At this early stage some
suspicion of the stability of the husband's affection
seems to have occurred to the young wife; and we
find him reassuring her in lines addressed to "Delia"
—the name by which Sir Lucius addressed *his*
flame :

> ' "Ask'st thou 'how long my love shall stay,
>   When all that's new is past?'
> How long?—Ah, Delia, can I say
>   How long my life will last?
> Dry be that tear—be hush'd that sigh;
> At least I'll love thee till I die!"'

Sheridan now entered as a student at the
Temple (on April 6th, 1773), but was not likely to
be very successful at the bar, or to show much application. There was, indeed, another resource for
the young pair—Mrs. Sheridan's lovely and much-
admired voice, which would have brought them a
competence. But they were fixed that she should
no longer sing in public. Her husband has obtained
much credit for this act, principally on the strength of
Dr. Johnson's praise. 'We talked,' says Boswell,
'of a young gentleman's marriage with an eminent
singer, and his determination that she should no
longer sing in public, though his father was very

earnest she should, because her talents would be
liberally rewarded. It was questioned whether the
young gentleman, who had not a shilling in the
world, but was blest with very uncommon talents,
was not foolishly delicate or foolishly proud, and his
father truly rational without being mean. Johnson,
with all the high spirit of a Roman senator, exclaimed, " He resolved wisely and nobly, to be sure.
He is a brave man. Would not a gentleman be
disgraced by having his wife singing publicly for
hire ? No, sir, there can be no doubt here." '

This was creditable to Sheridan, and shows that at
that early period he had high-souled instincts, not
to be extinguished for many years by extravagance
and pecuniary difficulties.

Boswell has confounded the two fathers ; for, as
we have seen, Mr. Sheridan was not on terms with
his son. But it will be remembered that this dis-
taste to singing in public was all the young lady's,
though approved and encouraged by Sheridan. He
was an actor's son, and was now writing for the
stage, and was presently to be a manager—things
not very remote, after all, from ' appearing in public.'
Mrs. Sheridan, on the contrary, was a romantic,
elegant creature, on whose nature this sort of
exhibition jarred. Her father had made some engagements for her in advance, notably at Oxford
and at Worcester ; but even these were not to be
kept, in spite of his remonstrances, which Sheridan

disposes of in a fashion that reads rather pedantic-
ally. ' "It would prove," he said, "of fatal consequence to our meeting. I hope Mr. Sheridan
will think his honour in some degree concerned in
fulfilling it." Mr. Storace, in order to enforce Mr.
Isaac's argument, showed me his letter on the same
subject to him, which begins with saying, "We must
have Mrs. Sheridan, somehow or other, if possible!"
This I conceive to be the very worst mode of application that could have been taken; as there really
is not common-sense in the idea that my *honour* can
be concerned in my wife's fulfilling an engagement
which it is impossible she should ever have made.
Nor (as I wrote to Mr. Isaac) can you, who gave
the promise, whatever it was, be in the least charged
with the breach of it, as your daughter's marriage
was an event which must always have been looked
to by them as quite as natural a period to your right
over her as her death. As to the *imprudence* of
declining this engagement, I do not think, even
were we to suppose that my wife should ever on
any occasion appear again in public, there would be
the least at present. For instance, I have had a
gentleman with me from Oxford (where they do not
claim the least *right* as from an engagement), who
has endeavoured to place the idea of my complimenting the University with Betsey's performance in the
strongest light of advantage to me. This he said,
on my declining to let her perform on any agree-

ment. He likewise informed me, that he had just left Lord North (the Chancellor), who, he assured me, would look upon it as the highest compliment, and had expressed himself so to him.'

All this time his father's displeasure was weighing on him, and he speaks in rather a touching way of his anger against him : ' There is but one thing that has the least weight upon me. But time, while it strengthens the other blessings we possess, will, I hope, add that to the number You will know I speak with regard to my father. Betsey informs me you have written to him again. Have you heard from him ?' All which is 'natural, simple, and affecting' enough.

'Sheridan,' said old Lady Cork to Moore, ' was then an ugly, awkward-looking man.' The Duchess of Devonshire was anxious to have Mrs. Sheridan to sing at her house, but did not like to have him—a " player," as she called him.' She was re-minded of this some time after by Lady Cork on her keeping a house two months unoccupied, which she had taken at great expense at Bath, and alleging for her reason that she and her party were detained from day to day at Chatsworth by the agreeableness of Sheridan's conversation. *

* The beautiful but ill-fated Duchess became involved in debts to money-lenders, which she concealed from her husband. We find she engaged Sheridan to interpose as to her note for £400, which had passed into the hands of others. One Cocker was going to law with her to recover £200 which he had paid on her account. — MS., British Museum.

Thus already had they set out on that course of pleasure which was by-and-by to prove so fatal to them. There were parties in Orchard Street, and a music-room or studio, built out at the back, furnished 'occasion fair' in giving agreeable parties when the sisters sang together.

The attractive Mrs. Sheridan drew the sympathies and admiration of many, among others of Sir Joshua Reynolds, whose portrait of her as St. Cecilia, before referred to, was exhibited at the Academy of 1775. 'Most simple and beautiful,' was Mr. Walpole's criticism—faint praise, however, for what was one of the master's finest works.* The sittings brought about a great intimacy, and we find from Sir Joshua's note-books that he often dined with the young pair. He did not paint Sheridan's likeness till the year 1789, then giving the 'counterfeit presentment' which fixes the popular idea of his features. Thus serious is the responsibility of a painter. 'Praise,' said Walpole again, 'cannot over-state the merit of this portrait. It is not canvas and colour; it is nature. All is the unaffected manner and character of the admired original.'

* This devotional picture of Mrs. Sheridan was to have its little history. It remained with Reynolds for over fifteen years, when Sheridan conceived a wish to possess it, and asked Reynolds to dispose of it to him. The cordial answer he received was characteristic of that charming, graceful nature :

'DEAR SIR,—I have, according to your orders, bespoke a very rich frame to be made for Mrs. Sheridan's picture. You will

At this happy time, when they were starting on their married life in London, full of life and promise, we see in the newspapers many evidences of the interest taken by the public in the young pair. Thus, in the *Morning Post* of February, 1771 : ' Sheridan has taken a house in Orchard Street, Oxford Street, where he purposes, if his wife recovers, to give concerts twice a week to the nobility. Mrs. Sheridan has refused 1,200 guineas

easily believe I have often been solicited to part with that picture, and to put a price on it ; but to these solicitations I have always turned my deafest ear, knowing that you would not give your consent, and without it I certainly never should part with it. I really. value that picture at five hundred guineas. In the common course of business (exclusive of its being Mrs. Sheridan's picture), the price of a whole length with the children would be three hundred. If, therefore, for the consideration of your exclusive right to the picture I charge one hundred and fifty guineas, I hope you will think me a reasonable man. It is with great regret that I part with the best picture I ever painted.'

This was true. It was certainly one of the most interesting and sympathetic of his greater works, matching with ' The Tragic Muse.' He was always thus inspired by women of genius, and added in return this tone of sympathy to his work. The picture passed to Sheridan ; and once, in the thick of his embarrassments, he seems to have raised money on it. He then lent it to be exhibited, whence, with other pictures, it was seized by Burgess, his attorney, who ' had a lien on it.' Sheridan was much distressed at this, and longed to have it back, and with this view *borrowed* £100 from Linley to release it (Mr. Moore hints there was something awkward in this transaction), but it seems to have fallen again into Burgess's hands. After many vicissitudes, the picture has found a home at Bowood, Lord Lansdowne's seat.

for twelve nights at the Pantheon, 1,000 guineas for the oratorios, and 1,000 guineas for Giardini's concerts.' In 1783 it was rumoured that Mrs. Sheridan, Mrs. Tickell, and Miss Linley were 'expected to be honoured with the Queen's desire to sing at the private concerts at Buckingham House'—and they accordingly performed there.

In 1779, the early flush of her husband's triumphs, we find a glimpse of her for a moment, just as she appeared to the volatile Fanny Burney.

'Mr. and the Misses Cholmondeley and Miss Forrest were with her!' she cries out; 'but who else, think you?—why, Mrs. Sheridan! I was absolutely charmed at the sight of her. I think her quite as beautiful as ever, and even more capti-vating; for she has now a look of ease and happiness that animates her whole face. Miss Linley was with her; she is very handsome, but nothing near her sister : the elegance of Mrs. Sheridan's beauty is unequalled by any I ever saw, except Mrs. Crewe. I was pleased with her in all respects. She is much more lively and agreeable than I had any idea of finding her; she was very gay, and very unaffected, and totally free from airs of any kind. Miss Linley was very much out of spirits; she did not speak three words the whole evening, and looked wholly unmoved at all that passed. Indeed, she appeared to be heavy and inanimate.'*

° 'Diary and Letters of Madame D'Arblay,' vol. i., pp. 167-8.

When there was a question of appointing a
director or manager for the oratorios, a Mr. Stanley
came to Sheridan, saying he was desired by the
King to offer him the control. As the young man
had no voice nor knowledge of music, it would
have been odd to find him in such an office. No
doubt it was offered to him as a bait to secure
Mrs. Sheridan. He, however, proposed his father-
in-law, who, he said, had 'twenty Mrs. Sheridans
more' at home.*

* Now was read in the newspapers on March 17, 1775 this
announcement : ' Mrs. Sheridan was delivered of a son, yesterday.'
This was the account of the arrival of the well-known 'Tom'
Sheridan.

CHAPTER VI.

'THE RIVALS,'—1775.

BUT all this time Sheridan had a store of brilliant resources that none of his friends credited him with, or even suspected. Who could have believed that this gay and rather frivolous youth was lightly and carelessly putting together a comedy which was destined for over a hundred years 'to keep the stage,' as it is called—a high exceptional honour which, out of the thousands of excellent British plays, has been attained by not half a dozen pieces.* He was now busy with 'The Rivals,' written, we are assured, within six weeks or two months, and reflecting the spirit and vivacity which such eagerness or haste might supply.

Mr. Harris, who was then manager of Covent

* The select list of plays which have attained the greatest popularity may be held to include 'Hamlet,' 'The Lady of Lyons,' 'She Stoops to Conquer,' 'The Hunchback,' 'Money,' 'The Rivals,' and 'The School for Scandal.' Of course, half a dozen more could be added, such as 'Macbeth,' 'As You Like It,' perhaps 'The Road to Ruin,' and 'The Man of the World.' These are mere revivals ; the first-named are always being acted.

Garden Theatre, asked him to write a piece, and was delighted with it when complete, guaranteeing its perfect success, assuring the author that 'the least shilling he would get would be six hundred pounds.' He selected as the subject of his drama Bath incidents and characters, and his own recent adventures. These, of course, would be scarcely familiar to the London public. But most writers will admit that such personal experience supplies a spirit and vividness of treatment, with an air of reality. The result has been a distinct gain, and his ardour prompted him to complete the whole in a few weeks.

Later, when he had to seek a subject, it became a matter of labour and tedious years. Mr. Sheridan's sister, writing from Bath, says she was told it was his own story, and therefore called 'The Rivals.' 'But,' she adds, 'I do not give any credit to this intelligence.' Such a rumour might well astonish Bath folks. In the piece, as we have said, are to be found the incidents of the recent escapade— the romantic Lydia, the 'Maid of Bath ;' the elope- ment, planned, though not carried out ; the rivals ; and the duel. Sir Anthony was his own dictatorial father ; Acres, Mathews ; Sir Lucius, Captain Paumier, and Mrs. Malaprop, probably some vul- garian of the place. The jealous and desponding Faulkland is founded on himself, and long after- wards he used to tease his wife with the same morbid suspicions and imaginings. These, however, only supplied outlines and hints to be treated *secundum artem.* For while he drew hints from his own temper for Faulkland, he also presented himself to the Bath public as the gay and gallant Absolute, though it was scarcely loyal to represent the character he intended for Mathews, as a coward.

The play, first produced on January 17th, 1775, was performed again on the 18th, and then 'withdrawn.' On its tenth representation it had a new prologue ; the epilogue was believed to be by Mrs. Sheridan. It was next brought down to Bath, where, naturally enough, it met with extraordinary success, to the delight of the Linley family.

Sheridan was exceptionally favoured in this caste —an interesting one for many reasons. Three or four of the players had performed in Goldsmith's comedy, Shuter having, indeed, saved 'The Good-natured Man,' but had been satirized by Churchill, as one who ' never cared what he left out or what he put in.' Quick was to be later styled 'the retired Diocletian of Islington,' by Charles Lamb. Woodward was a comedian of much *esprit* and power, as may be seen from his vigorous portrait in the Garrick Club. He had opposed Sheridan's father in Dublin with a rival theatre, and all but ruined both. Lewis became later a graceful, spirited comedian, and his picture adorns the National Gallery. Miss

Barsanti, or Mrs. Daly, was wife of a quarrelsome,
dissipated Irish manager; and Mrs. Lessingham was
to have later a strangely tragic and adventurous
history.

On the first night the play proved almost a
failure, owing, it was said, to the too vulgar inter-
pretation of the Irish baronet, by Lee. But this
was not the real reason, for Bernard, the actor, then
passing through London, attended the first performance, and sets us right on this point.

'It was so intolerably long,' he says, 'and so
decidedly opposed in its composition to the taste of
the day, as to draw down a degree of censure which
convinced me, on quitting the house, that it would
never succeed. It must be remembered that this
was the English "age of sentiment," and Kelly and
Cumberland had flooded the stage with moral poems
under the title of comedies, which took their views
of life from the drawing-room exclusively, and
coloured their characters with a nauseous French
affectation. "The Rivals" was an attempt to over-
throw this taste, and to follow up the blow which
Goldsmith had given in "She Stoops to Conquer."
My recollection of the manner in which the former
was received, bears me out in the supposition. The
audience on this occasion were composed of two
parties—those who supported the prevailing taste,
and those who were indifferent to it and liked
nature. The consequence was that Faulkland and

Julia (which Sheridan had obviously introduced to conciliate the sentimentalists) were the characters which were the most favourably received; whilst Sir Anthony Absolute, Acres, and Lydia were barely tolerated; and Mrs. Malaprop (as she deserved to be) was singled out for peculiar vengeance. To this character alone must be attributed the partial failure of the play. She was denounced as a rank offence against all probability (which in dramatic life is possibility)—as a thing without parallel in society—a monstrous absurdity which had originated with the author. Who can imagine for a moment that Mrs. Malaprop, a lady residing at Bath, the emporium of fashion and good taste, visited by, and about to be connected with, the family of a baronet, could have displayed such an ignorance of language. Again, nothing can be more unfounded than the reason which is commonly assigned for the first night's failure of the play, namely, the acting of a Mr. Lee in Sir Lucius O'Trigger. I remember his acting very well; it was very indifferent, particularly to the audience, who cared as little about Sir Lucius as did Lydia; it was his juxtaposition with Mrs. Malaprop that brought him into notice—her disease was infectious, and contaminated all that came into her society. It was therefore not less false than ungenerous in Sheridan (who originated this excuse) to transfer to the back of an unfortunate actor, a fault which was inherent to his own composition.

' Of the acting of the night (seen under so much disadvantage), that which made the greatest impression on me was Shuter's, in Sir Anthony—the character fitted him like his clothes; all the others I have seen better performed since. Lewis was not at home in Faulkland ; a serious sentiment was never upon friendly terms with his lips. Woodward would have played Acres better than the Captain, though not better than Quick. John Bannister's has been the best of any ; but Shuter was inimitable in the full and racy humour which so peculiarly characterized the acting of the " Old School." '*

He had the good sense and courage to accept the verdict of the public, and the play was actually withdrawn for revision—a step for which he informs us there was ' no precedent known on the stage.' In his preface he frankly explains the reasons of this temporary failure as owing to haste and undue length. The haste was owing to the season being far advanced, and the necessity of having the play brought out at once.†

* Sheridan was so pleased with Clinch, the new ' Sir Lucius,' that he adapted for his benefit, when he was poor and distressed, a piece, in two acts, called ' St. Patrick's Day.' This is said to have been written in forty-eight hours !

† He altered his prologue, a dialogue between a serjeant-at-law and an attorney, full of law allusions and ' quillets,' to explain the withdrawal of the play :

SERJ. 'How's this ? The poet's brief again ? Oho !
        Cast, I suppose.

When the piece was presented to Mr. Harris it was at least 'double the length of any existing comedy,' and the experienced manager suggested cutting it down. 'His feelings, however, for the vanity of a young author, got the better of his desire for correcting, and he left many excrescences remaining, because he had assisted in pruning so many more. Hence he thought that the first night's experience would help him to remove many more.' This preface is a very pleasing lively production, in which he frankly confesses his utter inexperience of the stage, his youth, and general faults.

Here he attributes the failure on the first night to the envy of the established writers, 'puny critics who scribble at every author who has the eminence of being unconnected with them.' And as they are usually 'spleen-swollen' from a vain idea of increasing their consequence, there is a petulance and illiberality in their remarks which should place them 'beneath the notice of a gentleman.' He also took

---

ATT.   Oh, pardon me, no, no ;
           We found the Court, o'erlooking stricter laws,
           Indulgent to the merits of the cause.
           By judge's smile, unused to stern denial,
           A rule was granted for another trial.
SERJ. Then, harkye, Dobble, did you mend your pleadings ?
           Errors no few we've found in our proceedings.
ATT. Come, courage, sir, we did amend our plea ;
           Hence your new brief and the *refreshing* fee.'
Here spoke the young law-student, and wittily, too.

notice of the attacks on Sir Lucius, which he seemed to think arose from its being assumed to be a reflection on the Irish, when he made a manful declaration of his nationality, declaring that 'if it added one spark to the decaying flame of attachment to that country, he was happy if his comedy failed :' a pardonable flight of extravagance.* All which helps to form for us the image of himself as he was then, full of sprightliness and ardour, and eagerly rushing on to seize fortune.

In certain notes which the clever author made long after, in a copy of his play, he makes some judicious criticism, which must have struck many others besides, and which forcibly applies to all his work.†

* Strange to say, Sheridan always affected to make little of this early effort, declaring it was one of the worst plays in the language, and he would give anything had he not written it. Goldsmith's comedy, 'She Stoops to Conquer,' had been produced but two years before, and its gifted author had died in the April of the year 1774. Like Sheridan's play, this had nearly been wrecked, owing to the too great extremes to which the farce had been carried ; but though the tearful drama still reigned, and the 'Clementinas,' 'Almeidas,' and 'Braganzas' were being brought out, the efforts of those cheerful Irishmen, Goldsmith, Murphy, and Sheridan, succeeded in shaking the supremacy of gloom and declaimed sorrows.

† 'Upon Mrs. Malaprop's quotation from Shakespeare, " Hesperian curls," etc., he writes, " Overdone—fitter for farce than comedy." On Acres' classification of oaths, "This we call the oath referential," etc., "Very good, but above the speaker's capacity." ' But this better applies to many of his characters,

The chief merits of the comedy are in the unbounded spirit and vivacity with which it is written,
the fertility with which the various phases of character are worked out, and the pleasant plot.   In vain
do sober critics protest, as they pronounced in the
case of 'Pickwick,' that the whole is too farcical,
travelling beyond the restraints of art ; the public set
such dry rules aside, and enjoy it more than ever.*

---

such as Fag, and to Trip's speeches in 'The School for Scandal,'
the latter, with real wit, offering 'post-obits' on his master's winter
clothes, with other financial pleasantry quite out of place and
keeping in a valet's mouth.   Yet it is odd that with this consciousness of the matter being 'above the speaker's capacity,' he should
have continued to adopt so undramatic a course.

Not so long ago it was revived at the Haymarket with great
magnificence, as an attempt to reproduce a picture of Bath
manners and society, the stage being filled with figures, chairmen,
dances taking place at the Assembly Rooms, etc.   The result was
the reverse of what was expected, the comedy and characters being
overpowered by the accessories.   It would seem that in the case
of pieces full of wit and sparkling dialogue, all this decoration
detracts and distracts.

* It was in this play that the clever author commenced his
system of 'borrowing' passages.   Suspicion is, indeed, excited by
his declaration in the preface that he had read or seen few plays,
that his wish was to avoid the appearance of plagiary.   For 'pleasant
images,' he adds, 'faded ideas, float in the fancy, and the imagination often becomes suspicious of its offspring, and doubts whether
it was created or adopted.'   We shall find that he had read and
seen plays to some purpose, and had adopted offspring pretty
freely.   But it must be owned that this was contrived with prodigious skill.   From Murphy's 'All in the Wrong,' produced some
sixteen years before, he obtained substantial assistance, for in this
piece there is also a Beverley, which puts us on further inquiries.

The following from a little collection — the
Theatrical Magazine — seems to offer a most

Does not this passage between Sir William and Mr. Blandford, the
father of Belinda, suggest Sir Anthony and Mrs. Malaprop?

'SIR W. Why, yes, Mr. Blandford, I think everything is settled.

'MR. B. Why, then we have only to acquaint the young people
with our intentions to conclude the affair.

'SIR W. That is all, sir.

'MR. B. As to my girl, *I don't mind her nonsense about Beverley.
She must do as I will have her.* . . . Why, here is my daughter.
Well, my girl, Sir William and I have agreed that you are to prepare
for marriage, that's all.

'BEL. Marriage with Mr. Beverley!

'MR. B. Mr. Beverley.

'BEL. But, sir——

'MR. B. But, madam, I will be obeyed. *You don't like him,
you say. But I like him; that's sufficient for you.* . . . *What did
you say? You mutiny, do you? Don't provoke me.* You know,
Belinda, I am an odd sort of man *when* provoked. Look you
here. Mind what I say. I won't reason with you about the
matter, *and if you offer to rebel, I'll cut you off with a shilling. I'll
see you starve, beg an alms,* live miserable, die wretched, if I should
find you an undutiful girl at last. So this one word for all.
(*Exit.*).'

Faulkland and Julia, with the agonizing doubts of the former,
are also copied, in part, from Beverley and Belinda. 'It is your
character,' says his friend Bellmont; 'instead of enjoying the
object before you, you are ever looking back to something past, or
conjecturing about something to come, and are your own self
tormented.'

In a conversation with Belinda, in reproaching her with being
at a party in his absence:

'I could learn, since, the spirits you were in the whole evening, though I enjoyed nothing in your absence. I could hear the
sallies of your wit, the sprightliness of your conversation.'

spirited estimate of this bright comedy, which has so 'increased the gaiety' of the nation :

' Sheridan was gifted with a sort of mental alchemy, which gave all the characters of the drama on which he exercised its power a golden hue. He was a most inveterate plagiarist, and yet to the casual observer he scarcely ever appears to have borrowed an idea. There is scarcely an original character in the whole of his compositions ; but all the personages of his plays are so skilfully brought out as to appear novelties to nine-tenths of the playgoers and readers of the day. To confine ourselves to " The Rivals," —Sir Anthony is the testy old father, with additions and corrections, who has figured in comedy from the days of Plautus ; Faulkland is almost a fac-simile of one of the lovers in " All in the Wrong ;" the gay young spark, Captain Absolute, who intrigues, cracks jokes, and dupes his daddy, is " as old as my grandmother ;" Mrs. Malaprop is another version of Dogberry ; Sir Lucius and all the O'Flahertys are cousins-german ; Fag is a grandson to Brush ; Lydia is one of the romantic young hussies who have made one in almost every novel and play for three hundred years past ; Julia is a character we have often met

---

She answers :

' You alarm me with these fancies, and you know I have often told you you are of too refining a temper ; you create for yourself imaginings, misunderstandings.

' BEV. Now she is seeking to break off.'

with in print, and now and then in real life ; and
Lucy a waiting-maid of the most approved fashion.

'Although all the *dramatis personæ* of this comedy
are stale on the stage, it unquestionably is one of the
most pleasant stock-pieces that the theatres possess.
It is full of life, humour, interest, and wit. We can
laugh at it to-night, and desire to see it again a
month hence. The fable, the incidents, the *dénoue-
ment*, are all excellent ; and few comedies possess
so many characters for the display of first-rate
abilities. Sir Anthony affords full scope for the
powers of a Dowton, a Munden, a Farren, or a
Fawcett—we say nothing of the old school ; Liston,
Harley, and even Mathews may well delight in Bob
Acres ; Captain Absolute was a fit and proper gallant
to be represented by Charles Kemble or Elliston in
their prime ; Young is right in deeming it no condescension in him to enact Faulkland ; Johnstone
was always delighted to play Sir Lucius ; Fag is
almost equal to Brush, which Jones plays so
inimitably ; Jordan, Kelly, and Vestris have each
gloried in performing Lydia Languish ; Davison was
ever proud of Julia ; and what old gentlewoman of
comic parts would ever desire a better character than
delicious Mrs. Malaprop ?'*

* At Bath, Mrs. Siddons condescended to play Mrs. Candour,
and did so with much intelligence.

CHAPTER VII.

THE author of this piece, with his charming wife, at once became celebrated and *recherché*; their society was sought everywhere, and they passed at once into a life of excitement. Mrs. Sheridan sang at musical parties, while her husband was busy with a thousand venturous schemes. He meditated a reply to Dr. Johnson's pamphlet on 'Taxation no Tyranny.' He was writing pamphlets and sketches of plays. For Harris, too, he had sundry commissions to adapt and alter various of the old comedies—a task he seems to have performed with tolerable success—besides obtaining a familiarity with the general tone and treatment and style of wit of those masters of comedy, Wycherley, Congreve, and Farquhar. It may be well conceived that his brilliant success at once fixed him in the dramatic course he had undertaken, and we presently find him busy working at an opera for Mr. Harris, based on 'The Country Wife.' This was the well-known 'Duenna,' which has been pronounced the best English opera. It was curious that he should not have thought of following up the vein he had struck on, and have thus fettered himself by the cramping restraints of an artificial form of entertainment.* But it may be suspected that the reason mentioned before was at the bottom of this choice, viz., that he was indebted to reality and experience for his comedy. Now he would have to cast about for a subject.

Long after, Sheridan stated that he had never seen Garrick act till the close of his career, and added that this was owing to his father, who assured him that he himself was the first actor of the age. It was therefore superfluous to see inferior performers. This amusing mixture of vanity and littleness shows also how dutiful a son was Sheridan. When he did see Garrick, he of course confessed to his surprising genius, though he would joke on the performance of 'King Lear,' exclaiming, when asked his opinion, 'Oh, the Leer, the Leer!'

In truth, one of the persons most likely to be attracted by the young writer was Mr. Garrick ; and how pleasantly intimate they now became will be

* Thus happily described by his friend Colman : ' In an opera, the dialogue is refreshed by an air every instant. Two gentlemen meet in a park, for example, admire the place and the weather, and, after a speech or two, the music strikes up. One of the characters takes a genteel turn or two on the stage during the symphony, and then breaks out :

' " When the breezes
Fan the treeses." '

seen from the following, addressed by Sheridan to
him.   He had now gone to live at Great Queen
Street :

'I have been about finishing the verses which
were to have followed you to Althorp every day
since you left town ; and as idle as such an employment is, I have been diverted from it by one thing
or other still more idle even than rhyming.   I believe
I shall give up all attempts at versifying in future,
for my efforts in that way always bring me into some
foolish predicament : what I write in a hurry, I
always feel to be not worth reading ; and what I try
to take pains with, I am sure never to finish.   However, such as it is, the poem shall salute your return,
and it will then have the advantage of finding you
less at leisure to be critical ; though indeed, but that
I am not sure of your even receiving this at Althorp,
I would endeavour to acquit myself of my promise,
though something after the time.   I mean to be
vastly civil to female talent of all sorts, and even to
the affectation of it where the person is very handsome (for the grace of Venus, which passes all
understanding, atones for an abundance of frailty),
and my bards shall be very easily recompensed.

> ' " In due proportion she rewards their toils,
>   Bows for a distich—for a stanza smiles ;
>   Familar nods an epigram attend ;
>   An ode will almost rank you as a friend ;
>   A softer name fond elegy bestows ;
>   But nearest to her heart a sonnet flows."

'I need not attempt to write you any news. I hear everywhere how valiantly you are fighting Cumberland's battles for him. I hope the bugle meets with due honour.'

This partiality of Garrick's was even extended to Sheridan's intimates, and he took interest in helping Richard Tickell, his brother-in-law. Through Sheridan's introduction the latter became acquainted with the great actor.* In one of his

* Two letters from Tickell attesting this interest, also show the intimacy between young Sheridan and Garrick. Tickell held a Government office :

'SIR' (wrote the latter, in May, 1778),—Allow me to express my gratefulness for the kind manner in which (Mr. Walsingham and Mr. Sheridan inform me) you have mentioned the little trifles I took the liberty to send you. It is very good of you to see these exertions in a favourable light ; I must attribute your commendations much more to your *feelings* than your *judgment.* You have heard of my embarrassments, and you do not think ill of the motives and principles which involved me in them. Something, too, Mr. Walsingham mentioned, of your wish to speak favourably of me to Lord North and the Chancellor. This thought gave me the greatest satisfaction. I know, indeed, it is too much to wish for ; yet I must own there is no recommendation I should more rejoice to be honoured with than that of Mr. Garrick. To rise by any appearance of merit would enhance the value of good fortune ; and your praise would certainly raise me in the opinion of every-one. I hope you will forgive my intruding on you, but I was anxious to acknowledge the politeness you have shown me, and to assure you of my respect and esteem.'

'SIR,—I received your very obliging letter, and am sensible how letters we find a very significant allusion to his friend Sheridan, which reveals his character at this time :

'I am sorry Mr. Sheridan could think so lightly of those points as to treat either my difficulties or your wish to overcome them with indifference. He has too much sense not to know and justly prize your friendship and patronage ; *but he should not check your good intentions towards another*, who, without any of *his* advantages, is oppressed with misfortunes he has never known.'

This little insidious stroke, perhaps the result of jealousy, was characteristic ; but it has not a pleasant flavour in so young a man.

The success of 'The Rivals,' it might be thought, would have led Garrick to wish to secure the services of its brilliant author for his own theatre. It seems that there had been some misunderstanding between them, which may have prevented such a connection. This we find from a letter addressed by Dr. Linley to Hoadley, the former being embarrassed between the claims Garrick had on his musical services, and

---

kindly you have interested yourself in my welfare. I have written to Mr. Sheridan to thank him for having mentioned me to you. Your explanation of his expressions has entirely removed my hasty and ill-grounded fears.'

There are many of these letters from Tickell to Garrick, always wanting 'something to be done.'

those of his son-in-law. The doctor thus excused himself:

' I have engaged to assist my son-in-law Sheridan in composing an opera, which he is to bring out at Covent Garden this winter. I am a good deal distressed that from some misunderstanding between him and Mr. Garrick, he is not connected with Drury Lane house; for though I believe they are now on very good terms, yet Sheridan thinks he has been so honourably treated by Mr. Harris, that he ought not to keep anything he has hitherto written from him. However, I hope Mr. Garrick will not take anything amiss in my assisting him on this occasion ; for it is a matter of absolute necessity that he should endeavour to get money by this means, as he will not be prevailed upon to let his wife sing. Mr. Garrick's extraordinary genius and merit, the noble fortune he deservedly possesses, and the universal sense he must know the world has of his just claim to every attention and respect, I doubt not has inspired him with that enlarged sentiment, which I think he with particular propriety is entitled to assume, of being the patron and protector of dramatic genius, in what place or shape soever he may find it ; and in this opinion I rest satisfied that he would rather promote, than discourage, my assisting Sheridan.'

This was meant to be shown or repeated to the

great man ; and he later addressed the same excuse
to the great man himself.   He referred, of course,
to ' The Duenna,' then in progress ; and so nervous
was the Doctor as to the danger of offending his
patron and employer, that he wrote again to him on
September 28th, 1775, in the following deprecatory
strain.   He felt that if the opera proved a success
at Covent Garden, it must, of course, draw audiences
away from Garrick's Theatre :

' There is a circumstance, because relative to
myself in the good opinion I wish you should
preserve of me, that I must mention, otherwise I
know not if I ought.   It is, that as often as I am
called upon, I have promised to assist Sheridan in
compiling—I believe it is the properest term—an
opera, which, I understand from him, he has engaged
to produce at Covent Garden this winter.   I have
already set some airs which he has given me, and he
intends writing new words to some other tunes of
mine.   My son has likewise written some tunes for
him, and I understand he is to have others from Mr.
Jackson, of Exeter.   This is a mode of proceeding
in regard to his composition I do not by any means
approve of.   I think he ought first to have finished
his opera with the songs he intends to introduce in
it, and have got it entirely new set.   No musician
can set a song properly unless he understands the
character and knows the performer who is to exhibit

it. For my part, I shall be very unwilling for either my own name, or my son's, to appear in this business, and it is my present resolution to forbid it; for I have great reason to be diffident of my own abilities and genius, and my son has not had experience in theatrical compositions, though I think well of his invention and musical skill. I would not have been concerned in this business at all, but that I know there is an absolute necessity for him to endeavour to get some money by this means, as he will not be prevailed upon to let his wife sing—and indeed at present she is incapable—and nature will not permit me to be indifferent to his success. You are deservedly at that point of fame which few of the great geniuses the world has produced ever arrived at, above the reach of envy, and are the protector of dramatic merit, in what place or shape soever you find it, and I look up to you as the Patron and Director of both theatres, virtually, if not officially. I hope Sheridan has done nothing to forfeit the protection you have hitherto shown him, and that you believe me to be with sincerity, sir,' etc.

There is some shrewd criticism in this letter, which is not without other interest.

The truth was, this scrappy or 'hand-to-mouth' mode of writing was with Sheridan an inspiration. He could seldom write soberly. Another reason may have been, that he had a number of plaintive and effective songs lying by him, even including those amatory ones addressed to his wife, which, *more* Sheridan, he turned to profit.

But while working for the manager who had brought him forward, he was now actually maturing his plans for securing the rival theatre, which it was known would presently be in the market. It is extraordinary to think of so young a man, who had been only a short time in London, reaching to such a position.

The opera may have been an old effort recently furbished up, and was founded on an incident in ' The Country Wife.' Eager, pressing letters passed between him and his father-in-law, which reveal the practical and mechanical way in which the songs were written to order :

' I want Leoni to show himself advantageously in the six lines beginning " Gentle maid." I should tell you, that he sings nothing well but in a plaintive or pastoral style ; and his voice is such as appears to me always to be hurt by much accompaniment. I have observed, too, that he never gets so much applause as when he makes a cadence. Therefore my idea is, that he should make a flourish at " Shall I grieve thee ?" and return to "Gentle maid," and so sing that part of the tune again.'

Again : ' I want Dr. Harrington's catch, but as the sense must be the same, I am at a loss how to put other words. Can't the under part (" A smoky house,"

etc.) be sung by one person, and the other two
change ? The situation is—Quick and Dubellamy,
two lovers, carrying away Father Paul (Reinold) in
great raptures, to marry them: the Friar has before
warned them of the ills of a married life, and they
break out into this. The catch is particularly calculated for a stage effect ; but I don't like to take
another person's words, and I don't see how I can
put others, keeping the same idea ("of seven squall-
ing brats," etc.), in which the whole affair lies.
Mattocks' I could wish to be a broken, passionate
affair, and the first two lines may be recitative, or
what you please uncommon. Miss Brown sings
hers in a joyful mood : and, for variety, we want
Mr. Simpson's hautboy to cut a figure, with replying
passages, etc., in the way of Fisher's " *M'ami, il bel
idol' mio*," to abet which I have lugged in " Echo,'
who is always allowed to play her part.'

There is humour in these notions, and they show
a thorough acquaintance with the *technique* of such
things. Everything was pressed on at an express
speed ; the music, words, and rehearsals were done
at high pressure. ' Every hour's delay is a material
injury to the opera and the theatre.'

The parts were all written '*as we go on*,' which was
to be a favourite mode of working with Sheridan.
The rehearsals took place at Orchard Street. Dr.
Linley seems to have discharged his portion of
the duty admirably. The music was considered

charmingly tuneful. It is not generally known that Linley's clever son contributed no less than four numbers to the score.

The opera was brought out on November 21, 1775, with a rather obscure caste, of which only two or three—Mrs. Mattocks, Quick, and Mr. Green —are known to fame. The piece had an extraordinary success, and was acted seventy-five times in a single season; then thought to be as great 'a run' as that of a whole year in our day. It was of course not wholly original, but was a gay and pleasing performance. So undoubted was its success, that Garrick, oddly enough, revived Mrs. Sheridan's piquant comedy as a counter-attraction.

Sheridan's father was still irreconcilable, and Mr. Moore describes a rather touching incident, showing how the son felt this treatment :

'Having received information from an old family servant that his father (who still refused to have any intercourse with him) meant to attend, with his daughters, at the representation of the piece, Sheridan took up his station by one of the side scenes, opposite to the box where they sat, and there continued, unobserved, to look at them during the greater part of the night. On his return home, he was so affected by the various recollections that came upon him, that he burst into tears, and, being questioned as to the cause of his agitation by Mrs. Sheridan, to whom it was new to see him returning thus saddened from the scene of his triumph, he owned how deeply it had gone to his heart, " to think that *here* sat his father and his sisters before him, and yet that he alone was not permitted to go near them or speak to them." '

·Suddenly an impending and very serious change in theatrical management was to offer a new chance to the young author. Garrick, now sixty years old, wearied out with the quarrels of his actresses, and suffering from painful disorders, had made up his mind to lay down the reins of office. When ' The Duenna' was in rehearsal, in October, the first idea of Sheridan's venturing to succeed him had been broached, though with but faint hopes of success. Sheridan had actually proposed the matter to him, and was positive he could make good his share of the venture; but he was sceptical as to Garrick's retiring or parting with his share, though ' he seemed to come closer to the point in naming his price.' Not until the end of December did Garrick finally make up his mind, declaring that he would be willing to entertain Sheridan's offers, subject to a previous offer to Colman.

Sheridan had conceived his scheme on the largest and boldest scale. He had bethought him of his wealthy friend Ewart, the brandy merchant, and brought him, by appointment, on Thursday, the 28th of December, to meet Mr. Garrick. He determined, also, to introduce his father-in-law. Then, for the first time, the actor 'seemed to mean business,' no doubt impressed by the substantial character of this purchaser, for Ewart was put forward as the responsible party. The result of that interview was a direct offer to Colman.*

After which, Sheridan received the following :

'Mr. Garrick presents his compliments to Mr. Sheridan, and as he is obliged to go into the country for three days, he should be glad to see him upon his return to town, either on Wednesday about six or seven o'clock, or whenever he pleases. The party has no objection to the whole, but chooses no partner but Mr. G.—Not a word of this yet. Mr. G. sent a messenger on purpose (*i.e.*, to Colman). He would call upon Mr. S., but he is confined at home. Your name is upon our list.'

'*According* to his demand,' wrote Sheridan to Linley, 'the whole is valued at £70,000. He appears very shy of letting his books be looked into, as the test of the profits on this sum ; but says it must be, in its nature, a purchase on speculation. However, he has promised me a rough estimate, of

---

* Made on December 29, 1775. 'He (Garrick) had seen a gentleman of great property, who had no objection to the price, viz., £35,000, for my part. He desired an immediate answer.' Colman, however, declined, on the ground that it was only Mr. Garrick's share that was offered. 'I immediately and most determinately say "No." I would not for worlds again sit on the throne of Brentford with any assessor except yourself.'

his own, of the entire receipts for the last seven years. But, after all, it must certainly be a *purchase on speculation* without *money's worth* being *made out*.

' This is all I can say on the subject till Wednesday, though I can't help adding, that I think we might *safely* give £5,000 more on this purchase than richer people. The interest is valued at £5,500; while this is *cleared*, the proprietors are *safe*—but I think it must be *infernal* management indeed that does not double it.'

Alas! 'infernal management' was to reduce the property to the lowest imaginable value!

By the first week in January, 1776, all was arranged, for Garrick was explicit and straightforward. It must be said that it does not bespeak Garrick's usual sagacity that he should have selected so young a man as his successor, clever as he was. From his intercourse with him he must have gathered a good idea of his character, love of pleasure, etc. But no doubt Sheridan's seductive manner and his lovely wife—' The Saint,' as Mr. Garrick called her —had turned the scale.

His rough estimate of the profits for the last seven years amounted to £7,000 a year on the whole property, or 10 per cent. The new partners were to contribute on this scale. Ewart was to furnish £10,000 ; Linley, £10,000; Sheridan, £10,000 ; and a Dr. Ford, £5,000. Total, £35,000. Lacy,

Garrick's partner, of course remained in the venture, representing £35,000 ; but his moiety was encumbered with a mortgage of £22,000 to Garrick, which it was suggested they should take over.* The new partners were desirous of getting control over Willoughby Lacy, who was an embarrassed man and obstructive person, and whose active interest in the theatre was really very small. Their taking Garrick's place in reference to the mortgage would give them this control.

'The sooner the arrangement was concluded the better,' wrote Mr. Sheridan. And the reason he offered was characteristic, as his confidential connection with the other house was *'peculiarly distressing till I can with prudence reveal my situation ;*

* There was also a curious charge upon the theatre, for which a claim was made early in 1776 by the Walpole family :

'Be it known, therefore, to you and your associate, Mr. Lacy, that my brother Robert Walpole having, in November, 1761, entered into certain articles of agreement with you both for the annual repayment of £315 in lieu of certain advantages arising to him by virtue of certain letters patent granted to yourself and Mr. Lacy under the Great Seal in the month of October, 1761, hath signed a declaration reciting that he entered into the above-mentioned agreement for the sole proper use and benefit of myself, my executors, administrators, and assigns, which declaration I have in my possession, together with the assignments relative to this matter. It appears by the agreement, that the first payment commenced on the 25th day of December, 1774, consequently one annual payment was due in December last.

'I am, sir, your most obedient and humble servant.

'P.S. Lady Walpole desires her compliments to Mrs. Garrick.'

and such a treaty, however prudently managed, cannot be long kept a secret.' In other words, if it were broken off, he would lose his friend Harris. Here we have certain indications of slight *shiftiness*, which was to characterize all his life. On the most confidential terms with the manager, who had helped to make the success of both his pieces, he was now secretly preparing to oppose him. He was also at the moment arranging, in anticipation, with his father-in-law, how they were both to control the theatre.

'For getting well paid for it you may lay aside every doubt of not finding your account in it; for the fact is, we shall have nothing but our own equity to consult in *making and obtaining any demand for exclusive trouble.* Leasy is utterly unequal to any department in the theatre. He has an opinion of me, and is very willing to let the whole burthen and responsibility be taken off his shoulders. But I certainly should not give up my time and labour (for his superior advantage, having so much greater a share) without some exclusive advantage. Yet, I should by no means make the demand till I had shown myself equal to the task. My father purposes to be with us but one year; and that only to give me what advantage he can from his experience. He certainly must be paid for his trouble, and so certainly must you.'

On June 24, 1776, the contract was concluded. Mr. Ewart had withdrawn, and Dr. Ford agreed to take his place, thus increasing his venture to £15,000. There had been much speculation as to where Sheridan, a young adventurer in town without a shilling, had procured his resources. Mr. Moore thinks there was something 'mysterious and even miraculous' in his contrivances. But it must be considered that he would have had little difficulty in raising the money on his share, which might be valued at £1,000 a year at least in a flourishing theatre, in which his reputation as a successful writer in the very flush of that success might be a guarantee of profitable management. In fact, Linley found no difficulty in raising *his* £10,000 on his share. Miss Sheridan, however, states that her brother raised no money himself, and that her father found a person in Bath who lent him the money at 4 per cent. The truth was, the security, as Sheridan said, was 'very clear,' and on a share in a patent or monopoly money could always be raised. But it will be seen that this was the mode in which Sheridan found the money, as in the deeds a mortgage to Ford for £7,700, and another to Abary Wallis, Garrick's solicitor, are charged against Sheridan's share. Thus he had only £1,300 to make up. Oddly enough Linley seemed inclined to remain at Bath, until his son pointed out to him that so serious a stake required his presence and personal exertions.

When all was signed and sealed, Linley wrote to

thank the retiring manager in a rather fulsome or romantic strain :

'My heart tells me I ought not to defer acknowledging, and thanking you most sincerely for the friendship you have shown to me and Sheridan, in permitting us to purchase a part of your share in the patent of Drury Lane Theatre. The loss to be sustained by the public, by your quitting the stage, will be truly felt, but cannot justly be described ; no person, I may boldly say, will ever appear after you, but with diminished lustre. You are a centre star of glory on this stage of the world ; and that you may long shine a light to us that walk in darkness, and then retire but to "new trick your beams and flame in the forehead of the morning sky" of the next, is the sincere wish and prayer of your ever obedient and most devoted humble servant,

'THOMAS LINLEY.'

The two families were to benefit by the new enterprise. Mr. Sheridan, as we have seen, was to be stage-manager. Later, Mrs. Linley was to superintend the wardrobe. This function she executed with a jealous economy that was said to verge on penuriousness.* It was reported that she

* It was also told, that when Sheridan asked his friend Jekyl to look at his dresses for Richard Cœur de Lion, he having seen the play in Paris, Mrs. Linley interposed, saying they had a capital dress for 'Richard,' in which Mr. Smith had often played the character. She was thinking of the Shakespearian Richard.

used to dock a tragedian's flowing train with a view to securing scraps of material sufficient to cover a footstool, or even a pincushion.

The campaign opened under the new management on September 21, 1776, with 'New Brooms,' a sort of jocular prologue, written by Colman. The first season promised badly; nothing, we are told, but empty boxes. The management was under the direction of Linley, who was succeeded by Younger, then by King. Linley supplied music for 'The Tempest,' and friends, like General Burgoyne, had their plays produced.

It was noted, however, that the new managers showed great incapacity in selecting what was likely to attract the public. They seemed to have no idea of novelty or energy, content with producing old pieces—adaptations like Shakespeare's 'Tempest,' with music written specially by Linley. Another injudicious selection was a re-casting of 'The Relapse' by Sheridan, re-named a 'Trip to Scarborough,' in which he had determined to give a leading part to a new actress.

One of his first acts as a manager had been the engagement of a beautiful woman whose life and adventures were later to attract much attention. This was Mrs. Robinson, a foolish, excitable, and exceedingly vain creature, to whom Mr. Garrick had not been unwilling to give a trial. He, however, went out of office before he could give effect to his

wishes, and she renewed her attempt when Sheridan
was in command. The young manager, she more
than insinuates, was smitten with her charms. She
was living in Newman Street, when one day Mr.
Brereton entered, bringing with him Sheridan.
'At his earnest entreaty,' she says, 'I recited some
passages from various plays; the gentleness of his
manners encouraged me.' He praised her lavishly.
It was settled that she should appear at Drury Lane
as Juliet. Mr. Garrick took the greatest interest in
her, and rehearsed Romeo with her till he was
exhausted with fatigue ; and on the first night sat
in the orchestra to applaud and encourage her.

The announcement of the 'Trip to Scarborough'
gave great dissatisfaction, and a cabal seems to have
been formed to damn it. The audience, it seems,
had expected a new piece, and finding it was only
an alteration or adaptation, began to hiss the
manager. 'Mrs. Yates, not liking it, quitted the
stage, and stood for some moments petrified,' says
Mrs. Robinson. 'Mr. Sheridan, from the wings,
desired me not to quit the boards. The late Duke
of Cumberland, from a stage-box, bade me take
courage. "It is not you, but the play they hiss,"
said his Royal Highness. "I curtseyed, and," adds
the vain woman, "*that curtsey seemed to electrify
the whole house*, for a thundering peal of applause
followed, and the comedy was suffered to go on."'

Sheridan presently wished her to appear in 'The

School for Scandal,' probably as Maria. 'But,' she admits, 'I was now so unshaped by my increasing size that I made my excuses. His attentions were now unremitting ; he praised my talents, and he interested himself in my comforts. When my infant died, and on the day of its dissolution, Mr. Sheridan called. I had seen many *proofs of his exquisite sensibility.* I had never witnessed one which so strongly impressed my mind as his countenance on entering my apartments. I had not power to speak. All he uttered was, " Beautiful little creature !" at the same time looking at my infant, and sighing with a degree of sympathetic sorrow which penetrated my soul.'*

* From a hint dropped by Miss Burney, to be quoted presently, it seems that he was already thought *volage*. Long after, in 1792, Mrs. Robinson, cast off by her protector, broken in health and fortune, had to fly from the country. In an unpublished letter, which I find in an old auction catalogue, she thus appeals to her former manager :

'July 23, 1792.

'You will perhaps be surprised to hear that, after an irreproachable connection of more than *ten years*, I am suffered to depart an *Exile* from my Country, and all my hopes, for a few paltry debts. I sail this evening for *Calais, alone*—broken-hearted. My state of health is too deplorable to bear description, and I am depressed in spirits beyond what my strength can support. I conjure you not to mention this letter to anyone, I am sufficiently humbled by the base ingratitude of the world, without the additional mortification of public exposure. Since Colonel Tarleton has suffered me to be thus driven a wanderer upon the mercy of an unfeeling world, after having endured every insult from his present low associate, I am resolutely determined never to accept of any favour from him.

Another acquaintance, made a little later, and welcomed with enthusiasm, was the vivacious Miss Burney, whom he pressed to furnish him with a play for his theatre. He thus showed himself eager to secure talent. She describes the scene when she first met Mr. and Mrs. Sheridan, though vanity and something of affectation colours all. It was at Mrs. Cholmondeley's. Mrs. Sheridan had, of course, arrived by herself. She found her to be very 'clever and very interesting, and unlike anybody else.'

' Mr. Sheridan has a very fine figure, and a good, though I don't think a handsome, face. He is tall, and very upright, and his appearance and address are at once manly and fashionable, without the smallest tincture of foppery or modish graces. In short, I like him vastly, and think him every way worthy his beautiful companion.

' And let me tell you what I know will give you as much pleasure as it gave me—that, by all I could observe in the course of the evening, and we stayed very late, they are extremely happy in each other ; *he evidently adores her, and she as evidently idolizes him.* The world has by no means done him justice.

' When he had paid his compliments to all his

Will you, my dear Sheridan, do me the kindness to lend me ONE hundred pounds ? I will pay you, upon my honour,' etc.

A postscript commences, ' Pray don't tell Tarleton—he will triumph in my sorrows.'

Sheridan was not likely to have commanded the £100 asked for ; the letter probably lay unopened and unanswered.

acquaintance, he went behind the sofa on which
Mrs. Sheridan and Miss Cholmondeley were seated,
and entered into earnest conversation with them.

'And now I must tell you a little conversation
which I did not hear myself till I came home; it was
between Mr. Sheridan and my father.

' " Dr. Burney," cried the former, " have you no
older daughters ? Can this possibly be the authoress
of ' Evelina ' ? "

'And then he said abundance of fine things, and
begged my father to introduce him to me.

' " Why, it will be a very formidable thing to her,"
answered he, " to be introduced to you."

' " Well then, by-and-by," returned he.

'Some time after this, my eyes happening to meet
his, he waived the ceremony of introduction, and in
a low voice said :

' " I have been telling Dr. Burney that I have
long expected to see in Miss Burney a lady of the
gravest appearance, with the quickest parts."

'Of course I could make no verbal answer, and
he proceeded then to speak of " Evelina " in terms of
the highest praise ; but I was in such a ferment from
surprise (not to say pleasure), that I have no recollection of his expressions. I only remember telling
him that I was much amazed he had spared time to
read it, and that he repeatedly called it a most surprising book ; and some time after he added : " But
I hope, Miss Burney, you don't intend to throw
away your pen ?"

' " You should take care, sir," said I, " what you say : for you know not what weight it may have."

' He wished it might have any, he said ; and soon after turned again to my father.

' " Miss Burney," cried Sir Joshua, who was now reseated, " are not you a writer of verses ?"

' F. B. " No, sir."

' MRS. CHOL. "Oh, don't believe her. I have made a resolution not to believe anything she says."

' MR. SHERIDAN. " I think a lady should not write verses till she is past receiving them."

' MRS. CHOL. (rising and stalking majestically towards him). " Mr. Sheridan, pray, sir, what may you mean by this insinuation ? did I not say I writ verses ?"

' MR. SHERIDAN. " Oh, but you——"

' MRS. CHOL. " Say no more, sir ! You have made your meaning but too plain already. There now, I think that's a speech for a tragedy !"

' Some time after, Sir Joshua returning to his standing-place, entered into confab with Mrs. Linley and your slave, upon various matters, during which Mr. Sheridan, joining us, said :

' " Sir Joshua, I have been telling Miss Burney that she must not suffer her pen to lie idle—ought she ?"

' SIR JOSHUA. " No, indeed ought she not."

' MR. SHERIDAN. " Do you, then, Sir Joshua, persuade her. But perhaps you have begun something ? May we ask ? Will you answer a question candidly ?"

' F. B. " I don't know, but as candidly as *Mrs. Candour* I think I certainly shall."

'Mr. Sheridan. "What then are you about now?"

'F. B. "Why, twirling my fan, I think!"

'Mr. Sheridan. "No, no; but what are you about at home? However, it is not a fair question, so I won't press it."

'Yet he looked very inquisitive; but I was glad to get off without any downright answer.

'Sir Joshua. "Anything in the dialogue way, I think, she must succeed in; and I am sure invention will not be wanting."

'Mr. Sheridan. "No, indeed; I think, and say, she should write a comedy."

'Sir Joshua. "I am sure I think so; and hope she will.'

'I could only answer by incredulous exclamations.

'"Consider," continued Sir Joshua, "you have already had all the applause and fame you can have given you in the closet; but the acclamation of a theatre will be new to you."

'And then he put down his trumpet, and began a violent clapping of his hands.

'I actually shook from head to foot! I felt myself already in Drury Lane, amidst the hubbub of a first night.

'"Oh no!" cried I; "there may be a noise, but it will be just the reverse." And I returned his salute with a hissing.

'Mr. Sheridan joined Sir Joshua very warmly.

'"Oh, sir!" cried I, "you should not run on so—you don't know what mischief you may do!"

'Mr. SHERIDAN. "I wish I may—I shall be very glad to be accessory."

'Sir JOSHUA. "She has, certainly, something of a knack at characters;—where she got it, I don't know; and how she got it, I can't imagine—but she certainly has it. And to throw it away is——"

'Mr. SHERIDAN. "Oh, she won't—she will write a comedy—she has promised me she will!"

'F. B. "Oh! if you both run on in this manner, I shall——"

'I was going to say get under the chair, but Mr. Sheridan, interrupting me with a laugh, said:

'"Set about one? very well, that's right!"

'"Ay," cried Sir Joshua, "that's very right. And you" (to Mr. Sheridan) "would take anything of hers, would you not?—unsight, unseen?"

'What a point-blank question! who but Sir Joshua would have ventured it?

'"Yes," answered Mr. Sheridan, with quickness, "and make her a bow and my best thanks into the bargain."

'Now, my dear Susy, tell me, did you ever hear the fellow to such a speech as this!—it was all I could do to sit it.

'"Mr. Sheridan!" I exclaimed, "are you not mocking me?"

'"No, upon my honour! this is what I have

meditated to say to you the first time I should have the pleasure of seeing you."

' Afterwards he took my father aside, and formally repeated his opinion that I should write for the stage, and his desire to see my play—with encomiums the most flattering of " Evelina." '

The play was written, and sent to her dear friend Smelt for criticism. He condemned it utterly, and Miss Burney accepted his judgment.

' As my play was settled in its silent suppression, I entreated my father to call on Mr. Sheridan, in order to prevent his expecting anything from me, as he had had a good right to do, from my having sent him a positive message that I should, in compliance with his exhortations at Mrs. Cholmondeley's, try my fortune in the theatrical line, and send him a piece for this winter. My father did call, but found him not at home ; neither did he happen to see him till about Christmas. He then acquainted him that what I had written had entirely dissatisfied me, and that I desired to decline for the present all attempts of that sort. Mr. Sheridan was pleased to express great concern—nay, more, to protest he would not accept my refusal. He begged my father to tell me that he could take no denial to seeing what I had done—that I could be no fair judge for myself—that he doubted not but it would please, but was glad I was not satisfied, as he had much rather see pieces before their authors were contented with them than afterwards, on account of sundry small changes always necessary to be made by the managers, for theatrical purposes, and to which they were loth to submit when their writings were finished to their own approbation. In short, he said so much, that my father, ever easy to be worked upon, began to waver, and told me he wished I would show the play to Sheridan at once. This very much disconcerted me : I had taken a sort of disgust to it, and was myself most earnestly desirous to let it die a quiet death. I therefore cooled the affair as much as I conveniently could, and by evading from time to time the conversation, it was again sinking into its old state—when again Mr. Sheridan saw my father, and asked his leave to call upon me himself. This could not be refused. Well—I was now violently fidgeted, and began to think of alterations—and by setting my head to work, I have actually now written the fourth act from beginning to end, except one scene. Mr. Sheridan, however, has not yet called, and I have so little heart in the affair, that I have now again quite dropped it.'

Nothing more was heard of this piece. The authoress of ' Evelina ' was perhaps too diffuse for the stage.

About this time there came to Sheridan with a play a fretful dramatist of some repute, bearing a sort of introduction from Mr. Garrick. Cumber-

land, for he was the person, was a writer of reputation, and might have claimed respect on his own
merits.   But the manager seemed to choose the
occasion for a display of more than his usual carelessness and even rudeness; though he appears to
have invited him to send a production to the
theatre.   Cumberland approached him with due
respect. *   In conclusion, he handsomely offered not
to ask any honorarium if the play was unsuccessful.
Of these proposals, which he had himself invited,
the young manager took no notice ; and we find the
dramatist complaining bitterly to his friend of the
rudeness with which he was treated. †   There could

* His letter is amusingly characteristic of the future Sir Fretful :
'SIR,—I am informed by Mr. Garrick that you have been so
obliging as to express a readiness to receive a tragedy of my
writing, and to give it a representation if you find it deserving.
This unfortunate production is under such peculiar circumstances,
that I cannot omit expressing to you, in the most earnest manner,
my sensibility on this occasion.   I ought and should have despaired
of its merits, if I had not had a pretty long and intimate acquaintance with the stage, and what produces stage effect ; if I had not
given infinite pains and attention to this composition for very many
years; and, above all, if I had not been supported by the unanimous
suffrages of every person to whose judgment I have committed it.
I really say this to you, not for the sake of parade, but in the way
of excuse for persisting in any degree of self-opinion, after I had
received judgment against me.   I beseech you, therefore, sir, to
read it with as much malice as you are capable of, considering that
an author is an ill judge in his own cause.'

† 'Colman asked me naturally enough about my tragedy, which
he had heard was in Mr. Sheridan's hands ; I told him the short
story, and what you had done; I was forced to add, that having

be no excuse for such treatment.   But the truth was
that this strange being, noted for his sensitiveness,
his jealousy of others, his particular antipathy to the
rising dramatist, seems at once to have challenged
all that was obstructive and mischievous in a nature
as sensitive as his own.   What occurred at the first
reading was significant : ' I read the tragedy in the
ears of the performers on Friday morning ; I was
highly flattered by my audience, but your successor
in management is not a representative of your polite
attention to authors on such occasions, *for he came
in yawning at the fifth act*, with no other apology
than having sate up two nights running.   It gave
me not the least offence, as I put it all to habits of
dissipation and indolence ; but I fear his office will
suffer for want of due attention, and the present
drop upon the theatre justifies my apprehensions.'

Mr. Garrick seems to have advised Cumberland

---

written a letter on Friday se'nnight to Mr. Sheridan in the most
candid and fair terms I could devise, he had not to this moment
acknowledged the receipt of it, and we both agreed that such a
conduct must be altered, or would operate to his disgrace and ruin ;
in my particular it is of small consequence, though it is not easy
to put a case where his politeness was more called upon : let
his reply come when it will, it comes with no grace.   I beseech
you not to molest yourself one moment about it ; but my experience
with the world assures me that there is no man who can keep his
place in the goodwill and esteem of those he has to deal with, *if
he so totally throws off the forms of politeness*, which even a prime
minister cannot dispense with, and which we shall only excuse in
him from his ignorance of good breeding.'

to be forbearing and tolerant, advice which he tried to follow.

He writes: 'We have as yet had no rehearsal, nor can I tell when we shall. Thank you for your advice ; I persuade myself I have anticipated it, and shall certainly not lose the battle for want of temper : without some prudence and patience I should never have got the ladies cordially into their business, nor should I have avoided a jar with Mr. Smith.'

He had also 'called yesterday on Mr. Sheridan and quickened him, but all in good humour and perfect harmony, having strictly followed your good advice in all particulars.'

The piece was produced in due course ; but the manager was registering during its preparation the full tale of the eccentricities and ill-humours of the author, which he was to turn to account and to profit in his play of 'The Critic.' There is something unhandsome in this, for on the stage, if anywhere, *esprit de corps oblige.*

This irregular system, pursued without plan or purpose, must have brought the enterprise to ruin, but for one of those strokes of good fortune and genius which came to our hero more abundantly than to any other, in the course of a life.

CHAPTER VIII.

WE now arrive at one of the most important incidents
in Sheridan's career, the production of the ever-green
'School for Scandal'—perhaps the most popular and
firmly established of English comedies, which is
revived again and again with unfailing interest. Its
traditions are so well preserved that it is generally
respectably performed, so as to supply a fair idea of its
meaning and the author's intentions, giving enjoyment
to both actors and audiences. Its author, though
apparently careless and engrossed in pleasure, took
enormous pains in the composition, making endless
experiments and combinations before he could satisfy
his nice and critical taste. Innumerable little note-
books have been preserved filled with variations and
experiments of all kinds—sentiments, good things,
and little scraps of wit—combinations of plots and
characters attempted and rejected. No one suspected
that so great a piece was being so slowly and pains-
takingly elaborated. Mr. Moore believes that he
took the most ostentatious pains to convey the idea

that he had left everything to the last, and could
depend on his own ability to 'work against time.'
But he was so consistent in such habits of pro-
crastination that it is unnecessary to assume this
hypothesis of affectation and deceit.

The day of performance was actually announced
before all the parts were put into the actors' hands,
and they were served out in scraps and fragments.
It was natural that a composition so altered and
compounded should not have satisfied its author,
even at the last moment. *

On the very day of performance the play had
nearly been interdicted by the Chamberlain. Sheridan
himself, as Mr. Fraser-Rae was the first to point
out, related the incident many years later.   An
election was taking place, and it was thought that
the character of Moses might be applied to one of
the candidates.   This, even at the worst, would not
have interfered with the performances, as a few
touches would have changed this important character ;
but Sheridan hurried to Lord Hertford, then Lord
Chamberlain, and, with his usual persuasiveness,
laughed off the prohibition.

This famous, memorable night was May 8, 1777 ;
and the caste was a strong one.

---

* The last leaf of the prompter's copy has the well-known
' doxology,' as Moore calls it : ' Finished at last ! Thank God !
R. B. Sheridan.' Followed by 'Amen ! William Hopkins '
(the prompter).

The play was completely and triumphantly successful. Angelo, the fencing-master, relates that a friend of his, passing by Drury Lane towards the close of night, heard a tremendous noise which startled him, and which he found was the prolonged burst of applause which greeted the falling of the screen in the fourth act.

Mr. Garrick had been so interested in the new play that he had attended the rehearsals, and was 'never known to be more anxious for a favourite piece.' He was proud of the new manager. Sir George Beaumont met him in the lobby, as Mr. Cradock tells us, on the first night, 'and with sparkling eyes I remember he expressed his admiration of the play, and particularly praised the fourth act.' The occasion was also to be celebrated by an odd incident.

On this great night, as the author told Lord Byron long after, 'he was knocked down and put in the watch-house for making a row in the streets, and for being found intoxicated by the watchman.'

A few days after the first performance Mr. Garrick addressed the author in congratulatory terms :

'Mr. Garrick's best wishes and compliments to Mr. Sheridan. How is the Saint to-day ? A gentleman who is as mad as myself about yᵉ School remark'd, that the characters upon the stage at yᵉ falling of the screen stand too long before they speak ;—I thought so too yᵉ first night :—he said it

was the same on ye 2nd, and was remark'd by others;
—tho' they should be astonish'd, and a little petrify'd,
yet it may be carry'd to too great a length.—All praise
at Lord Lucan's last night.'

It was as profitable as successful. From that time
to the present hour it has kept its place on the
stage.*

* The 'author's nights' produced him £648. As the treasurer
said later, 'It damped the new pieces; and even a year later it would
bring £250, when the piece of the preceding night brought £160.'
Mr. Taylor, writing later to Garrick, said, he 'wished that Sheridan
would write no more, for nothing now goes down but "The School
for Scandal" and "The Duenna."'

The only newspaper criticism that I have been able to find
speaks of it in the highest terms: 'This is almost the first time
we ever saw a screen introduced, and a closet used, without exclaiming against the incidents as poor devices. Mr. Sheridan has
so adroitly placed each, and made both so naturally of advantage
to the conduct of the fable, that they appear by no means the
instruments of art or that kind of stage trick which the French
term *la fourberie du théâtre*." It was objected that there was too
much conversation at the opening; and a pit-critic was heard to
say on the first night of the scandalous coterie, "I wish these
people would have done talking, and let the play begin."'

Among his audience one night was Cumberland, who had
taken his children to see the comedy; and, as the story was told by
a gentleman, a friend of Sheridan's, who was close by, every time
the children laughed at what was going on on the stage, he pinched
them, and said, 'What are you laughing at, my dear little folks?
you should not laugh, my angels; there is nothing to laugh at;'
and then, in an undertone, 'Keep still, you little dunces.' Sheridan
having been told of this long afterwards, said, 'It was very ungrateful in Cumberland to have been displeased with his poor
children for laughing at *my comedy:* for I went the other night to
see *his tragedy*, and laughed at it from beginning to end.'

A sagacious observer, Murphy tells us, remarked to Garrick that this was 'but a single play, and, at the long-run, *will be but a slender help to support a theatre.* To you, Mr. Garrick, I must say, " the Atlas that propped the stage has left his station." " Has he ?" said Garrick ; " if that be the case, he has found another Hercules to succeed to the office." It is to be regretted,' continues Murphy, 'that his prediction has not been fulfilled. A few more such productions would, with propriety, have fixed on Mr. Sheridan the title of our modern Congreve.'

The comedy, when published, had prefixed to it the prologue furnished by Garrick, and also 'a portrait, addressed to Mrs. Crewe,' in which that lady's perfections were celebrated in elegant verse, and in the most extravagant terms of praise. The concluding lines were :

> ' And so each pallid hag with blistered tongue,
>   Mutters assent to all thy zeal has sung,
>   Owns all the colour just, the outline true,
>   Thee my inspirer and my model—CREWE !'

Later ' The Critic' was dedicated in prose to her friend Mrs. Greville. Fitzpatrick wrote the prologue.

Astonishing as was ' The Rivals,' as the work of a young man of only twenty-three, ' The School for Scandal,' written when he was only two years older, is yet a greater marvel. Whence did he draw that store of dramatic witty dialogue and ingenious intrigue ; and above all, that deep knowledge of stage-

11—2

craft, and what would delight and interest audiences of the most mixed character ?   That this was owing to the 'comedy cast' of his mind—his own airy appreciation of the delicate humours of character, fortified by his studies, seems likely enough. Whence he obtained his knowledge of the stage is more difficult to speculate.

Sheridan was truly fortunate in his company. In a happy passage Mr. Boaden, who seems to have witnessed these early performances, describes the effect : ' His company fortunately possessed every variety of elocution.   I think his comedy was better *spoken*, in all its parts, than any play that I have witnessed upon the stage.   And I can safely add that, as to the acting of it, every change, to the present hour, has been a sensible diminution of the original effect.   The *lingered sentiment* of Palmer— the jovial smartness of Smith—the caustic shyness of King—the brilliant loquacity of Abington—however congenial to the play, have long been silent. The first actors of "The School for Scandal" were imitated throughout the country, and some portion of *their* excellence, by frequent transmission, must reach a distant age.   Sheridan himself attended rehearsals, and fully approved the first exhibitors ; an advantage which should stamp the highest value upon their performance, and leave it, if possible, secure from innovation.'

As Lamb said, ' Never was piece so perfectly cast

as this manager's comedy.' The actors were of the 'Old Guard,' and of the 'School of Garrick,' as it was styled. King, the Sir Peter, was an admirable comedian, with an expressive face and figure, as one can see from Zoffany's fine picture of the scene of the 'Clandestine Marriage;' Yates, a veteran of reputation ; and Palmer, who had in his character something of the insincerity of Joseph.* Farren, who then acted Careless, was later to be the 'old Farren' of a past generation, and played Sir Peter with admirable force. There was also Smith, 'the genteel, the airy, and the smart ;' while Dodd, Parsons, even Baddeley, were all excellent in their degree.

The very name of Abington—the first of the Lady Teazles—brings up a tide of bright recollec- tions and jocund associations as we look on her rather pert and mischievous face, as portrayed in Sir Joshua's fine series of portraits. We think of her quarrel with Garrick, who styled her 'that worst of worthless women,' and of Johnson mustering a party to attend her benefit. Miss Pope, too, who owed her engagement with Sheridan to Garrick, was another of this matchless corps. While Miss Pris- cilla Hopkins, the prompter's daughter, and known behind the scenes as 'Pop,' was a pleasing per-

---

* Which prompted one of Sheridan's happiest replies. Palmer, after some act of deception, laying his hand on his heart, while he 'assured Mr. Sheridan,' etc., the other said, ' Why, Jack, *you forget that I wrote it !"*

former, afterwards selected with grotesque solemnity
by Mr. John Kemble as his wife.   But the testimony
of an eye-witness is worth the ' Dead Sea apples'
of conjectural praise ; and Lamb, in a familiar un-
rivalled passage (where, with infinite art, he also
lays down the true principle for rendering comedy),
has recounted for us the impressions of the time.*

* 'It is impossible that it should be now *acted*, though it continues, at long intervals, to be announced in the bills.   Its hero,
when Palmer played it at least, was Joseph Surface.   When I
remember the gay boldness, the graceful solemn plausibility, the
measured step, the insinuating voice—to express it in a word, the
downright *acted* villainy of the part, so different from the pressure
of conscious actual wickedness—the hypocritical assumption of
hypocrisy, which made Jack so deservedly a favourite in that character—I must needs conclude the present generation of play-goers
more virtuous than myself, or more dense.   I freely confess that
he divided the palm with me with his better brother ; that, in fact,
I liked him quite as well.   Not but there are passages—like that,
for instance, where Joseph is made to refuse a pittance to a poor
relation—incongruities which Sheridan was forced upon by the
attempt to join the artificial with the sentimental comedy, either of
which must destroy the other—but over these obstructions Jack's
manner floated him so lightly, that a refusal from him no more
shocked you, than the easy compliance of Charles gave you in
reality any pleasure ; you got over the paltry question as quickly
as you could, to get back into the regions of pure comedy, where
no cold moral reigns.   The highly artificial manner of Palmer in
this character counteracted every disagreeable impression which
you might have received from the contrast, supposing it real,
between the two brothers.   You did not believe in Joseph with the
same faith with which you believed in Charles.   The latter was a
pleasant reality, the former a no less pleasant poetical foil to it.
The comedy, I have said, is incongruous ; a mixture of Congreve
with sentimental incompatibilities : the gaiety upon the whole is

Nothing proves so forcibly that Sheridan possessed the true dramatic instinct and power as his treat-

buoyant ; but it required the consummate art of Palmer to reconcile the discordant elements.

'John Palmer was twice an actor in this exquisite part. He was playing to you all the while that he was playing upon Sir Peter and his lady. You had the first intimation of a sentiment before it was on his lips. His altered voice was meant to you, and you were to suppose that his fictitious co-flutterers on the stage perceived nothing at all of it. What was it to you if that half-reality, the husband, was over-reached by the puppetry—or the thin thing (Lady Teazle's reputation) was persuaded it was dying of a plethory ? The fortunes of Othello and Desdemona were not concerned in it. Poor Jack has passed from the stage in good time, that he did not live to this our age of seriousness. The pleasant old Teazle *King*, too, is gone in good time. His manner would scarce have passed current in our day. Joseph Surface, to go down now, must be a downright revolting villain—no compromise—his first appearance must shock and give horror. Charles (the real canting person of the scene—for the hypocrisy of Joseph has its ulterior legitimate ends, but his brother's professions of a good heart centre in downright self-satisfaction) must be *loved*, and Joseph *hated*. To balance one disagreeable reality with another, Sir Peter Teazle must be no longer the comic idea of a fretful old bachelor bridegroom, whose teasings (while King acted it) were evidently as much played off at you, as they were meant to concern anybody on the stage—he must be a real person, capable in law of sustaining an injury—a person towards whom duties are to be acknowledged—the genuine *crim. con.* antagonist of the villainous seducer, Joseph. Crabtree and Sir Benjamin—those poor snakes that live but in the sunshine of your mirth—must be ripened by this hot-bed process of realization into asps or amphisbænas ; and Mrs. Candour—oh, frightful !—become a hooded serpent. Oh ! who that remembers Parsons and Dodd—the wasp and butterfly of " The School for Scandal "—in those two characters ; and charming natural Miss Pope, the perfect gentlewoman as distinguished from ment of his personages. Sir Peter and Lady Teazle, if measured by the length of their speeches and by what they tell us, are but a short time before us. Yet we seem to know them and their history and characters thoroughly. It is done by a few masterly touches. Nay, there is even an abundance of suggestion which leads us on to speculation and discussion, as upon a real character.*

---

the fine lady of comedy, in this latter part—would forego the true scenic delight, the escape from life, the oblivion of consequences, the holiday barring out of the pedant Reflection—those Saturnalia of two or three brief hours, won from the world—to sit instead at one of our modern plays, to have his coward conscience (that, forsooth, must not be left for a moment) stimulated with perpetual appeals?'

* Witness this interesting letter of Miss Kelly's—Lamb's ' Divine Fanny Kelly.' When asked to undertake Lady Teazle, she made this appeal to the manager :

' I read Lady Teazle last night and again this morning with great attention, and I do not see the slightest difficulty to myself in performing the part. My view of her character is still the same. She appears to me anything but a fine lady ; indeed, there is not a line in the whole play which describes her either as a beautiful or an elegant woman ; but, on the contrary, as having been six months before a girl of limited education, and of the most homely habits. Now, if I could reconcile it to my common-sense, that such a person could acquire the fashionable elegance of high life in so short a period, I hope it is no vain boast to say, that having had the good fortune to be received for years past into society far above my rank in life, and having, therefore, had the best opportunities of observing the manners of the best orders, I must be a sad bungler in my art if I could not at least convey some notion of those manners in the personation of Lady Teazle ; but this, I repeat, is contrary to my common-sense view of her character. Still the town has been so long accustomed to consider her, through

Unfortunately the art of performing 'The School for Scandal' as a comedy seems a lost one. Often as it is revived, 'it cannot now be *acted*.' This will be seen by considering how ineffective seem the scenes where the leading *motif* of the play is put forward, where the Backbites, Lady Sneerwells, Mrs. Candours, etc., figure. The audience look at these characters as at curiosities in a museum ; their long-prolonged conversations and laboured, emphasized wit are unlike anything known or experienced. The real popularity of the piece rests on Sir Peter and his lady, Charles and Joseph. The late Mr. Horace Wigan used, indeed, to say that Sir Oliver was the best acting character in the piece, and is certainly popular with the audience. Yet Lamb dwells with rapture almost on the effect of the more ornamental characters, as played by Dodd and others, as though everything they said and did told. The truth is, our modern stage, with its elaborate effects, lights, mountings, and paraphernalia, overpowers this sort of witty dialogue. These parts, too, are put into the hands of inferior actors, who know not how to treat them ; their only mode is to 'labour them,' overdo and make them as grotesque as possible. In Sheridan's time there were the conversational coteries actually existing—all sorts of professional talkers.

the representation of Miss Farren, and all her successors in the part, in this and no other light, that I really tremble to attempt my simple reading of her character.'

Dr. Johnson is described at one of these parties talking for the public, to a single friend, while all the fashionable company stood crowded round his chair in rows, trying to catch a word. The theatrical audience had assisted at scenes of this kind, and were therefore familiar with what was before them on the stage. Again, this conversation was not meant to be absurd or grotesque, but to be natural, exhibiting the form and pressure of the time. Further, it was supported by first-rate comedians in the habit of acting together every night, and who had been trained by a round of such characters. They knew all the arts of making such points *tell*, without overdone emphasis. Their very bearing and tones betokened the characters. The later exaggeration has spoiled every one of the minor characters. The valet becomes an unnatural being, talking about ' post-obits on his master's clothes,' which never produces even a smile on the face of the audience.*

Another absurdity is certainly making Sir Peter no more than fifty ; but this is generally rectified in the performance, he being played invariably as, a hale and hearty old person of about seventy, but looking past sixty. What Sheridan intended to

---

* Such a valet, living with an impecunious master, would have picked up some of his jargon, using it in a wrong sense, and in all seriousness. This is the idea the player should keep before him. So with little Moses, exaggerated and made a character of, as in a 'Gaiety Burlesque.'

bring out was the *disparity* of some thirty years between the pair ; but, as Lady Teazle is generally played by a mature actress, the difficulty again recurs. Yet there can be little doubt that, for dramatic effect, the actors are right, as a man of forty or fifty would not display the uxorious senility which constitute the humour of Sir Peter.

It is a curious proof of the influence of the stage, that the interest in Charles Surface, so artfully heightened by contrast with that of his brother Joseph, should have made it a fashionable doctrine that this union of a good heart with extravagance was real virtue, instead of being an extenuation of follies. This was in the spirit of Congreve ; and it further seemed a plea urged by the author for his own failings. It was in keeping with Sheridan's ingenuity and readiness at devising clever shifts in his own favour, for there can be no doubt he would have benefited by this popular indulgence. *

* Even in the plays that were brought out by his friends, the changes were rung ; and his friend Richardson, in a comedy called 'The Fugitive,' inculcates the same 'pleasant but wrong theory :'

'OLD MANLY. Yes, my son too, an abandoned profligate.

'ADMIRAL. Nay, if that were all, there might be hopes. The early little irregularities that grow out of the honest passions of our nature are sometimes an advantage to the ripened man ; they carry their own remedy along with them ; and when remedied they generally leave the person wiser and better than they found him : wiser for his experience, and better for the indulgence which they give him towards the infirmities of others ; but a cunning, whining, preaching profligate—a sermon-maker at twenty—a fellow

Mr. Moore has given a very interesting and elaborate account of Sheridan's conception of the play, and his various experiments and re-castings of the plot. His method was exceptional. In the ordinary cases a story is suggested to the author, with perhaps some telling characters which he hopes to attach to the story, and with these materials proceeds to his work. Sheridan had in his mind various coteries of scandal at Bath and its attendant humours, as indeed his sister assures us, trusting to luck for the inspiration of a story. Rich and elaborate characters have often, in novels and dramas, supplied the author with a story ; and the phases of a single character often make a story, as in the instance of Macklin's Sir Pertinax. The mischief done by scandal would be fertile in suggestion, and he had written a good deal of his play on this foundation. But he plainly saw that this was not substantial enough as a motive of interest. He then sought to combine with it a story of a marriage ' between May and December,' with its natural attendant, the tempter, and the additional element of the contrasted brothers working it out. In this spirit he first conceived the idea of the retired tradesman, ' Old Teazle,' who was to be the obvious

---

that becomes a saint before he's a man—a beardless hypocrite—a scoundrel that cannot be content with common homely sinning, but must give it a relish by joining a prayer with it in his mouth— of such a fellow there can be no hopes.'

victim of a young wife thirty years younger. Here
he obtained a suggestion or two from his mother's
play, ' A Trip to Bath,' which also furnished him
with a title, ' The Trip to Scarborough.'

After every repetition this one objection strikes
us with greater force ; but it is radical and cannot be
removed, as it is impossible by any means, save by
the temporary withdrawal of Joseph, to get Sir Peter
to reveal the secret to Charles. Yet the scene is
contrived with such spirit that we overlook this
blemish. One of the finest and most lifelike touches
is Charles's reception of the news, and his eagerness
to ' have her out ' is truly dramatic and exciting, and
the best development of the situation. Sheridan
told Mr. Rogers that he ' was aware he ought to
have made a love-scene between Charles and Maria
in ' The School for Scandal,' and would have done
it, but that the actors who played the parts were
not able to do justice to such a scene.

But the play shows signs of the change of plan,
there being no distinct connection between the
doings of the scandalous coterie and the main plot,
saving their acting as a sort of chorus. *

---

* Mr. Moore minutely describes the different changes of even
the names of the characters, in which Sheridan was singularly
fastidious. An ill-chosen name, however, often seriously fetters
the imagination of even the ordinary author. He had thus
selected originally : Sir Rowland Harpur, —— Plausible, Captain
Harry Plausible, Freeman, Old Teazle (left off trade), Mrs. Teazle,
Maria. His first intention was, as appears from his introductory

In these difficulties he was not to rely on his
own resources; but, as usual, sought aid from others.
He thus ever helped himself to the intellect, as well
as to the cash, of others.

A few passages will show how diligently he has
made use of the ideas of his predecessors, and how
skilfully he has turned them to profit.　It has been
seen that he already owed something to Murphy's
comedy for his ' Rivals,' and he now turned to the
same source for various touches.　Thus, is not
Sir Brilliant's advice to Mrs. Lovemore like that of
Joseph Surface to Lady Teazle?　' Upon my word,
Mrs. Lovemore, for a fine woman like you to be the
dupe of your own false delicacy, an old-fashioned
kind of sentiment, a vulgar prejudice, an antiquated
principle of I know not what! renounce it altogether.
Vivez, ma'am ; do like the ladies of condition.'　Then
Wilkins, the servant, is surely Trip.　' I can't be for
ever a slave to your *second-hand* airs,' he says to the
maid.　' Yes.　You take care of your ladies' toilet,

speech, to give Old Teazle the Christian name of Solomon.
Sheridan was, indeed, most fastidiously changeful in his names.
The present Charles Surface was at first Clerimont, then Florival,
then Captain Harry Plausible, then Harry Pliant or Pliable, then
Young Harrier, and then Frank ; while his elder brother was
successively Plausible, Pliable, Young Pliant, Tom, and lastly
Joseph Surface.　Trip was originally called Spunge ; the name of
Snake was, in the earlier sketch, Spatter ; and, even after the
union of the two plots into one, all the business of the opening
scene with Lady Sneerwell, at present transacted by Snake, was
given to a character, afterwards wholly omitted, Miss Verjuice.

with their cast gowns, and so you descend to us with them. And then, on the other hand, there's my master. Because he claims to live upon the principal of his health, and so run out his whole stock,' etc.

But what has never yet been noticed is his cool appropriation of the characters of one of Colman's plays. Sir Peter and his wife being simply a replica of Lord and Lady Townly in ' The Provoked Husband.'*

* Here is the scene :

' LORD TOWNLY. Why did I marry ?——Was it not evident, my plain, rational scheme of life was impracticable, with a woman of so different a way of thinking ?——Is there one article of it that she has not broke in upon ?——Yes—let me do her justice—— her reputation——insupportable ! for on the pride of that single virtue she seems to lay it down as a fundamental point, that the free indulgence of every other vice this fertile town affords, is the birthright prerogative of a woman of quality——Yet, let me not be rash——Perhaps this disappointment of my heart may make me too impatient ; and some tempers, when reproach'd, grow more untractable——Here she comes——Let me be calm a while.

' (*Enter* LADY TOWNLY.)

' Going out so soon after dinner, madam ?

' LADY T. Lard, my lord ! what can I possibly do at home ?

' LORD T. What does my sister, Lady Grace, do at home ?

' LADY T. Why, that is to me amazing ! Have you ever any pleasure at home ?

' LORD T. It might be in your power, madam, I confess, to make it a little more comfortable to me.

' LADY T. Comfortable ! And so, my good lord, you would really have a woman of my rank and spirit stay at home to comfort her husband. Lord, what notions of life some men have !

The spirit of all this is the same as Sheridan's, and we need only turn to his early drafts of the play to see that he was much indebted to his predecessors.

'LORD T. Don't you think, madam, some ladies' notions are full as extravagant?

'LADY T. Yes, my lord, when the tame doves live coop'd within the pen of your precepts, I do think 'em prodigious indeed.

'LORD T. And when they fly wild about this town, madam, pray what must the world think of 'em then?

'LADY T. Oh, this world is not so ill bred as to quarrel with any woman for liking it!

'LORD T. Nor am I, madam, a husband so well bred, as to bear my wife's being so fond of it; in short, the life you lead, madam——

'LADY T. Is to me the pleasantest life in the world.

'LORD T. I should not dispute your taste, madam, if a woman had a right to please nobody but herself.

'LADY T. Why, whom would you have her please?

'LORD T. Sometimes her husband.

'LADY T. And don't you think a husband under the same obligation?

'LORD T. Certainly.

*   *   *   *   *   *

'LORD T. Now, then, recollect your thoughts, and tell me seriously why you married me?

'LADY T. Why, then, my lord, to give you, at once, a proof of my obedience and sincerity—I think—I married—to take off that restraint that lay upon my pleasures while I was a single woman.

'LORD T. How, madam! is any woman under less restraint after marriage than before it?

'LADY T. Oh, my lord, my lord! they are quite different creatures! Wives have infinite liberties in life, that would be terrible in an unmarried woman to take.

*   *   *   *   *   *

'LORD T. By heaven, if my whole fortune, thrown into your lap, could make you delight in the cheerful duties of a wife, I should think myself a gainer by the purchase!

It has always seemed a mysterious circumstance that Sheridan did not publish his comedy—a course

---

'LADY T. That is, my lord, I might receive your whole estate, provided you were sure I would not spend a shilling of it.

'LORD T. No, madam ; were I master of your heart, your pleasures would be mine ; but, different as they are, I'll feed even your follies to deserve it. Perhaps you may have some other trifling debts of honour abroad, that keep you out of humour at home ; at least it shall not be my fault, if I have not more of your company. There, there's a bill of five hundred ; and now, madam——

'LADY T. And now, my lord, down to the ground I thank you. (*Aside*) Now am I convinced, were I weak enough to love this man, I should never get a single guinea from him.

'LORD T. If it be no offence, madam——

'LADY T. Say what you please, my lord ; I am in that harmony of spirits, it is impossible to put me out of humour. [*Exit.*

*   *   *   *   *   *

'LORD T. Insensible creature! neither reproaches nor indulgence, kindness nor severity, can wake her to the least reflection ! Continual license has lull'd her into such a lethargy of care, that she speaks of her excesses with the same easy confidence, as if they were so many virtues. What a turn has her head taken ! But how to cure it ? I am afraid the physic must be strong that reaches her. Lenitives, I see, are to no purpose ; take my friends' opinion. Manly will speak freely—my sister with tenderness to both sides. They know my case ; I'll talk with them.'

Compare with this the two scenes between Sir Peter and his lady, particularly this passage :

'SIR P. Why did you marry me?

'LADY T. When you asked me if I could love an old fellow, who would deny me nothing, I simpered and said, "Till death."

'SIR P. Why did you say so?

'LADY T. Shall I tell you the truth?

'SIR P. If it is not too great a favour.

then invariable in the case of the most ordinary drama. Plays were written to be *read*, as well as acted ; and this was a fixed element in the author's profits. To a young man under such heavy pecuniary engagements, it must have been an object to secure five or six hundred pounds. This no doubt gave rise to the accusations of plagiarism, and that he had appropriated the play of ' a young lady who had died at Bristol '—a story which was actually accepted by Mr. Isaac Reed. All his other pieces were printed and sold ; and the excuse he gave a bookseller, that ' he had been trying for twenty years but could not satisfy himself,' is scarcely a likely one. It has been said, he feared his borrowings might be traced. Sheridan makes Sir Fretful allude to him in this spirit, declaring that he will never send a play to Drury Lane while he lives, because, he whispers, the manager ' writes himself ;' hinting at ' envy,' and adding, ' it is not always *safe* to leave a play in the hands of those who write themselves. They are sure to steal and disfigure your best thoughts,

---

' LADY T. Why, then, the truth is, I was heartily tired of all these agreeable recreations you have so well remembered, and having a spirit to spend and enjoy fortune, I was determined to marry the first fool I should meet with . . . . you made me a wife, for which I am much obliged to you, and if you have a wish to make me more grateful still, make me a widow.'

There is also a little remark of Lord Townly's, which proves that Sheridan had been reading the play, ' She may break my heart, but she shall not alter my hours.'

as gipsies do stolen children.' This rather absurd speculation is completely disposed of by the notes furnished by Mr. Moore.

As to Sheridan's borrowings from the classical comedy writers—Wycherley, Congreve, Farquhar —his obligations are very faint. Mr. Moore points out that there is a scene in the second act of ' The Plain Dealer ' which offered a suggestion, where a tattle-monger caps an allusion to the absent by some lively bit of disparagement. In ' The Double Dealer ' there is one short scene to which his obligation is more considerable ; in this, one of the characters is actually called Mr. Sneer. There is little in ' The Way of the World ' that suggests any such conveyings.*

It has been often repeated that our author was indebted to a story of his mother's, ' Sydney Biddulph,' for some of the incidents in this comedy. On reading through the novel, it must be said there is little to support the imputation beyond this, that the name of Faulkland is found in ' Sidney Biddulph.' A rich uncle also returns from the Indies much in the same way as Sir Oliver.

* ' Bishop O'Beirne showed Sheridan, in a " Life of Dr. Clarke," the following words : " She did command, because I *would* obey," as being the passage from which he had borrowed one of the lines at the end of " The School for Scandal." Sheridan was angry at the imputation. They used to annoy him about his plagiarisms from Wycherley, till he at last swore he had never read a line of Wycherley.'—*Moore's Diary.*

From Sir John Suckling Sheridan certainly borrowed Charles Surface's lively song. It will be
found in 'The Goblins,' but cannot be decently
quoted in its entirety :

> ' A health to the nut-brown lass,
>   With the hazel eyes—*let it pass.*
>   She that hath good eyes
>
> *   *   *   *
>
>   Let it pass, let it pass,
>   As much to the lovely grey.
>
> *   *   *   *
>
>   I pledge !   I pledge !   Ho ! some wine !
>   Here's to thine, and to thine !
>   The colour was divine,
>   But oh, the black, the black !'*

Again, it has been said that the idea of the two
contrasted brothers was taken from the 'Tom Jones'
and ' Blifil ' of Fielding ; but this, also, is far too
general. The hypocritical man of sentiment is a
common type, and has been presented on the stage
and in novels repeatedly.

The triumph of the whole play is the well-known
screen scene, treated with such art as to overpower
all the obvious incomprehensibilities and even
absurdities of the situation. We always ask, why
could not Joseph deny himself to visitors who not only
invade his library, but hold him in such slavery that
he must leave his guests and *go down to visitors* to
the hall ; while Lady Teazle is left behind the screen,

---

* The name of 'Lady Sneerwell' is taken from one of
Fielding's pieces.

her husband and his own brother remaining in the room ? There was even a closet in the room, where the lady might have been concealed. Indeed, no one of Joseph's cunning, or no one of ordinary sense, would have left so explosive a combination behind him.*

Though the obligation to 'Tom Jones' for the two Surfaces is of a shadowy kind, there can be little doubt that Sheridan owes the suggestion of this most telling scene to that wonderful work. It is surely drawn from that other screen scene at 'Molly Seagrim's,' which Sheridan, with exquisite art, 'adapted' to modern society.

Exception has often been taken to the unfeeling scoffing of Charles Surface after the discovery on the falling of the screen, when he gibes in succession

* Of this screen incident, however, Cumberland wrote handsomely enough, and furnished the best excuse that could be offered : ' I could name one now living, who has made such happy use of his screen in a comedy of the first merit, that if Aristotle himself had written a whole chapter professedly against screens, and Jerry Collier had edited it with notes and illustrations, I would not have placed Lady Teazle out of earshot to have saved his ears from the pillory ; but if either of these worthies could have pointed out any expedient to have got Joseph Surface off the stage, pending that screen, with any reasonable conformity to nature, they would have done more good to the drama than either of them has done her.' There is a picture of the 'screen scene' in the Garrick Club, which has a true air of quiet comedy, contrasting with the farcical exaggerations thrown into it in our time. It seems to be four ladies and gentlemen behaving as those in their rank would do, in a very painful situation.

at the various characters, who stand patiently to hear
him.   This, I believe, is really owing to the exaggerations of the actors, who, as the author said, never
can have too much of a good thing, and have
emphasized the speech into undue importance.   It
was intended as a bit of the lightest raillery, in
a pleasant spirit, to take off the seriousness of
the situation.   It now becomes quite earnest, which
is 'out of key.'   Similarly, the auction scene is
dealt with in too realistic a spirit, the model being
a genuine auction ; whereas it was a bit of persiflage.
But all such things are 'bits of fat' dear to the
actor's heart.

Owing to the present realistic mode of delivery,
many of the epigrammatic passages and allusions fall
flat, or seem unintelligible ; as when Mrs. Candour
says : ' But, sure, you would not be quite so severe on
those who only report what they hear ?'   To which
Sir Peter replies : 'Yes, madam, I would have law
merchant for them too ; and in all cases of slander-
currency, whenever the drawer of the lie was not to
be found, the injured party should have a right to
come on any of the indorsers.'

One might appeal to the experienced playgoer if
this has not always sounded far-fetched and laboured.
The first draft might almost seem more likely to *tell :*
' People who utter a tale of scandal, knowing it to
be forged, deserve the pillory more than for a forged
bank-note.   They can't pass the lie without putting

their names on the back of it. You say no person has a right to come on you because you didn't invent it ; but you should know that, if the drawer of the lie is out of the way, the injured party has a right to come on any of the indorsers.' So with the scenes of scandal, into which the 'gags,' as they are called, have been introduced profusely. The true sympathetic centre of the play is found in the scenes where Sir Peter and his lady and the two Surfaces figure. The scandalmongers belong to an age of conversation. Yet one might imagine an ideal performance of the play even in these days ; the conditions being a small theatre, meagre but adequate scenery, subdued costume, and the actors trained to deliver their witty speeches with a gay, airy intention.

One of the most curious incidents connected with the piece was Kemble's taking the fancy to play Charles Surface ! This well-meant attempt was the source of much jesting. A gentleman whom Kemble had seriously affronted—the great actor was in his cups—agreed to pass it over on condition that he would never play the character again.*

* On the other hand, Lamb was enchanted with him. 'I remember it was then the fashion to cry down John Kemble, who took the part of Charles after Smith ; but, I thought, very unjustly. Smith, I fancy, was more airy, and took the eye with a certain gaiety of person. He brought with him no sombre recollections of tragedy. He had not to expiate the fault of having pleased beforehand in lofty declamation. He had no sins of Hamlet or of Richard to atone for. His failure in these parts was a passport to success in one of so opposite a tendency. But, as far as I could

The successful comedy was now transferred to
Bath, where Mr. Palmer, of coaching notoriety,

judge, the weighty sense of Kemble made up for more personal
incapacity than he had to answer for.   His harshest tones in this
part came steeped and dulcified in good humour.   He made his
defects a grace.   His exact declamatory manner, as he managed
it, only served to convey the points of his dialogue with more
precision.   It seemed to head the shafts to carry them deeper.
Not one of his sparkling sentiments was lost.'

Mr. Taylor describes him when this idea of playing Charles
Surface first occurred to the great tragedian : 'When I called on
him one morning, he was sitting in his great chair with his night-
cap on, and, as he told me, cased in flannel.   Immediately after
the customary salutation, he said, "Taylor, I am studying a new
part in a popular comedy.   What do you think of Charles, in 'The
School for Scandal'?"   "Why," said I, "Charles is a gay, free,
spirited, convivial fellow."   "Yes," said he, "but Charles is a
gentleman."   He tried the part, but his gaiety did not seem to the
town to be of "the right flavour."   It was said by one of Mr.
Kemble's favourable critics in a public print, that his performance
was "Charles's restoration ;" and by another, that it was rather
"Charles's martyrdom."'

To make the issue certain, he seems to have applied to Topham,
a newspaper editor, through Mrs. Wells, a well-known actress of
beautiful face but indifferent reputation, for favourable press
notices.   The lady, many years later, annoyed at being refused
free admission by Kemble, published the correspondence.

'I have taken the liberty,' he wrote, 'to put Mr. and Mrs.
Samuel and Mr. Bonner on the free list, and hope you will have
the goodness to give orders to your people to speak favourably
of the Charles, as more depends on that than you can possibly be
aware of.'

Mr. Topham wrote to Mrs. Wells :

'Cowslip Hall, Suffolk.

'DEAR PUD,—I received your letter, where you mentioned
Kemble's wish to be puffed in Charles.   You may inform Mr.

brought it out with an excellent caste, while the
author himself superintended the rehearsals, and
took immense pains with the production.

'The principal members of our green-room,' says
Bernard, the Bath actor, 'were Edwin, Dimond,
Diddear, Blisset, and Rowbotham (Henderson was
now engaged at Covent Garden). Most of these
persons were men of ability and worth (Mr. Dimond
in particular).' He gives a pleasant account of
Sheridan's labours in the preparation of the play,
and of his careful diligence, which contrasts with
his later carelessness and reckless inattention, when
he would leave portions of the dialogue unfinished
to the very night of performance. 'Such was
Sheridan's particularity, that he took a fortnight
to get up the play, and drilled all the servants and
underlings himself: nothing, however, could be more
pleasant or polite than his manner of doing so. In
his sensitiveness as an author, he never lost sight of
his propriety as a gentleman. The person that gave
him the most trouble was Edwin, who was continually forgetting his business, making wrong exits,
entrances, and crossings. Sheridan, with the utmost
good humour, put him right every morning. "Good
God! Mr. Edwin," Sheridan would exclaim, "there

Este from me, I will not sacrifice the credit of my paper for all
the admissions in Europe to puff either the Siddonses or the
Kembles in comedy.'

you go again !—you've lost your situation, sir !"
Mr. Palmer was on the stage, and Edwin, cock-
ing his eye on him, replied, " I hope I'm not discharged !" '

The play has been translated into many languages,
and is highly esteemed in Germany, where it is often
acted at the classical theatres. Even in Sheridan's
day Schroëder, the German actor, told Kelly ' that
he went to London for the purpose of seeing " The
School for Scandal," previous to translating it. He
understood English perfectly, and spoke it with
fluency. During the time he was in London he
went (as he told me) every night " The School for
Scandal" was performed, and placed himself in the
middle of the pit. He gave the most unqualified
praise to the English actors, as being true to nature.
He regretted not having had the good fortune to
see Garrick ; but he had a very fine picture of him,
which he showed me.'

The King and Queen were always partial to the
comedy, and ' Sir Peter' was a special favourite of
his Majesty's. When the manager was once attending their Majesties to their carriage, the King said
to him, ' I am much pleased with your comedy of
" The School for Scandal," but I am still more so
with your play of " The Rivals ;" that is my favourite,
and I will never give it up.' Her Majesty at the
same time said, ' When, Mr. Sheridan, shall we have
another play from your masterly pen ?' He replied

that 'he was writing a comedy, which he expected very shortly to finish.'*

It was in this brilliant season of 'The School for Scandal' that the compliment was paid Sheridan of being elected a member of 'The Club,' Johnson, his proposer, declaring that a man who had written two of the best comedies in the language ought to be a member.† In a prologue to a play of Savage's, produced at his theatre, Sheridan had alluded in very handsome terms to the Doctor. We find his name also among those who signed the famous 'Round Robin' as to Goldsmith's epitaph.

* The original autograph MS. of 'The School for Scandal' is, or was, in the possession of Sir George Chetwynd, to whom it came through Chetwynd, who was licenser at the time it was produced. It had a narrow escape of being destroyed, having been sent to a binder on whose premises a fire broke out. It was long supposed to have been burnt. There are a few erasures and alterations. It was stated in the papers, that on the morning of the first performance, Mrs. Sheridan had been delivered of a son ; while at night, 'Mr. Sheridan's Muse was delivered of a bantling likely to live for ever.'

† 'On March 14, 1777, Fox in the chair. Present : Fordyce, Gibbons, Garrick, Reynolds, Johnson, Adam Smith, and Burke.' Mr. Tom Taylor, who copied this entry, says it is an illustration of the value of traditions ; for there was a current story at the Club that Sheridan had dined there but once, and then did *not pay for his dinner*. The truth is that he dined over thirteen times.

CHAPTER IX.

THIS brilliant success notwithstanding, the discordant elements in the management continued to work to the serious prejudice of the theatre. Both managers were men of pleasure ; Lacy having but little power owing to his heavily mortgaged moiety, his partners were determined to allow him as little influence as they well could. It was natural, therefore, that matters should speedily come to a crisis.

The extravagant son of an extravagant father, this Willoughby Lacy lived in a wasteful spendthrift style down at Isleworth. He had married a person of great beauty, and, it was noted, ' had driven her to the altar in a splendid coach and four.' He had a town house and a country one. His friend Angelo recalled joyous meetings at the Thames mansion (later occupied by Mrs. Walpole) ; one specially given to celebrate the host's birthday, which wound up with a ball and supper. Here were the Sheridans and Colmans, Captain Thompson, and other jovial wits ; and Mr. Ewart, the son of Sheridan's old friend, 'then,' goes on Angelo, 'famed in gallantry for eloping with the daughter of the wealthy old Manship, an East-India director—his friend Richard Brinsley, as the story went, playing the part of coachman in that real drama of fashionable life. I remember, moreover, the high spirits of all the guests at the supper-table ; and Mr. Colman, in the fervour of argument with Captain Thompson, mounting the table, and declaiming with great energy. Our orgies lasted until day (with the exception of a few of the more sober guests, who departed earlier), when, about five o'clock, our party of *bons vivants* sallied forth to the garden, it being a bright summer morning. Sheridan and I had a fencing match ; and Jerry Orpin, brother of Mrs. Lacy, for a wager jumped from the lawn, his clothes on, into the stream, and swam backwards and forwards across the Thames. I could relate more of this protracted festival, but such frolics may not be worth recording.'

Unfortunately matters were not helped by the autocratic and ignorant rule of the elder Sheridan. The direction of so large an establishment required the greatest tact and flexibility for its exercise. But everyone concerned in the direction seemed unfitted for his duties. An occasional piece, called 'The Camp,' was brought out, written by Sheridan, apropos of the Volunteers' movement, and in which, with much lack of tact, their martial efforts were ridiculed.

'At this impending moment,' it was asked in the newspapers, ' is it wise, is it honourable, in a poet of such talents as Mr. Sheridan, to vilify and throw disgrace on the national character ; to sink the virtue of courage in its own esteem, and hold it forth in colours that tend to make us shun and despise instead of admiring it ? *Bombast* is much more pardonable than *burlesque.*'*

Before the year 1776 was out, the managerial quarrels were to become a scandal. Lacy, who felt his treatment, and seems to have been an obstructive personage enough, contrived a plan for selling a portion of his share to two partners, Captain Thompson and Langford, an auctioneer, who would, of course, come into the management. Sheridan discovered the plot in time, and, acting with great promptitude, frustrated it. He took counsel with Garrick, and contrived a bold, and, as it proved, successful *contre-coup*. He details to his friend his manœuvres for bringing Lacy to reason. The letter shows that Garrick favoured these schemes. It is all told in a pleasant and amusing strain.

* In 1794, Lord Howe's victory, which became known as the 'Glorious First of June,' suggested to Sheridan another occasional piece. No sooner had it occurred to him, than it was prepared at his usual express speed. Some little model ships were fashioned by the stage carpenter, and the Duke of Clarence, a good-natured seaman, came down specially to the theatre, to see that all was nautically correct. Sheridan, during the rehearsals, was in the boxes actually scribbling the dialogue, and handing it down as fast as it was written.

' My dear sir,' he wrote on October 15, 1776, ' I have never been to the theatre nor interfered with the business of it since I saw you, a resolution which at first appeared precipitate even to our own party, and particularly to our friend Wallis. However, they are now convinced that it was positively the only step which could have prevented Lacy's signing with the parties, or have put us on the footing which I hope we shall be on after a meeting we are to have to-morrow. I was convinced that everything had passed between Lacy, Thompson, and Langford, on Friday, except the actually having executed the deeds, and I had reason to think that the next day was appointed for this to be done. It was not to be supposed that argument, or indeed any consideration whatever, would prevail with Captain T. to quit his hold (when he had so much at stake) if he could by any means maintain it : the only method, therefore, which the exigence admitted of, was to convince those who were to find the money that they were going to embark their property in a vessel that was on flames ; and by thus dividing his share, he would ruin the whole of it. Accordingly, after I left you, I wrote a long letter to Langford and Thompson, stating the injustice and illegality of the business, and informing them of my determination if they persisted in it. This Mr. W. delivered to Langford before five o'clock. At eight, I sent Hopkins to Lacy with a more formal and written notice to provide for the business and management by himself. He scarcely believed till then that I would actually do this, and sent Hopkins back to me, etc., but as I would not talk even relative to the theatre, he returned to L., who was in great confusion. Mrs. A. having refused to play, and " The Christmas Tale " (not being ready from the evening rehearsal, which had waited for my coming) being stopped, at twelve " Richard " and the pantomime were fixed, the performers not having heard anything of our change. The next day (which I am convinced was the day they would otherwise have signed and sealed on) Hopkins found them all three in great confusion and perturbation ; Mr. Langford particularly, on hearing from H. that he did not think he could keep the house open a week. However, T. spirited them as much as possible to stand to the business ; but (as I suppose Langford began to have qualms about advancing the money) it was determined to try what a civil letter to me would do, which they sent, hoping to be friendly, with a compliment to my abilities and so forth ; and at night, and again on Sunday morning, Lacy sent by Hopkins to entreat I would return to the management, and that he would do everything in his power to procure matters to be settled to my satisfaction, and would give up the point if he could prevail on them. As I was aware of this, and felt on what secure ground I stood, I still declined hearing anything on the subject ; so that they soon found that the whole of their stock, after changing their play several times, was reduced to the *Committee*, and that after Tuesday they had not one play which they could perform. This appeared to have a great effect in settling the matter, and in consequence (though our meeting yesterday ended in nothing) we were to-day very friendly together, and received a positive promise that the point should be given up, and Mr. Lacy's word that he would never part with his share, or any part of it, but to us. We are to meet at night at Mr. Wallis's, where we are to receive a letter from Captain T. and Mr. L. renouncing the business, though I do not expect we shall come to the point till to-morrow. I have seen none of the performers (purposely) except Mr. Smith and Mr. King, who called on me in Orchard Street, since the affair happened. King has acted particularly well. However, from one motive or other, almost all the principal performers declined playing, on various pretences ; even one or two, who I believe he thought would stand forward, have been taken ill : indeed there never was known such an uncommonly epidemic disorder as has raged among our unfortunate company. It differs from the plague by attacking the better sort first ; the manner, too, in which they are seized, I am told, is very extraordinary : many who were in perfect health at one moment, on receiving a billet from the prompter to summon them to their

business, are seized with sudden qualms, and, before
they can get through the contents, are absolutely
unfit to leave their rooms ; so that Hopkins's notes
seem to operate like what we hear of Italian poisoned
letters, which strike with sickness those to whom
they are addressed : in short, if a successful author
had given the company a dinner at Salt Hill, the
effects could not be more injurious to our dramatic
representations.   And what has been still more
alarming is, that those who being indisposed sent for
our doctor, found themselves on the first visit (an
effect which doctors often produce) worse than they
were before, with this difference only in the process,
that instead of learning his patient's case, he related
his own.   However, I hope we shall be able to procure a *bill of health* very soon ; and as their confinement stands entirely on the ground of their dislike
of playing under they know not whose management,
I shall be particularly cautious that there shall be no
precedent for sickness, as I have been from giving
any authority for it ; and indeed I believe they were
most of them actuated by the same considerations
and obvious foresight of the event, which had influenced me to desist from any part in the direction.
. . . The business of the house is all stopped, by
Lacy's desire, sooner than let it be known to his
proposed partners (which another play, the effect of
my interfering, must have informed them of) that we
were already agreed on our old terms ! We dine

together to-day at Wallis's, when the affair *must* be decided ; but I will not keep this, as Mr. Wallis will have time more fully to inform you of the event, as I speculate on rehearsing "The Christmas Tale" at ten o'clock for Friday. I have run this vile scrawl (which I beg you will excuse, being written in haste) to such a length, I have scarcely room to say how much we feel your friendship in this business.'

The lively sketch of this theatrical ill health is characteristic of Sheridan's humour ; but it was significant that he should have preferred the enjoyment of his dangerous victory to the true interests of the theatre and of the public. Nothing could be more prejudicial than the spectacle afforded of the disorder on the stage to which he alludes, and which tended to develop yet further. There was something unscrupulous in thus stirring up the actors to rebel.

As it was reasonably asked in one of the newspapers : ' Is there a precedent in the annals of the theatre, where the acting manager deserted the general property, left the house, and seduced the actors from their duties—why? forsooth, because he was angry. Is not such conduct actionable ? In any concern of common property, Lord Mansfield would make it so. And what an insult to the public, from whose indulgence and favour this conceited young man, with his wife and family, are to receive their daily bread ! Because Mr. Lacy, in his opinion, had used him ill—his patrons and benefactors might go

13—2

to the devil! Mr. Lacy acted with great temper and moderation ; and, in order that the public might not be wholly disappointed, he brought on old stock-plays—his brother-manager having robbed him of the means and instruments to do otherwise, by taking away the performers.'*

* The influence of a person of Sheridan's character was not unlikely to affect those who were under his authority, and his own shiftiness and devices were often found reflected in the players under his rule. Thus, it was curious that the original Joseph Surface should have been personated, and admirably personated, by the well-known Palmer—'Plausible Jack'—whom Elia has presented to us so delightfully. Kelly gives the following amusing illustration of his elaborate and needless deceptions :

'About two months afterwards he was engaged to go to Reading, to act for a benefit, but he did not go ; and wrote to the poor actor, for whom he was to perform, that he could not leave town, because Mrs. Palmer was just brought to bed ; his letter was read from the stage to the audience. When I heard of it, I congratu-lated him upon the possession of a partner who increased his family every two months. But Plausible Jack, all his life, was blessed with inventive faculties.

'I remember there was a new comedy to be performed at Drury Lane, the name of which I do not now remember, in which Palmer had the principal part ; it was very long, and the day before, at rehearsal, he did not know a single line of it. On the day the play was to be acted, the boxes all engaged, and a crowded house expected, Palmer sent word that he was taken dangerously ill, and that it would be at the risk of his life if he were to play that night. His letter was not sent to the theatre until three o'clock, when all was confusion, from the lateness of the hour at which the intelli-gence was received. Mr. Sheridan was at the box-office, and I was with him, when Powell, the prompter, brought him the letter. When he had read it, he said to me, "I'd lay my life this is a trick of Plausible Jack's, and that there is nothing the matter with

Discipline was now completely relaxed or totally lost, and the players, ill-controlled or neglected, took airs and absented themselves on the most frivolous excuses and in disorderly fashion. What failing theatre could present a more disastrous spectacle than the following, a picture drawn by the despairing prompter, Hopkins!—

'I have been silent thus long in hopes to have sent you an account of the new pantomime, which

---

him, except indeed not knowing a line of the part he has to act to-night. Let you and I call upon him, and I am sure we shall find him as well as ever."

'He lodged in Lisle Street, two doors from my house, and, finding the street-door open, I walked upstairs, where I found him seated at table with his family, in the middle of dinner, in seeming excellent health and spirits. I told him to clear away the table, for Mr. Sheridan would be there in two minutes to see him; "and," said I, "he swears there is nothing the matter with you, and that you have shammed sick only because you are not perfect; if he find himself right in his surmises, he will never forgive you for putting off the play."

'"Thanks, my best, my dearest, valued friend," replied Palmer; " I'm sure you'll not betray me."

'I assured him I would not, and in a moment he was in his bedroom, enveloped in his dressing-gown, with a large woollen night-cap on his head, and a handkerchief tied under his jaw, stretched on a sofa. As Mr. Sheridan entered the room he began groaning, as if in the most excruciating torture from the tooth-ache. Never did he act a part better on or off the stage. Mr. Sheridan was really taken in; advised him to have his tooth extracted, and then to study his part and get perfect in the new play. We went away, and I kept his secret till the day of his death.'

is again obliged (on account of the scenery's not being ready) to be deferred till Friday. This delay has been attended with very bad houses, having nothing ready to perform but the common hackneyed plays, as you will see by the papers. We played last night " Much Ado about Nothing," and had an apology to make for the change of three principal parts. About twelve o'clock Mr. Henderson sent word he was not able to play. We got Mr. Lewis from Covent Garden, who supplied the part of Benedick. Soon after Mr. Parsons sent word he could not play. Mr. Moody supplied the part of Dogberry ; and about four in the afternoon Mr. Vernon sent word he could not play. Mr. Mattocks supplied his part of Balthazar. I thought myself very happy in getting these wide gaps so well stopped. In the middle of the first act, a message was brought me that Mr. La Mash could not come.'

In short, the poor prompter was at his wits' end. It was extraordinary to find the brilliant young manager even thus early displaying this reckless carelessness.

The excellent Garrick, now in his declining days, must have often bitterly regretted the entrusting of his fine property to such hands. Instead of a secure dependence for his old age, he had to see it gradually drifting into insolvency. Affairs now became so involved, that notice was sent to him in

May, 1778, to the effect that for the future they could not pay him his interest ($£2,200$), until the debts and charges of the theatre had been paid. Garrick remonstrated with excellent temper, saying that it was only ' reasonable' that he should be paid, but he must now give them notice of foreclosure. He complained, too, of the rude, unceremonious manner in which he had been treated. All which led to renewed hostility, and paragraphs appeared in the papers reflecting on Garrick, which Linley was obliged to confess were written by him.*

* 'Dear Sir,' he wrote from Norfolk Street, 20th May, 1778,— 'Mr. Sheridan came to me yesterday, and informed me that you are offended by a paragraph which has appeared in the *Morning Chronicle*, and of which you entertain suspicions that it was written by me, in consequence of one which has been published in the same paper reflecting upon Dr. Ford and myself, accusing us of absurdity in our theatrical conduct, and of ingratitude towards *you*. As I trust I cannot tell a lie, therefore for my own satisfaction and your *true* information, I take the earliest opportunity of saying that it was I who wrote it, and that I meant it as a general reply to the paragraph first published, and to many others which have aimed with the like honest and benevolent intent. I am certain —unless the words are perverted from their *true* meaning—there is nothing said that conveys any idea that does not place *you* in a *respectable* situation ; and if I had not *laughed* in my turn, I must have taken no notice at all of what appeared to me to have been inserted with no good intent : nor do I understand upon what ground any person should, thus unprovoked, treat me in so unjust and contemptuous a manner as that paragraph does ; and as I never take liberties of this kind with any person whatsoever, I think I have a right at least to laugh at, if not resent, any such behaviour towards myself. I never thought that *you* wrote the first paragraph, but I thought it very possible some humorous

Stung by which treatment, Garrick wrote to demand his money :

'Aug. 16th, 1778.

' GENTLEMEN,

'The rudeness of your letters, which is always the sign of a bad cause, I shall pass over with the utmost contempt ; but as you have proposed to my friend Mr. Wallis, and my brother, an arbitration, I cannot, as an honest man, refuse to meet you upon any ground. I therefore desire that your attorney will, without delay, in concurrence with Mr. Wallis, settle and prepare this matter, and that all other correspondence may cease between you and

'Your humble servant,

' D. GARRICK.'

Apologies, however, were made, and the matter patched up, as it is called, for the present. Indeed, Garrick's sweetness of disposition and temperate good sense were never better displayed than in the course of these transactions. He had attended rehearsals, and given valuable hints to some of his old friends and favourites, until he was driven away

---

sally of yours or Sheridan's—which had I heard, I am sure I should have enjoyed—might have suggested the malicious and impertinent turn given it to some retailer to a newspaper It is evident that no inconsiderable degree of insolence, profligacy, and imposition prevails in the theatre, when the proprietors dare not correct a servant for misconduct without being *Chronicled.* I beg pardon for thus intruding on you, but I wish not to conceal any action of mine from you.'

by the coarse jealousy of old Mr. Sheridan, now glad to show his power. The following good-humoured protest, addressed to the son, speaks for itself :

'Pray assure your father that I meant not to interfere in his department : I imagined (foolishly indeed) my attending Bannister's rehearsal of the part I once played, and which your father never saw, might have assisted the cause, without giving the least offence. I love my ease too well to be thought an interloper, and I should not have been impertinent enough to have attended any rehearsal, had not you, sir, in a very particular manner desired me. However, upon no consideration will I ever interfere again in this business, nor be liable to receive such another message as was brought me this evening by young Bannister. You must not imagine that I write this in a pet : let me assure you, upon my honour, that I am in perfect peace with you all, and wish you from my heart all that you can wish.'

But this was not all. The actors were even encouraged to treat the veteran player with studied insolence, and at the Theatrical Fund Dinner he met with actual rudeness. King, however, sent his old manager some excuses :

'I am certain there was not an actor at that table who does not hold you, your name and opinions, in the highest veneration ; nor has there been one of them, that I have heard of, who has not expressed concern and surprise, on hearing you had found anything amiss in their conduct *towards you.* That we were insufferably dull, I most readily acknowledge ; that *I* was hurt, on entering the room, at seeing Palmer and Wrighton there, I freely confess ; the former having just before dishonoured the body by a degrading plea in a public court, and the latter having broken a solemn engagement made with one manager (whom he left in the utmost distress) for no other reason than because he could enter into a new one with another on terms more advantageous.'

Garrick, wounded, but forgiving, answered him with his usual gentleness :

' Though you would not *seek* me, I have sought you this morning. You are a male coquette, Mr. Thomas, but have such winning ways with you, that we readily forget your little infidelities. I must confess that my reception at the Fund Dinner was as surprising as it was disagreeable and unexpected. I seemed to be the person marked for displeasure, and was almost literally sent to Coventry. Though I ventured among you after a very severe illness, and had dressed myself out as fine as possible, to do all the honour I could to the day and the Committee, I never was more unhappy for the time : however, let it be forgotten ; and, when we meet, let not a word be said of what is past. Poor old Drury! It will be, I fear, very soon in the hands of the Philistines.'

In which foreboding he was too soon to be justified.

At last Lacy, who was now intending to follow the stage as a profession, was induced to dispose of his shares to Sheridan himself. This other 'miracle' was performed towards the close of 1778. He was said to have paid Lacy at the rate of £45,000, a rise of £10,000 on the value of the property in two years. The arrangement, however, was of a somewhat complex character, as Sheridan himself disposed of his share to Ford and Linley at an advanced price, 'so as to make up each of theirs a quarter.'* Sheridan thus became the largest single proprietor, holding half the property. Ford, having previously £15,000, gave for only a portion of Sheridan's share £7,500, thus holding £22,500 in all; while Linley must have paid considerably more.†

Garrick did not live to receive half his capital, nor indeed was the mortgage paid off till fifteen years after his death, when the new shareholders

---

* Moore's 'Sheridan,' i. 263.

† Lacy's moiety was actually purchased for 31,500 guineas, and two annuities of £500 each—one for Lacy's wife, the other for Langford's. He was also to have the privilege of putting twenty persons on the free list, and of selling his annuity as he pleased. In the year 1800, a writer says that 'Mrs. Lacy is now, with a large family, in very distressed circumstances. The writer of this sketch is in possession of very curious particulars with respect to the transfer of the Lacy property in the theatre to Mr. Sheridan.'

had to discharge it. His claims then amounted, with interest, to nearly £30,000.*

It was in the year 1779 that the kind friend who had so applauded 'The School for Scandal' passed away. The greatest of English actors was interred in Westminster Abbey. At the funeral Burke pointed out how appropriately the statue of Shakespeare seemed to point down to his grave—a happy idea which Sheridan instantly 'conveyed' and appropriated for the 'Monody' he wrote, and which, with an eye to business, he caused to be delivered for many nights on the boards of his theatre. Of this several editions were sold.†

* Mr. Moore wonders again and again where Sheridan contrived to raise these thousands of pounds. It is not difficult to discover his method, from the accounts and charges of his theatre. He let Garrick's mortgage lie over; he received nearly £11,000 from Linley, who mortgaged his share to Mr. Wallis for that amount. Linley seems to have also mortgaged it for nearly £4,000 to Ford. Sheridan also mortgaged his share for £5,000; and eked out the balance with annuities—his favourite mode of raising funds.

† The idea this imparted was thus dressed up:

'The throng that mourn'd as their dead favourite pass'd,
The grac'd respect that claim'd him to the last;
While Shakespeare's image, from its hallow'd base,
Seem'd to prescribe the grave and point the place.'

While the basis of the whole—the record of the actor's glories being transitory and precarious, when compared with the enduring one of the painter—was actually suggested by some lines of the deceased player he was celebrating.

It is pleasant to find Sheridan at this time doing many good-natured acts, one of which was giving a benefit to 'Tom Davies,'

After this serious effort Sheridan now turned to a higher subject that was to supply to the theatre, and with singular ease of effort, yet another production—one destined to the rare and enviable lot of keeping the stage. He possessed the happy gift, so often found in careless but clever men, of discerning a good opportunity, and of striking out profitable and apropos ideas. A couple of years had elapsed since the great success of his comedy, and he was prepared with a new venture. This seems

---

at which Mr. Taylor was present, who noted his mouthing voice—'as curs gnaw a bone.' Davies, in his preface to the 'Life of Garrick,' gratefully acknowledges this assistance: 'Your kindness shown to me at a time I most stood in need of your friendship can never be blotted from my remembrance. This is a subject which I could, with delight, enlarge upon ; but I am convinced, from the constant pleasure you feel in conferring favours, you would rather do a thousand generous actions than be told of one.' Sheridan also furnished many prologues, epilogues, and, when asked, brought out Savage's play.

There is an amusingly characteristic incident connected with the dedication of the Monody. He had inscribed it effusively to Lady Spencer, Garrick's friend, a person deservedly admired : 'To her whose approbation of this drama, and whose peculiar delight in the applause it has received from the public, has been to me the highest gratification derived from its success, I dedicate this play.' More than thirty years afterwards, Lord Byron saw him take up the 'Monody;' when he lighted on the dedication to the lady, he flew into a rage, and exclaimed 'it must be a forgery, that he had never dedicated such a thing to a d——d canting, etc., etc., and so went on for half an hour— abusing his own dedication, or the object of it.' Truly, a scene worthy of his own Sir Fretful.

to have been a production that had been lying by him, for we find him, in one of his letters to Linley, written long before, alluding to a two-act piece which he was preparing. The ever-amusing 'Critic,' or 'A Tragedy Rehearsed,' may be considered something of an adaptation of previous pieces by the Duke of Buckingham, Fielding, Murphy, and others, and, indeed, the subject has always been tempting to the wits. The 30th of October was fixed for the performance, but on the 27th the piece was not complete. Managers and actors became seriously uneasy, and all entreaties were found useless. At last, one night, when a rehearsal was going on, King whispered to Sheridan to come out, as he had something important to tell him. In a room with a fire blazing, sandwiches and wine on the table, he found Linley, and they both half jocosely and half seriously assured him it was vital that the piece should be completed at once. Tempted by the inviting prospect, Sheridan suffered himself to be *locked in*, and actually accomplished his task.

Mr. Adolphus, who had seen the play, was enraptured with Miss Pope's playing of Tilburina, which, he said, could 'never be forgotten by those who had seen her, or adequately conceived by those who had not.' There was a clever young actor, who had been instructed by Garrick, just then beginning to attract attention—Bannister—who made an immense deal of Don Ferolo. Holcroft declared to

Adolphus that he could 'furnish a key to the piece' —as in the case of the 'Rehearsal'—by selecting the passages burlesqued from contemporary authors.*

It is said that Sheridan's brother-in-law, Tickell, helped him, and there is a certain likeness in the style to passages in the 'Anticipation' of the latter. The passage where Puff gives an account of his various modes of advertising is beyond question suggested by Shift's account of himself in 'The

---

* A couple of specimens of Sheridan's borrowings or adaptations from the Duke of Buckingham will serve to show how wholesale was his system :

'SCENE.—*Enter* SIR WALTER RALEIGH *and* SIR CHRISTOPHER HATTON.

'SIR CHRIST. H. True, gallant Raleigh——
'DANGLE. What, they had been talking before ?
'PUFF. Oh yes, all the way as they came along.'

Compare 'The Rehearsal' :

'PHYS. Sir, to conclude——
'SMITH. What, before he begins ?
'BAYES. No, sir ; you must know they had been talking of this a pretty while without.
'SMITH. Where ? in the tyring-room ?
'BAYES. Why, ay, sir.   He's so dull.'

So with Lord Burleigh's famous 'Shake of the head' :

' *Enter Four Patriots from different Doors, who meet in the Centre and shake Hands.*

'SOUR-WIT. These patriots seem to equal your greatest politicians in their silence.
' MEDLEY. Sir, what they think now cannot well be spoke, but you may conjecture a good deal from their shaking their heads.'

Minor.' Mr. Moore, indeed, rather tolerantly alludes to these borrowings, saying that 'such coincidences, whether accidental or designed, are at least curious.'

It was in this lively piece that the veteran Cumberland found himself held up to ridicule, portrayed to the life, with all his sensitiveness, jealousies, rage, and other peculiarities. This was not strictly loyal towards 'an author of the House.' Not since the days of Foote had this odious system of personality been tolerated. The likeness was striking and unmistakable. Sir Fretful's inviting criticism, while at the next moment he rejected it, seems to have been drawn from Sheridan's own experience of the sensitive writer, who had invited him to judge his play 'with as much malice as he was capable of, an author being but an ill judge in his own cause.' The bitterness of the portrait was really unwarrantable, and becomes surprising in a person like the author, naturally good-natured.*

* Among the Sheridan papers in the British Museum there is an account for October 5, 'the author's night,' in which 'The Critic' was performed, with 'As You Like It.'

	£	s.	d.
First account	200	17	0
Second account	35	0	0
After-money	0	6	6
	236	3	6
Deduct charges of the house .	73	10	0
Balance	162	13	6

This series of three remarkable plays, the best comedy, best opera, and perhaps the most popular and enduring burlesque in the language, completes Sheridan's dramatic labours, for what he did later was little more than translation and adaptation. It is amazing to think that these three *chefs-d'œuvre* were produced in succession within the short space of half a dozen years. Such success, so brilliant and so lasting, is unexampled, and is the highest proof of Sheridan's talent.*

Among his papers were found rough drafts and stray sketches of two other pieces—'The Forresters,' and a comedy on the subject of affectation. The former, of which Mr. Moore gives some specimens, was intended for an opera, and seems to have been taken from the German. Its tone is thoroughly German, and it is not at all in Sheridan's manner. 'Affectation' seems to have been conceived in the spirit of 'The School for Scandal;' and he appears to have followed the same mode of compo-

---

* The following are the dates of performance of Sheridan's series of plays :

'The Rivals'	. .	January 17, 1775.
'St. Patrick's Day'	.	November, 1775.
'The Duenna'	. .	November 21, 1775.
'Trip to Scarborough'	.	February 24, 1777.
'The School for Scandal'	.	May 8, 1777.
'The Camp'	. .	October 15, 1778.
'The Critic'	. .	October 30, 1779.
'Pizarro'.	.	May 24, 1799.

sition, by first securing some fashionable folly of
society for treatment, and trusting that a plot and
characters could be fitted to it later. This would
probably have been a failure, for the reason given
in the case of ' The School for Scandal,' that mere
witty sayings are not sufficient to give dramatic
strength.*

But besides these sketches there are actually in
existence some finished pieces, undoubtedly the
work of Sheridan, and which clearly show that he
was inclined to renew his former triumph if he could,
but that he had exhausted his vein, or lacked the
spring and enthusiasm necessary for success. Thus,
in the year 1808, when he was treating with Jones,
a pleasant 'airy' comedian from the Dublin theatre,
he was, as it were, engaging himself by the odd
agency of a bet to take up the old pursuit. At the
One Tun Tavern he bet two gentlemen five hundred

* The specimens preserved of this comedy are pleasant :

' A man intriguing, only for the reputation of it, to his confidential servant : "Who am I in love with now?"—"The newspapers give you so and so ; you are laying close siege to Lady L.
in the *Morning Post.*" " I forgot to forget the billet-doux at
Brooks's "—" By-the-bye, ain't I in love with you ?"   An old
man, who affects intrigue, and writes his own reproaches in the
Morning Post, trying to scandalize himself into the reputation of
being young.' So with the sketch of a fat woman, who in sitting
can only lean against her chair—'rings on her fingers, and her
fat arms strangled with bracelets, which belt them like corded
brawn—rolling and heaving, when she laughs, with the rattles in
her throat, and a most apoplectic ogle—you wish to draw her out
as you would an opera-glass.'

guineas that, provided the latter joined the direction, he would, within three years, produce a five or three-act play. Many years ago there came into the hands of the late Mr. P. G. Patmore three dramas which really appear to be of Sheridan's composition. The reasons for this view are almost convincing. The dramas were obtained *from a pawnbroker*, with whom poor Sheridan had pledged them! He could have obtained no money on MS. pieces written by others. They may be said certainly to be in his writing, for though Mr. Patmore tells us the body of the play is in the handwriting of a copyist, many hundreds of *blank spaces* were left in it, of all lengths, from that of a single word to several lines, and Sheridan filled in every one of these blanks with his own hand, together with many hundreds of corrections, additions, etc. One of these pieces was the youthful fragment of 'Jupiter,' or 'Ixion,' at last completed and fitted for the stage. 'The second, which, from its subject, I am rather doubtful about, is a fairy opera on King Arthur and Queen Mab, etc., full of songs, and evidently written to be set to music. The last is a musical after-piece entirely in his handwriting, in which occurs this pretty song:

' "LAURA.

' " Melancholy, friend to grief,
　　Ever o'er my bosom reign;
　To my sorrows bring relief,
　　And thyself inspire my strain.

14—2

' " When thy sadness can impart
 All its healing, soft'ning powers,
Then thy tears are to the heart
 Like the falling dew to flowers.

' " Happy he whose peaceful day
 In retirement gently flows !
From the busy world away,
 All thy balmy calm he knows.

' " Then he hopes alone in thee
 Some relief from care to find,
Seeking no society
 But his memory and mind." '

There was also ' The Forresters,' before alluded to, of which he would say in company, ' Wait until you hear my "Forresters." ' It was fortunate, on the whole, that these pieces were not brought forward, as the unbroken line of success might have been interrupted. Still there is no knowing but that the burlesque of ' Ixion,' if regularly shaped for the stage under pressure, as it would have been, might have proved an extraordinary success.

Here, then, we conclude this, perhaps, most interesting portion of Sheridan's career, from which we may lament that he was ever drawn aside.

CHAPTER X.

We shall now turn to survey Sheridan in a yet more pleasant aspect, as he enjoyed himself 'on town,' surrounded by gay and humorous friends, and giving full vent to his fund of spirits and good-humour. A very amusing record it will prove. He had surrounded himself with a number of intimates—a sort of 'jovial crew'—with whom he delighted to associate. These were of a congenial sort. And here, before surveying him in this part of his career, we may take note of an objection latterly made by the charitably fastidious as to the impolicy or injustice of 'lifting the veil,' as it is termed, supposed to hang before the weakness of the eminent. Clamour of this sort has in our own day followed the remarkable account given by Mr. Froude of Thomas Carlyle, and the author has disposed of the objection in an admirable vindication. It might be urged that our age is one of detail, when broadly abstract estimates are found barren by the public, and conveying little. The question would require the space of an essay to deal with fully ; but it may be said in the case of Sheridan that these extravagancies and failings *are* his life, and seemed to prompt every incident of it. Again, as to those tales and 'anecdotes' so often retailed, and making the staple of his adventurous course, we may note an objection that has been taken by ardent advocates and extenuators of his follies. Mrs. Norton, Mr. Fraser-Rae, and others, are positive that three-fourths of the anecdotes recorded are fictions, or coloured to his prejudice. This too partial view cannot be supported. These stories, an essential portion of his life and character, are given on the evidence of persons of character who knew him intimately, such as Taylor, Kelly, the Kembles, Boaden, etc. They are all circumstantial, with names, dates, and places, and they are in exact keeping with his admitted failings. Why, therefore, should they not be accepted ?

Among his associates were Richard Tickell, before introduced at Bath ; 'Joe' Richardson ; and his brothers-in-law the Linleys ; while the two charming sisters Linley seemed to inspire all their quips and pranks. For, not yet had the early romantic tenderness of Sheridan and his wife begun to grow worn. She was still the centre and the inspiration of all the rather boyish pastimes which were the delight of the coterie. The chimes were heard at midnight in

Orchard Street. The two sisters were bound together by an extraordinary affection; whilst the brothers-in-law were always on excellent terms.

Mr. Taylor, who knew both well, and was a keen observer enough, contrasts their characters rather happily. He shows, too, that there is something laborious and uncertain in the life of the professional joker.* 'It was supposed,' says Taylor, 'by some of their friends, though not of the most discerning, that Sheridan was jealous of the conversational powers of Tickell, who displayed great wit, humour, and an appropriate delineation and characteristic diversity of character in his "Anticipation," and poetical spirit in his "Wreath of Fashion," and more in his "Charles Fox, partridge-shooting, to John Townshend, cruising." He was peculiarly spirited and entertaining in conversation.'†

* Who has touched this topic so happily as one who was a professional joker himself — Sydney Smith? 'No pecuniary embarrassments,' he says, 'equal the embarrassments of a professed wit: an eternal demand upon him for pleasantry, or consciousness on his part of a limited income of the facetious; the disappointment of his creditors, the importunity of duns, *the tricks, forgeries, and false coin he is forced to pay instead of gold.*'

† A whimsical circumstance occurred during a short visit which he paid at Oxford, to the head of one of the colleges. 'Dining in the common room, an old member of the University, who was very deaf, observing the effect of his lively sallies on the company, and hearing that his name was Tickell, asked the gentleman who sat next to him, and who was a wag, whether that was the Mr. Tickell who had been the friend of Mr. Addison. The gentleman told him it was the same person. The old member then expressed

When the first Mrs. Tickell died, her husband was in an agony of grief, and signified to his friend Richardson that it was his intention to have engraved on her tombstone his solemn unalterable purpose to remain single for the rest of his life. His friend earnestly dissuaded him from this step, for he knew his rather volatile character. He urged that if it were immediately inscribed, it might be considered the effusion of temporary grief; whereas if he waited a twelvemonth or so, it would have the air of a settled determined purpose. Tickell yielded to these prudent considerations, waited for the twelvemonth, and married another lady. This friend incidentally and pleasantly mentions a ' characteristic ' of Tickell's habitual conduct. ' It was a

great regret that he sat at such a distance, and was too deaf to hear the brilliant effusions of Mr. Tickell's genius, particularly, too, as he might also hear some original anecdotes of his immortal friend, the author of " Cato." The wag, to console him, promised that whenever Mr. Tickell uttered anything of striking humour, or told an interesting anecdote, he would relate it to him. The wag gave a hint to the company of the old member's misconception. Whenever a laugh was excited by what Tickell said, the old gentleman resorted to his waggish friend to know what he had heard. The wag either invented a *bon mot*, or told a ludicrous incident, which perhaps delighted the former even more than if he had heard Tickell's real effusion. This whimsical entertainment continued till the humour was no longer diverting to the party ; and the object of this hardly allowable jocularity retired, proud that he had been in company with the friend of Mr. Addison, but lamenting that he could only profit by his wit and humour at secondhand.'—*Taylor's ' Records.'*

common trick of his,' he says without surprise, as if
it was a proper step, 'when supping at a coffee-
house with a friend, to quit the room upon some
pretence for a few moments, and leave the friend to
pay the reckoning. This habit was certainly not
the effect of meanness or of parsimony in Tickell,
but of a waggish humour ;' which ' waggish humour '
was quite after ' the higher manner ' of his brother-
in-law ; and indeed there was a singular likeness in
their modes, manners, and humours. This pleasant
circle was described in polished lines by Tickell,
who lavishes praise and compliment on the various
members—the 'wit of Fitzpatrick,' 'the friendly
sneer' of 'good-natured Devon'—and thus intro-
duces his friend :

> ' Of wit, of taste, of fancy, we'll debate,
> If Sheridan for once be not too late.'

This was the age of verses of society, written in a
spirit of much grace and elegance, by almost everyone that pretended to cleverness. The ' Dodsley
Collection,' with its continuation in many volumes,
the ' New Foundling Hospital for Wit,' and such
productions, attest this cultivated taste. We should
wonder now if ' a copy of verses ' were sent by a
gentleman to a lady, or handed round the clubs or
saloons, written on the model of Pope.

This agreeable joker, however, Moore heard from
friends of his, was a disagreeable, unpleasant fellow in
domestic life, and showed some jealousy of Sheridan.

These two singular beings used gravely to repre-
hend each other upon their faults and failings,
Tickell reproving his friend for his careless, dissipated life, and Sheridan inveighing against the
thoughtlessness and frivolity of the other! When
one of Tickell's numerous daughters was growing
up, a dispute arose between them as to her education. Sheridan and his wife were eager to adopt
her and superintend her life, and the question
was taken up by Sheridan in an oddly eager way;
but Tickell did not incline to the idea, and proposed
sending her to a boarding-school under the care of
a Miss Leigh, or Lee—a plan that was violently
opposed by Sheridan, who pressed the value of
home education. He was angry when he found
his plan was rejected, urging that 'she was deprived
of natural affection.' Tickell urged his own paternal
claims with due gravity. 'All such renunciation of
my unalienable right as *a fond parent*,' he laid down,
'I considered as totally out of the question. I cannot think Kitty is deprived of maternal affection;
still less why, if she were so deprived, Sheridan's
interference was necessary.' Not long after, Mr.
Tickell married the Miss Leigh to whom his
daughter had been sent.

Another friend, 'Joe' Richardson, offers an illustration of the curious disturbing fascinations offered by
the stage. This clever man, originally a politician,
had a seat in Parliament, and was the ally of Fox,

Lord Fitzwilliam, the Duke of Portland, and other distinguished persons. He became a barrister, with sagacity and power of cross-examination which promised him success. Then, unhappily, he became the friend of our hero, and this fatal influence, of course, drew him away from all serious labour and business. He now began to write plays, and produced 'The Fugitive' with some success. But it had been well for him if he had kept to the bar.

In the early days of their connection this trio seemed to enjoy life like schoolboys. They revelled in the invention of practical jokes, and in keeping up fast and furious fun at country-houses. It is extraordinary to think of this mercurial state of mind in full-grown men of middle life, with families, and engaged in serious enterprises. It is impossible not to relish one trick played at Richardson's expense by Sheridan. Having had a hackney-coach in employ for five or six hours, and not being provided with the means of paying for it, he happened to espy Richardson in the street, and proposed to take him in the coach some part of his way. The offer being accepted, Sheridan lost no time in starting a subject of conversation, on which he knew his companion was sure to become argumentative and animated. Having, by well-managed contradiction, brought him to the proper pitch of excitement, he affected to grow impatient and angry himself, and saying that 'he could not think of staying in the same coach with a person that would use such language,' pulled the check-string and desired the coachman to let him out. Richardson, wholly occupied with the argument, and regarding the retreat of his opponent as an acknowledgment of defeat, still pressed his point, and even hallooed 'more last words' through the coach-window after Sheridan, who walked quietly home. What amuses here is the adroit knowledge of character displayed by the performer, and the turning of the foibles of human nature to his own profit.[*]

The Irish Bishop, Dr. O'Beirne,[†] a clever ecclesiastic, a friend of statesmen, and possessing

[*] So with his contriving an ambuscade for his friend Tickell. 'Having covered the floor of a dark passage, leading from the drawing-room, with all the plates and dishes of the house, ranged closely together, he provoked his unconscious playfellow to pursue him into the midst of them. Having left a path for his own escape, he passed through easily ; but Tickell falling at full length into the ambuscade, was very much cut in several places. The next day, Lord John Townshend, on paying a visit to the bedside of Tickell, found him covered over with patches, and indignantly vowing vengeance against Sheridan for this unjustifiable trick. In the midst of his anger, however, he could not help exclaiming, with the true feeling of an amateur of this sort of mischief, " But how amazingly well done it was ! " '—*Moore.*

[†] The history of this prelate is a curious one. He had been a Roman Catholic, but accidentally meeting two political Dukes at an inn on the road, so pleased and entertained them that he was induced, on promise of patronage, to give up his creed and attach himself to their party. He eventually became Bishop of Meath.

some wit, for he was a contributor to 'The Rolliad,' seems to have been a favourite 'butt' of Sheridan's, who ridiculed his Irish pronunciation in some pleasant rhymes.

On this prelate, then a clergyman, a very pleasant and original form of jest was practised, at which it is impossible not to smile. It used to be related by the victim himself.

'I have had the advantage,' says Moore, 'of hearing the joke from the person on whom it was inflicted. The Rev. Mr. O'Beirne having arrived to dinner at Sheridan's country-house near Osterley, where, as usual, a gay party was collected, consisting of General Burgoyne, Mrs. Crewe, Tickell, etc., it was proposed that on the next day (Sunday) the reverend gentleman should, on gaining the consent of the resident clergyman, give a specimen of his talents as a preacher in the village church. On his objecting that he was not provided with a sermon, his host offered to write one for him, if he would consent to preach it ; and the offer being accepted, Sheridan left the company early, and did not return for the remainder of the evening. The following morning Mr. O'Beirne found the manuscript by his bedside, tied together neatly (as he described it) with riband, the subject of the discourse being the "Abuse of Riches." Having read it over and corrected some theological errors, such as "it is easier for a camel, *as Moses says*," etc., he delivered the sermon in his most impressive style, much to the delight of his own party, and to the satisfaction, as he unsuspectingly flattered himself, of all the rest of the congregation, among whom was Mr. Sheridan's wealthy neighbour, Mr. Childs. Some months afterwards, however, Mr. O'Beirne perceived that the family of Mr. Childs, with whom he had previously been intimate, treated him with marked coldness ; and, on his expressing some innocent wonder at the circumstance, was at length informed, to his dismay, by General Burgoyne, that the sermon which Sheridan had written for him was, throughout, a personal attack upon Mr. Childs, who had at that time rendered himself very unpopular in the neighbourhood by some harsh conduct to the poor, and to whom everyone in the church, except the unconscious preacher, applied almost every sentence of the sermon.'

Unhappily these jovial times were to be succeeded by the embarrassments which inevitably attend the *viveur's* life. The three lively friends had to encounter their proper share of pecuniary difficulties. So early as 1787, Tickell had to give security for £250, the arrears of an annuity charged on Sheridan's share. In 1792 we find Richardson describing his negotiations with a creditor. 'Wright's bill of £500,' about which a prosecution had been commenced, was ' stopped by an injunction,' the creditor declaring that he would only give time on £2,000

being put into a shape of practicable use and payment immediately ; for the rest he would take security.

We have a piteous letter from Richardson, who
complains that after being assured by Sheridan that
he was to be assisted, he was left in the lurch.
Driven to desperation he wrote : 'In four days I
have a *cognovit* expires for £200. *I can't suffer my
family to be turned into the street if I can help it.* I
have no resource but my abilities, such as they are.
I certainly mean to write something in the course of
the summer. As a matter of business and bargain
I *can* have no higher hope about it than that you
won't suffer by it. However, if you won't take it
somebody else *must*, for no human consideration
will induce me to leave any means untried that may
rescue my family from this impending misfortune.
For the sake of convenience you will probably give
me the importance of construing this into an incendiary letter. I wish to God you may, and order
your treasurer to deposit the acceptance accordingly ;
for nothing can be so irksome to me as that the
nations of the earth should think there had been any
interruption of friendship between you and me.'

This does seem something like an incendiary
letter. His chequered course did not last long.
He fell into bad health, and died on June 9, 1803, of
breaking a bloodvessel, when only forty-seven years
old. At his funeral, which was at Virginia Water,
a most singular, half-grotesque incident occurred,

which illustrates more than anything the character of
Sheridan. It is described by one of the mourners :

'The funeral ceremony was to take place at one
o'clock in the day, but we did not reach the ground
till a quarter after, and were surprised and grieved
to find that the funeral rites had been performed.
Mr. Sheridan was particularly affected, and traversed
the churchyard in great anxiety. He said to me as
we walked together, " Now this disappointment will
be imputed to me, and it will be said in town by all
our mutual friends that it was owing to Sheridan's
d——d negligence, which he could not shake off,
even to pay respect to the remains of his dearest
friend." I left Mr. Sheridan, and inquired of the
reverend gentleman what was the cause of this hasty
interment, as greater latitude ought to have been
allowed to friends who had to come twenty miles to
attend on the mournful occasion, and who had
arrived within a quarter of an hour after. The
clergyman said it was owing to the undertaker, who
alleged that he had another funeral to attend at a
distant place. I then asked the clergyman if the
ceremony could properly be repeated, as we were all
bitterly disappointed that we were prevented from
testifying our grief by partaking in the last offices of
respect to the remains of a valued friend. The
clergyman seemed to pause, and as I knew that my
interference could be little likely to affect him, I
hastened to Mr. Sheridan, and told him there was a

possibility that the ceremony might be repeated.
Mr. Sheridan then ran to the clergyman, telling him
who he was, and earnestly entreating, if there were
no impropriety in the measure, that the ceremony
might again take place to satisfy the feelings of himself and his friends. The clergyman said that he
was only the curate to his father, the vicar, and
could not without authority comply, but would consult his father, and if he consented, return immediately, properly attired, to repeat the ceremony. In
a few moments he appeared, dressed for the occasion.
We then adjourned to the church, in which the
funeral service was partly performed, and the remainder at the side of the grave, without removal of
the coffin.

'It is difficult to describe the sort of mournful
exultation with which Mr. Sheridan said he could
now venture to face his friends in London, conscious
that he had not failed in any respect to do honour to
his departed friend. We dined at Bedfont on our
return to town, and Mr. Sheridan entered into an
eulogium on his deceased friend, of whom he spoke
with sincere emotion and affecting eloquence. As soon
as we entered Conduit Street, he manifested great
emotion, and in the agony of his feelings *struck his*
head against the door of the nearest house, exclaiming
that he had lost his dearest friend, and there was
now nobody who could enter into his domestic cares
and be a confidential agent, when occasion might

require, between himself and Mrs. Sheridan. I endeavoured to soothe his feelings, and on parting with him at his own door, he designated me as " Joe Richardson's Legacy."

'The scene in the churchyard would have been diverting also on a less melancholy occasion ; for in our hurry to attend the melancholy ceremony, not knowing it had already been performed, we put on the mourning cloaks without regard to their size, so that Mr. Sheridan had one that hardly reached to his knees, and Dr. Coombe, a very short man, had one so long that he trampled upon it, and nearly tumbled at every step. Naturally conversing on the subject of our departed friend in the coach, as we returned, Mr. Sheridan expressed his determination to write an epitaph on Mr. Richardson ; and Dr. Coombe, who professed particular knowledge of stones, declared that he would select a durable one for the inscription. The epitaph, however, was never written, and the stone was never found.'

Mr. Richardson left a widow and four daughters, who were reduced almost to beggary. Thus every incident was in keeping with convivial traditions. Nor was the end of Sheridan's other friend and 'co-drinker' less unfortunate. The brothers-in-law, once so intimate, became estranged, and Mr. Taylor noted that even at Richardson's funeral they were on bad terms. And here it must be laid down as a melancholy factor in Sheridan's life, that there was hardly a single person with whom he had ever been intimate that he did not alienate or injure. This seems a harsh saying, but it is a truth that is almost forced on the chronicler of his life ; and the reader, if he make his way through these pages, will find himself adopting the same conclusion. There was this consistency, at least, in all his inconsistencies.*

Another member of the family (for members of the Linley family came often to London, and

---

* 'Tickell could not have been happy in his second marriage. The lady was a beauty, and brought some fortune. They kept a coach, an extravagance which her fortune and his income as a Commissioner of the Stamp-office could not support. His wife expected him to be constantly with her ; and when he wanted to take a walk with a friend, she importuned him to ride in the coach with her. At length he became embarrassed in his affairs, and desponding in his temper, and he, who was once all vivacity, sank into such melancholy and dejection as to render it doubtful whether his falling from the parapet at Hampton Court Palace was wholly accidental.'

It is a melancholy consideration that almost immediately after his death, a near relation, who had been apprised of his desponding state, came with ample means to relieve him from all his necessities.

'The second Mrs. Tickell, it is said, found a less indulgent husband in her second marriage, and sank into a despondency like that which attended the last days of her former partner.'

Messrs. Robson and Kerslake, the booksellers, of Coventry Street, have shown me a curious volume, or scrap-book, that belonged to one of the Miss Tickells. She seems to have been in high favour with the Princesses of the Royal Family. The book has some water-colour and other sketches by Gainsborough, and some by her brother, who was in the Navy.

contributed to the reign of frolic) was Ozias Linley, Minor Canon in Norwich Cathedral—'Hozey,' as his brother-in-law Sheridan styled him—and a most eccentric personage. His fits of absence of mind developed into something grotesque, and furnished innumerable stories :

'One Sunday morning. as he was riding through the Close, on his way to serve his curacy, his horse threw off a shoe. A lady, whom he had just passed, having remarked it, called out to him, " Sir, your horse has just cast one of his shoes." " Thank you, madam," returned Ozias ; "will you then be kind enough to put it on ?" Upon another occasion, having dismounted in the course of his journey, for the purpose of exercise, he hung his horse's bridle on his arm, concluding that he would follow; but the bridle had been put on carelessly, and the animal having disengaged it from his head, began to browse very comfortably, and at his leisure. In the meanwhile Linley walked on, the bridle still on his arm, to a turnpike-gate, where he offered the usual payment for his horse.'*

But William Linley, brother of the mercurial prodigy, was of the true convivial type. He held

---

* So fond was the Rev. Ozias of music that he resigned his living to pursue his art, and on May 5, 1816, was appointed organist to Dulwich College, where he died in March, 1831. His brother William lived until 1835. Their portraits are to be seen in the gallery—interesting faces both.

some office in India—given to him by Fox, no
doubt at Sheridan's instance—whence he had come
over, seduced by the hope of being advanced by his
versatile brother-in-law. He lived with his mother
and family in Southampton Street, Strand, and soon
was drawn into the social clubs and jovial coteries that
were to be found about Covent Garden, especially at
the Beef Steak Club, where his simple nature furnished infinite food for merriment to the wags of the
place.

Exquisite amusement was furnished by a novel
in three volumes, which poor Linley had been ill-
advised enough to publish, and for which Sir Richard
Phillips gave him the large *honorarium* of £30. It
was called 'Ralph Reybridge,' and a specimen of
it which the merciless wight who brought the book
read to the club, entitled 'The Recognition,' ended
in this singular form.

The hero, coming to an hotel, started when he
saw the waiter; and, 'looking more observantly in
his face, every trait of which had been long familiar
to him, exclaimed with the greatest emotion :

'"Eh—eh—it cannot be—yes, it must be—it is
Rumsby !"

'"Yes, Reybridge, it is Rumsby," returned the
waiter, and threw himself into our hero's arms. It is
your own Rumsby !"'

An oil-painting in the exhibition of that year, is
marked in the catalogue thus : 'Ralph Reybridge

recognising his friend Rumsby in the disguise of a waiter, at the Falcon Inn.' So that it appears to have been a favourite scene of the author's.

Sheridan's share in another of his ventures, illustrates the happy carelessness of the manager. 'Poor Linley, many years ago, had written a musical farce, in two acts, called "The Pavilion," which was acted at Drury Lane, and had set the songs to some exquisite music of his own composition; but placed it in Sheridan's hands, that the dialogue might receive a few touches from so great a master. Sheridan undertook the task with his usual good-nature, which, as everyone knows, was inexhaustible in all kinds of promise. The piece was cast, and the night fixed for its representation; but it was only by incessant importunities that the author could recover the MS. in time for a rehearsal. It was returned with no correction or alteration whatever, save the slight addition of a very middling joke upon the lover's valet. In answer to his master's reproof of his negligence, the fellow makes a remonstrance upon the irksome and incongruous duties that were cast upon him:

' "There," says he, " had I not fifty verses to write for you upon your finding Miss Louisa Dangle's garter? Had I not at the same time your coat to brush, your boots to polish, your hair to dress, and to carry the poetry, with the garter enclosed, to Miss

Dangle's maid—and was not all this to be done in a single hour ?"

' His master replies :

' " Yes, you blockhead, and you marred the whole by your cursed confusion of head, and precipitancy of action ; for you ran in a violent bustle to Miss Dangle, burglariously entered her dressing-room, and brushed her riding-habit *vi et armis;* then curled her hair by sheer force with cold curling-irons ; and, after all, inscribed the verses to me, and enclosed the garter in the envelope."

' This, which is certainly not in the best antithetic style of Sheridan's comedy, was, by the critics of the pit, who never dreamed that Sheridan had furnished it, considered as a miserable attempt on the part of the author to mimic the manner of that great comic writer, and probably conduced much to the failure of the piece. When Sheridan was told of the mischief which his slight contribution had effected, he replied with infinite coolness :

' " It's the very thing I wished ; the farce was so replete with absurdities, that I thought there was no harm in hazarding one absurdity more. Bill Linley has a good situation in the Company's service—why does he not go back to India ? If his d——d farce had succeeded, we should have had him here for the rest of his life, scratching his head in a garret, or twiddling his thumbs in the green-room, instead of saving rupees enough to come back and loll in his carriage." '*

* Linley's absurdities and oddities are in the pleasantest vein of comedy, and no doubt profited his brother-in-law.

A brother club-man described amusingly his established notions and prejudices, which 'no ratiocination can reach, no refutation shake,' 'and the perfect composure with which he hears them confuted every day, conceding every time the whole series of propositions by which the confutation is achieved; and then, when his opponent has done talking, calmly asserting his right to remain in the same opinion as before.'

'I think I can convince you,' said his opponent to Linley, 'if you are candid.' 'I am candid,' rejoined the other, 'but not to be convinced.' 'I will begin, then. Will you not allow that in all civil communities, each individual has a right to worship his Creator in the mode he thinks best, if, in so doing, he does not disturb the peace and order of society?' 'Certainly,' was his reply. 'If, then, the Catholics claim that very right, ought the civil magistrate to punish them?' 'Oh! no, my good fellow—certainly not.' 'Well then—is there anything in their holding transubstantiation, or in kneeling to saints, or in making confessions, that can promote rebellion against the laws, or disobedience to the authority of the state?' 'Oh! by no means. Let them believe what they like.' 'Then do you not think,' continued the other, 'that if there is a decided majority of these enthusiasts in Ireland, this valuable member of our empire is now, or may be, soon endangered?' 'Assuredly.' 'Why, then, would it not be better to give them relief?' 'Why, yes, I admit all that; but I must still keep to my opinion—that Catholic emancipation would overturn Church, State, and everything.'

'There was something truly comic in the disappointment of this ingenious disputant, when he found the most willing admission of all his premises, without the slightest inclination to concur in his conclusion; and that he had thrown away so much good logic upon an intellect that never submitted to its jurisdiction, and suffered no argument to come within the precincts of its preconceptions.'

The convivial life of this time, however, merits consideration, as it was totally different from that of our own day, was pursued on system, and had a serious influence on the business of life. It had a particular bearing on the relations of persons connected with the stage, the dramatists and purveyors of jokes particularly, who appeared to be stimulated by the companionship of actors, managers, critics, and others. These were found at the various clubs, which latter were, indeed, rather taverns than clubs, and on the model of the village 'free-and-easy.' Here persons came to laugh and drink; and here the dubious reputation of being a three or six bottle 'man' was earned. The extent to which inebriety flourished is astonishing, and it was contrived that sobriety and drunkenness might be reconciled, so as to be a sober, respectable citizen by day, yet a drunkard by night. It was thus with the grave Mr. John Kemble, who was repeatedly found intoxicated at these clubs, and sat up all night at 'The Finish.' There were a vast number of these drinking resorts—the '*Je ne sçai quoi,*' 'The Keep the Line,' and the most celebrated, 'The Beef-steak.'*

Linley imparted to Mr. Thomas Moore some interesting materials for his work.

* A good description of these places will be found in the 'Memoirs of Mr. Adolphus,' who describes the curious characters who frequented them.

A most extraordinary combination of character, combining the clever, ardent politician, the skilful, vigorous debater, and earnest partizan, with the habits of an almost professional debauchee of the school of Wilkes and Sandwich, was the well-known Earl of Surrey, afterwards Duke of Norfolk. This odious being was also celebrated for his love of beefsteaks, and of club-room joviality ; and his gross person and gross manners and habits leave an unpleasant idea of what the 'man of pleasure' was then considered. 'Nature,' says Wraxall, 'which cast him in her coarsest mould, had not bestowed on him any of the external insignia of high descent. His person, large, muscular, and clumsy, was destitute of grace or dignity, though he possessed much activity. He might, indeed, have been mistaken for a grazier or a butcher.'

Another of these bacchanals, one also among the beautiful Mrs. Sheridan's many admirers, was the well-known *viveur* and song-writer, Captain Morris, who, on his 'suit being rejected,' it was said, 'took to drinking and conviviality in despair.' This poor creature appears a melancholy spectacle, with his specially written songs and chanted compliments : nothing is more piteous than the *farceur* or con-vivialist grown old and *passé*, who has outlived all his friends, or rather acquaintances, and even his own jokes and stories.*

* The captain feasted on the smiles of royalty, which cast him

The poor captain at last fell into poverty, obtained
a pension from the Regent, and his great patron and
co-beefsteak-eater, the gross Duke of Norfolk, had
quite forgotten him, when at some midnight orgie
Kemble, in a half-grotesque remonstrance, bade him

---

off at last, when, as a lean and slippered pantaloon, he sang of
himself:

> 'I am an old bacchanal quite worn out,
> Once leader of many a jolly bout ;
> But the game's all up, and the show's gone by,
> And now an old bore and a twaddle am I.'

A chant unique in its candour. To him, however, the world owes
one pleasant and oft-quoted line in praise of Pall Mall :

> 'In town let me live, then, in town let me die,
> For in truth I can't relish the country, not I ;
> If one must have a villa in summer to dwell,
> Oh give me the sweet, shady side of Pall Mall.'

He would troll such gross flattery as this :

> 'Rise, and fill to my toast, and this darling of Fame,
> Who restored to the world its great order and frame,
> Whose firm British virtue still braved the storm's blast,
> Till he brought to his feet the world's tyrant at last.
> George the Fourth, of Great Britain, whose wise-ordered plan
> Redeemed the lost blessings of earth and of man.'

We owe to him also the bacchanalian 'reason fair, to fill again,'
and the praise of beef :

> 'While thus we boast a general creed
> In honour of our shrine, sir,
> You'll find the world long since agreed
> That beef is food divine, sir.
> And British fame still tells afar
> This truth where'er she wanders,
> For wine, for women, and for war,
> Beefsteaks make Alexanders.'

give practical effect to his sympathy. The result was that the Duke gave him a cottage near Dorking, where he died when ninety-three years old.

But it was to be expected that Sheridan's connection with the stage should bring him in contact with yet another jovial circle, a band of wits who lived by the stage. Of these some wrote plays, others prologues ; others, again, advised as to rehearsals, etc. They formed an exceedingly amusing coterie of dramatists, Members of Parliament, actors, and men of business. In these days, and for at least fifty years before, the theatre was open to all writers of ability ; and any clever person with a tolerable recommendation was certain to be received by the manager, and secure of having his piece considered. Nay, the manager was always in want of, or looking out for, new pieces ; and a play by an untrained dramatist, but with a good plot or idea, could be put into shape by the aid of the manager, and served to ' draw ' for the few nights necessary. This happy era for ' outsiders ' was owing to the short ' runs ' which were then in vogue, of eight or nine nights, and which made it indispensable for the manager to have successive novelties. The age of Sheridan was therefore fruitful in dramatists, who were stimulated by the ceaseless demand.*

* The habit, too, of putting familiar characters on the stage, and the toleration that was extended to this caricature, made it easier for the dramatist to work, as, following the example of Foote, he

Among these friends of Sheridan were Miles Peter Andrews, M.P., an eminent powder manufacturer at Dartford, Frederick Reynolds, Cobb, Taylor, Topham, Merry, Kelly, and others. Andrews was an amusing companion; as his friend Reynolds described him : 'Young, very prepossessing in his appearance ; popular, as a writer of epilogues, and other dramatic compositions ; rich, in the possession of a large income arising from his gunpowder mills at Dartford and Faversham ; mixing in the most fashionable society ; extremely hospitable : and truly original.'

Cobb—secretary at the India Office, member of the Beefsteak Club, and writer of comic operas of a pleasant sort, such as ' The Haunted Tower,' and ' The First Floor '—was another of these eccentrics. Him Sheridan succeeded in drawing into, or rather *engulphing* in, the theatre. This was a clever and much-respected person. He was fond of music, and sang with great taste and impressive spirit. His farces are marked by humour without extravagance. At the desire of Mr. Sheridan, he wrote a prelude

acquired a knack of drawing or generalizing from life, which in one full of rattling humour and good spirits, like the Reynoldses and O'Keefes, became an easy task. The age, too, indeed, offered so many varied, singular, and original topics of oddity and eccentric characters, that it was scarcely wonderful that English comedy flourished and diverted audiences with Protean shapes of humanity which now would seem far-fetched and out of drawing, for the reason that there are no such originals known to the audiences.

on the removal of the Drury Lane company of actors to the King's Theatre, preparatory to the rebuilding of the former. This prelude was written, but one whimsical stroke was introduced by Mr. Sheridan. One of the characters, describing the difficulty of removing the scenes, etc., from Drury Lane Theatre, said that there was so pelting a storm in Chandos Street, that they were obliged 'to carry the rain under an umbrella.' One of his friends, Mr. Marsh, a facetious barrister, who wrote an account of the clubs of his time, thus describes him at the 'Steaks,' and the good-humoured way in which he took his friends' bantering: '"Cobb!" said Arnold, "what a misnomer it was to call your opera 'The Haunted Tower.' Why, there was no *spirit* in it from beginning to end!" "Yes," exclaimed some other desperate punster (I cannot now recall who it was), "but Cobb gave one of his pieces the most appropriate title possible, by calling it 'Ramah Drûg;' for it was literally *ramming a drug* down the public throat." "True," rejoined Cobb; "but it was a drug that evinced considerable power, for it operated on the public twenty nights in succession." "My good friend," said Arnold, triumphantly, "that was a proof of its weakness, if it took so long in working." "Arnold, you are right," retorted Cobb: "in that respect, *your* play" (Arnold had brought out a play which did not survive the first night) "had the advantage of mine; that was so powerful a drug, that it was thrown up as soon as it was taken!" '

Sheridan's witty conversation and repartees have been often celebrated. An actor, who one night officiated as secretary at a convivial meeting of the 'Steaks,' amused himself by setting down some of these flashes, and thus gives an idea of the general tone of his jesting. It seems rather a laboured kind of merriment :

' TOPHAM. "Fox was very powerful last night." WOODFALL. "His arguments were unusually clear, and well connected." SHERIDAN. "Yes ; his tongue's like a time-glass ; the longer it runs, the clearer it gets." ANDREWS. "Then, he's not like a cask of madeira." SHERIDAN. "No, or he'd have died long ago by tapping." MERRY. "And yet he's been tapped pretty often." SUETT. "Talking of tapping, gentlemen, I had an aunt (Heaven rest her bones!) afflicted with the dropsy, who was tapped seventy-five times in one week." A general laugh. CAPT. M. (an M.P.). "Suett, was your father an actor?" SUETT. "No; he was a tailor." MERRY. "Then he did more for his customers than the captain will for the Constitution—he mended their breaches." SUETT. "To one thing, gentlemen, may I crave your attention ? I know who *was* my father." SHERIDAN. "A wise child!" ANDREWS : "And a true believer." BEARCROFT. "We must take his word as to that ; for we can't produce evidence to the contrary." . . . ANDREWS. " Kemble played ' Hamlet ' with great effect on Monday." TOPHAM. " Once or twice, I thought he forgot himself." SHERIDAN. " You mistake ; he forgot his audience." ANDREWS. " He never forgets *you*, Sheridan." SHERIDAN. " Not on a Saturday." . . . SOMEBODY. " Can't we have a glee ? Here's Dignum and Sedgwick, but not Kelly." CAPTAIN BAKER. " I like Kelly ; he's a sociable, manly fellow." ANDREWS. " I question his manhood ; he's inclined to Crouch." . . . . . SOMEBODY. " What could have induced —— to blow his brains out ?" SHERIDAN. " A desire to contradict the world, who said he never had any." . . .'

I shall close this record of strange figures with a sketch of a singular character among the many singular characters of the time, viz. a clergyman, the Rev. Henry Bate Dudley, afterwards a baronet. This person was connected with the *Morning Herald*, and has a claim on the grateful world of fashion for establishing the now flourishing *Morning Post*.

He was, perhaps, the best specimen of the type known by the edifying title of the ' Bruising Parson ;' was intimately connected with managers, actors, etc., and wrote pieces himself. He was also an intimate friend of Garrick's, and despatched by him on a mission to report on the merits of an obscure country actress, Mrs. Siddons, then playing in the country. It is creditable to his judgment that he should have at once seen and reported her merit.

Other adventures of this extraordinary person were made up of brawls, boxing-matches, quarrels in and out of newspapers, libellous writings abundant, duels, and general violence ; yet all the time he maintained the clerical character, strictly enforced his title of ' Reverend,' and through Court interest was appointed to a good living in the country, to the disgust of the ordinary, with whom he was presently engaged in serious conflict, all which was accepted by the society of the day in a tranquil if not indifferent fashion. We may introduce him in connection with Sheridan's friend ' Joe Richardson,' who was a co-proprietor with him of the *Morning Post.* Mr. John Taylor, who was also concerned in that paper, thus describes this incident in the management of the paper :

' Sir Henry, then the Reverend Henry Bate, was thwarted by the other proprietors of the *Morning Post* at a general meeting. Mr. Richardson had remained silent. Irritated by their opposition, Mr. Bate *called them all a parcel of cowards, and withdrew.* Richardson thought it incumbent on him to demand from Mr. Bate an exception from the imputation of cowardice which he had thrown upon the proprietors. I dined with Richardson at the Rainbow Coffee-house next day, for the purpose of his addressing a letter to Mr. Bate, requiring that exception. Richardson's letter was, perhaps, some-what too lofty for the temper of such a man as Mr. Bate, and the answer was not conciliatory. Another letter was written by Richardson, but in such softened terms as to draw a more pacific answer from Mr. Bate. I believe a third letter followed, with no better effect; and the conclusion was, that the parties were to meet the following morning at five o'clock in Hyde Park. I was the bearer of all Mr. Richardson's letters to Mr. Bate, who then lived in Surrey Street, Strand. My anxiety for the welfare of Mr. Richardson prevented my going to bed, and I waited in the Park the result of the meeting. A coin was tossed for the first fire, which fell to Mr. Bate, who wounded his antagonist in the right arm, and rendered him unable to return the fire. Mr. Bate then, as I understood, came forward, and said that if Mr. Richardson's letter had been written in a less commanding style, this event would not have happened, and that he had no hesitation then in saying that he would otherwise most willingly have exempted Mr. Richardson from any such imputation as he had applied to the other pro-prietors, holding him in respect and esteem. Thus the matter ended, and Mr. Bate and Mr. Richardson afterwards were always on the most friendly terms. Mr. Denis O'Brien was the second to Mr. Bate, and Mr. Mills, a surgeon, the friend of Mr. Richardson, his second.

'Mr. Bate related to me a circumstance that well illustrates the character of an Irish duellist, which ought to be carefully distinguished from that of an Irish gentleman. He said that once being apprehensive that a dispute between him and another gentleman would terminate in a mortal contest, and being unprovided with arms, he asked a Mr. Brereton, with whom he had long been acquainted, to lend him a brace of pistols. Mr. Brereton seemed delighted with the request, as if it was a great favour conferred upon him, and brought the weapons, of which he spoke with high commendation, as if admirably constructed for the purpose. It happened that the adverse party made a satisfactory explanation to Sir Henry, and he returned the pistols, stating that he had fortunately had no occasion to use them. Mr. Brereton expressed much discontent that his pistols should have been borrowed for nothing, and then observed that Sir Henry had sometime before uttered some words that had offended him, and that he had often determined to demand an explanation. Sir Henry assured him that he never could intend to offend him, and had no recollection of having said anything that could possibly displease him. This courteous assurance, however, by no means appeased Brereton, who seemed to be rising into violent emotion. "Oh! I perceive what you are at," said Sir Henry. "There, I'll take this pistol and you take the other, and we will settle the matter immediately." Finding Sir Henry so resolute, Brereton said, "Ah! I see you are a man of spirit ; and as you are an old friend, let us shake hands, and the matter is over." '*

It was with distractions such as these, and compromises of this edifying description, that we find Sheridan carrying on the management of the great establishment in Drury Lane. The theatre, indeed, seems to have been conducted, to use a common phrase, in a sort of 'happy-go-lucky' way, the extraordinary ingenuity of the director being ever exerted, not to prevent, but to *repair* his blunders. Wonderfully, too, had he been favoured by various strokes of good fortune, not the least of which was the discovery of the greatest of English actresses and her distinguished brother. Yet Mrs. Siddons he had nearly lost by his carelessness and indifference ; and when secured, as it will be seen, he took little trouble to retain her or encourage such a stay of his house. It is well known that when he first came

---

* It was curious, too, that the 'Bruising Parson' should have been concerned in a duel something of the pattern of Sheridan's, and which arose out of a scuffle at Vauxhall, where the beautiful Mrs. Hartley had been stared at insolently by ' Fighting Fitzgerald ' and some other roysterers. A duel was arranged, which came off at a tavern, and at a subsequent meeting the 'gentlemen' were eager to settle it by boxing. A captain was brought to the tavern, whom the clergyman thrashed soundly, but it was later discovered that he was a professional bruiser dressed up as a gentleman. See ' The Vauxhall Affray, 1755,' for this curious picture of the manners of the day.

to take the theatre from Garrick he did not care to
re-engage her. It must be said, however, that the
impression she had made was slight. Her own
account of Sheridan's share in the matter is interesting, and, though significant of his character, shows
that she had, to a certain extent, failed :

' Mr. Garrick had promised Mr. Siddons to procure me a good engagement with the new managers,
and desired him to give himself no trouble about the
matter, but to put my cause entirely into his hands.
He let me down, however, after all these protesta-
tions, in the most humiliating manner ; and, instead
of doing me common justice with those gentlemen,
rather depreciated my talents. *This Mr. Sheridan
afterwards told me;* and said that, when Mrs.
Abington heard of my impending dismissal, she told
them they were all acting like fools. Whilst I was
fulfilling my engagement at Birmingham, to my utter
dismay and astonishment I received an official letter
from the prompter of Drury Lane, acquainting me
that my services would be no longer required. It
was a stunning and cruel blow, overwhelming all my
ambitious hopes, and involving peril even to the
subsistence of my helpless babes. It was very near
destroying me.'

Now, knowing what we do of Garrick's invariably
truthful and honourable character, can we doubt
that he *had* named the actress to the new management? He had already shown his interest in her,

and her struggling position would have commended itself to his sympathy. Nor is it probable that had she been engaged, after such a *début*, she could have made a success, or had such an opportunity as was offered to her in her brilliant *rentrée*. But that Garrick depreciated *her* is most unlikely. We can almost hear the ingenious and amiable Sheridan in the first whirl of success transferring the whole blame to other shoulders.

When Mrs. Siddons had retired again to comparative obscurity, and was playing at Bath and Bristol, she had to be rediscovered; and so obscure was she then, that Mr. Taylor, when at Bath in 1779, had drawn Garrick's attention to 'an excellent actress which has appeared here this season (a Mrs. Siddons), who I really think is as much mistress of her business as any female I ever saw; I have attended to her with the most critical attention I was master of, and I declare my opinion of her to be all that my ideas can reach. Her Portia, Belvidera, and other pathetic parts in tragedy, are, I think, exquisitely fine. You have seen her on your stage. Am I right or not?'

But this hint seems not to have been attended to. It was reserved for 'old' Mr. Sheridan to bring her talent to his son's theatre. His granddaughter, Mrs. Le Fanu, relates how this occurred:

'While at Bath for his health, Mr. Sheridan sen. was strongly solicited to go to the play, to witness

the performance of a young actress, who was said
to distance all competition in tragedy. He found,
to his astonishment, that it was the lady who had
made so little impression on him some years before
in the " Runaway ;" but who, as Garrick had declared, was possessed of tragic powers sufficient to
delight and electrify an audience. After the play
was over he went behind the scenes, to get introduced to her, in order to compliment her. He said.
" I am surprised, madam, that with such talents you
should confine yourself to the country ; talents that
would be sure of commanding, in London, fame and
success." The actress modestly replied that she
had already tried London, but without the success
which had been anticipated ; and that she was advised
by her friends to be content with the fame and profit
she obtained at Bath, particularly as her *voice* was
deemed unequal to the extent of a London theatre.
Immediately on his return to London, he spoke to the
acting manager of Drury Lane, strenuously recommending her to him. Upon her being engaged, he
directed her, with a truly kind solicitude, in the choice
of a part for her first appearance. With the usual
preference of young and handsome actresses for a
character of pomp and show, she inclined to that of
Euphrasia, in " The Grecian Daughter ;" but the
juster taste of Mr. Sheridan determined her in
favour of the far more natural and affecting character
of " Isabella ;" and the judgment with which the

selection was made was amply confirmed by the
bursts of rapturous applause. The kindness of Mr.
Sheridan, which did not stop here, but showed itself
in every possible way in her behalf, was gratefully
acknowledged by the object of it ; who, when at
the height of her professional prosperity, was wont
to term him " The father of my fortune and my
fame." '

The extraordinary success of her second *début* at
Drury Lane has been often described. She was a
welcome and precious addition to the theatre. At
her performances, we are told, ' Mr. Sheridan was
seen weeping in the boxes,' in company with all the
world.

The appointment to office at Drury Lane had
happily reconciled Sheridan to his father, another
evidence of his affectionately filial disposition—his
most redeeming merit—having long forgotten the
rather unforgiving harshness with which he had
been treated. This office the father retained but
for a short time. He had not abandoned his old
hobby of elocution, and we find him then treating the
public to lectures on his favourite topics.*

---

* Thus, in April, 1781, it was announced that Mr. Thomas
Sheridan projected a course of lectures on the 'Art of Reading,'
at the King's Tavern, Cornhill. Two guineas for the course of
eight lectures, and each subscriber to be entitled to one copy of
his 'Rhetorical Grammar and Dictionary,' now sold at a guinea
and a half. 'As the chief benefit to be expected from this course
will arise from the subscribers having copies of the lectures in

He also gave a course of ' Historical Prelections '
at Hickford's great rooms, which drew large
audiences, and even some members of the royal
family. Henderson the actor meeting him, in 1785,
at Angelo's house, Mrs. Angelo suggested their joining in 'Readings.' Angelo, the son, gives the following amusing account of the old actor, whose recitation
of the line ' None but the brave,' emphasized in half a
dozen different ways, must have been amusing enough:

' Henderson and he engaged Freemasons' Hall,
Queen Street, which was afterwards full every night.
Old Sheridan had a pompous emphasis ; his elocution was of the old school ; but as he was occasionally
spitting or taking snuff, it did not altogether so well
please. His day had passed by, *le rideau tombé.*
Henderson had a deal of comic humour, and used to
recite the tale of " John Gilpin " in excellent style. The
hall was always crowded, and whenever it was his

---

their hands, in order to supply those who are not in possession
of his former edition, a new one is now being prepared, price 6s.,
boards.'

And again :

' To the Public, and more particularly to Parents and Guardians.
—Mr. Sheridan senior, having now prepared all his materials
for carrying into execution his long-concerted plan for the general
improvement of elocution in both sexes by introducing the regular
study of our native language, and reviving the lost art of elocution,
wishes for an opportunity of delivering his sentiments at large on
these important subjects before an assemblage of such ladies as
may think themselves interested in the event of such an undertaking.'

turn to read, there was a general buzz of approbation. Being a constant attendant there, I could not but feel for poor Sheridan, whom I had known from a child, and whose esteem I had long experienced. The crowd was so great, many would not make room for him to pass along. Alas! that John Gilpin should put John Dryden's nose out of joint; that "Alexander's Feast" should cause coughing, blowing of noses, and scraping of the feet! But so it was. Even "None but the brave deserves the fair," where he most certainly excelled, did not excite attention. However, it succeeded as a pecuniary speculation.

'I am sorry to say my old friend's disappointment at his readings did not finish here. Considering himself the principal, and having taken the receipts, which were considerable, when the performance closed, he presented his colleague with a bank-note (I never heard the sum), as a present for his assistance, which he refused. As the readings were undertaken mutually, half was expected. This produced a quarrel; and my mother, who set them going, with much difficulty at last brought them back to a reciprocal accommodation. When she first mentioned Henderson's dissatisfaction, Sheridan assumed a tragic attitude, raising his arms and exclaiming, "My God, madam!" his favourite expression; "what! Dryden's Ode to be put in competition with Gilpin's trash! impossible!"'

'Notwithstanding the emoluments,' adds Mr. Taylor, 'Mr. Sheridan expressed some discontent, " For," said he, " I wanted the readings to be rather instructive than diverting, and calculated to attract the select and judicious ; but Mr. Henderson has frustrated my intention by *bringing in the whole town*." Those who knew the grave character of the elder Mr. Sheridan, and his fondness for his favourite subject, elocution, will not be surprised at his whimsical disappointment.'

For nearly fourteen years his son was to direct the old theatre which he had purchased from Garrick. He was altogether over thirty years in office, and surely a more curious record of eccentricity, shifts, neglect, and debt, desperate embarrassments encountered and surmounted, could not be conceived. It does credit to the fertility of his resources, that during that long period he should have contrived to keep the concern 'going,' and to have saved it from ruin. Unhappily, he only contrived this at the expense of others, whose all was engulphed, by listening to his seducing tongue. The chronicle is a mingled yarn of farce and tragedy. At the close of the year 1788 the theatre was in such disorder that the veteran actor King, who had succeeded the elder Sheridan as stage-manager, trained in the orderly and respectable discipline of Garrick, resigned his situation in despair. The public, forgetting the services of so

old a favourite, were inclined to lay the fault of
the disorder on him. He then came forward to
justify himself. He declared that he never had
proper authority over anything, or to do anything,
adding this very significant statement, 'that he
could not order the cleaning of a coat or a yard of
coffin-lace, both of which were often much wanted.'
He further informed them that 'there was something
undefined, if not indefinable, in his situation; in
consequence he had sustained many inconveniences,
and been liable to very disagreeable attacks; thus
being called to account by authors for non-perform-
ance of works he had never heard of, and being
arraigned for objecting to performers with whom he
had no power to treat. Should anyone ask what
was my post at Drury Lane, and add the further
question, "If I was not manager, who was?" I
should be found to answer, like my friend Atall in
the comedy, to the first, "*I don't know;*" and
to the last, "*I can't tell.*" I can only positively
assert *I was not manager.*' So free and easy a
communication as this would not have been tolerated under respectable management.

Having announced his retirement, King was
treated to the usual round of Sheridan's blandish-
ments. 'This gentleman,' says King, 'with great
cheerfulness and liberality, declared or wished that
I should return, and seemed very desirous to do his
utmost that I might be gratified.' King then asked

that his power might be defined, and this merely by
'a memorandum drawn by Mr. Sheridan in his own
words. This and much more was promised;
several *appointments* were made, *some of which were
kept, but in general when I met the gentleman, either
by appointment or otherwise, he was in a great hurry
or surrounded by company ;* so it was found impossible
to bring him to the point.' As a last resource, he
absented himself altogether. During the first night
Sheridan arrived, and not finding him, sent to say
he would call on him that very night; and the poor
player waited up *till past three* in the morning, but
no Sheridan came, on which he indignantly threw
up his post finally, and left town the next day.

The same powers of persuasion were now used to
get Kemble to assume the office, who in October,
1788, rashly agreed to take on himself a heritage
of annoyance and embarrassment such as he
never dreamed of. He and his gifted sister were
to be the principal victims of the manager. She
herself used to relate to Rogers, who often repeated
the story, an instance of the manager's singular
treatment of her. One night when she was driving
away from the theatre, he jumped into the carriage,
when she addressed him with that solemn gravity
which, like the 'ale story,' often brought a smile to
those looking on : ' *Mr. Sheridan, I trust you will
behave with more propriety;* if not, I shall have to
call the footman to show you out of the carriage.'

She added with equal gravity that ' Mr. Sheridan *did* behave himself.' When the carriage stopped, he jumped out, and hurried off as though he did not wish to be seen with her. ' Provoking wretch !' she would add.

Reports of his being engaged on a new piece were frequently circulated. There were paragraphs in the newspapers : ' Mr. Sheridan is engaged on a new comedy entitled ' Affectation ;' ' Mr. Sheridan is far advanced in his new comedy.' Many wondered that he did not work the vein that was so certain to bring profit, success, and fame. The Queen, as we have said, even asked if he were thus engaged ? He told her that ' he was actively about one.' But his friend Kelly meeting him next day in Piccadilly, said to him, on hearing the story : ' " Not you ; you will never write again ; you are afraid to write." He fixed his penetrating eye on me, and said, " Of whom am I afraid ?" I said, " You are afraid of the author of ' The School for Scandal.' " ' The author smiled, and seemed to admit that this was likely to be true. No doubt it was. But there was yet another reason. It was a different thing to write in the whirl of dissipation, and in the bright early day of hope and struggle, when he longed to secure fame and fortune.

CHAPTER XI.

But we are now arrived at the moment when this versatile and wonderful being was to enter on a new and more exciting career. His social gifts and dramatic successes had already introduced him to political coteries, such as Devonshire House; and at the time a clever man so introduced was certain to be offered a seat in Parliament. He had already become acquainted with the Prince of Wales. To Burke he had been made known at Johnson's Club; Windham and others he had met at Bath. It is quite clear, indeed, that before he entered Parliament, he was taking a share in the concerns of the party, and was on intimate terms with all its leading men. Lord John Townshend told Mr. Moore that he was the first to bring Fox and Sheridan together at dinner at his house, ' having told Fox that all the notions he might have conceived of Sheridan's talents and genius from the comedy of " The Rivals," etc., would fall infinitely short of the admiration of his astonishing powers which I was sure he would entertain at the first interview. The first interview between them (there were very few present, only Tickell and myself, and one or two more), I shall never forget. Fox told me, after breaking up from dinner, that he had always thought Hare, after my uncle, Charles Townshend, the wittiest man he ever met with, but that Sheridan surpassed them both infinitely; and Sheridan told me next day that he was quite lost in admiration of Fox, and that it was a puzzle to him to say what he admired most, his commanding superiority of talents and universal knowledge, or his playful fancy, artless manners, and benevolence of heart, which showed itself in every word he uttered.'* This was to prove for many years an enduring intimacy, until Sheridan's unstableness alienated this great friend.

Amongst Sheridan's papers were found sketches and fragments of political pamphlets: one on ' Absentee Landlords from Ireland,' with a proposal to impose penalties on such. All through his course, indeed, he was to show himself a vehement Irish patriot. But it was curious that he should never have set foot in his native country since the day he quitted ' Sam Whyte's' school in his childhood, though once he seemed likely to have a chance of

---

* It should be said, however, that this testimony was given under the influence of grief, and sent with an excuse for not attending his funeral. It will be seen from Lord Russell's ' Letters of Fox,' that Lord John Townshend held but a low opinion of Sheridan's character.

visiting it in an official way. At this time he also
wrote in a party paper called the *Englishman*.

The story of the mode of Sheridan's admission
to Brooks's Club has been repeated so often
without contradiction, that it might fairly be accepted as true. We have, however, a contemporary authority, that of Sir N. Wraxall, whose
version differs from others in its circumstantial air.
' The tricks of Scapin,' he says, ' could not boast of
more originality or ingenuity than did those of
Sheridan. They were current in every company,
and would of themselves fill a volume. Two members of the club held him in peculiar dislike : I
mean George Selwyn and the late Earl of Besborough. Conscious that every exertion would be
made to ensure Sheridan's success, they agreed not
to absent themselves during the time allotted by the
regulations of the club for ballots ; and as one black
ball sufficed to extinguish the hopes of a candidate,
they repeatedly prevented his election. In order to
remove so serious an impediment, Sheridan's friends
had recourse to artifice. Having fixed on the
evening when it was resolved to put him up, and
finding his two inveterate adversaries posted as
usual, a chairman was sent with a note, written in
the name of Lady Duncannon to her father-in-law,
acquainting him that a fire had broken out in his
house in Cavendish Square, and entreating him
immediately to return home. Unsuspicious of any

trick, as his son and daughter-in-law lived under his roof, Lord Besborough, without hesitating an instant, quitted the room, and got into a sedan-chair. Selwyn, who resided in the vicinity of Brooks's, in Cleveland Row, received, nearly at the same time, a verbal message to request his presence, Miss Fagniani (whom he had adopted as his daughter, and who afterwards married the present Earl of Yarmouth) being suddenly seized with an alarming indisposition. This summons he obeyed; and no sooner was the room cleared, than, Sheridan being proposed as a member, a ballot took place, when he was unanimously chosen. Lord Besborough and Selwyn returned without delay, on discovering the imposition that had been practised on their credulity; but too late to prevent its effect.'* That the device

* The date of his admission, as I find from the book at Brooks's Club, was November 2, 1780.

Sheridan, Mr. Trevelyan tells us, 'brought forth from its retirement the almost neglected volume, and turned it into something very like a private betting-book of his own. In 1794 he was responsible for eight bets running on subjects which varied in importance from the question whether the French had failed or succeeded in occupying Amsterdam, to the question of the shortest way from one house to another, viz., by Sackvile Street or Bond Street. He entered his last wager in 1795.'

Moore has quoted a number of these childish wagers from the betting-book at Brooks's. These are for large sums—500 and 200 guineas, and he nearly always offered odds. The 500 guineas bet, which was that Reform would be passed before 1796, he lost, as indeed it seems he generally did. Mr. Fyler, the Secretary of the Club, has been kind enough to furnish me with the following extracts from 'the Book:'

was of Sheridan's own conception we may be sure ;
yet, though we may smile at the joke, it does not
seem an edifying or even a gentlemanly mode of
gaining admittance to a private society.* This
introduced him to a yet more ' roystering ' society,

' 24th December, 1792.—Mr. Sheridan bets Mr. Stepney fifty
guineas that Great Britain is at war in three months from the date
hereof (any commencement of hostilities understood to be a
declaration of war).

' Mr. Sheridan bets Mr. Stepney twenty guineas to one that
Valencien (Valenciennes ?) is not taken at this time, viz., a quarter
past three o'clock, July 21, 1793.

' Mr. Wyndham bets Mr. Sheridan five guineas that no play is
performed on or before the 1st January next in the new theatre
now building in Drury Lane, 18th September, 1793.'

* The well-known ' Fighting ' Fitzgerald attempted to enter by
another device, but was not so successful as his countryman. The
scene is described humorously by Mr. Marsh. Another version
of the story of Sheridan's admission was that Selwyn was sent for
by the Prince of Wales to a room below-stairs to hear some
important story from Sheridan, which the latter seemed to have
invented for the occasion. During its progress, Sheridan received
news that the ballot was over, and that he was admitted. He left
the Prince to finish his story, who soon got involved, and at last,
bursting into a loud laugh, said he knew nothing of it, and confessed
the trick.

The death of the proprietor of this club inspired Sheridan with
an epitaph, which I believe is only to be found in that curious
work, Richardson's ' Recollections of Fifty Years,' and is little
known :

> ' Alas ! that Brooks returned to dust,
>   Should pay at length the debt that we,
>   Averse to parchment, mortgage, trust,
>   Shall pay when forced—as well as he.

17—2

and we now hear of him figuring in night adventures akin to those of the later trio, Tom and Jerry, and 'Bob Logic.'

In these days, as it was related to Rogers, Sheridan and Fitzpatrick and Lord John Townshend, coming out of Drury Lane, observed a handsome phaeton waiting. The party prevailed on the groom to let them get in for a moment, when they set off at full speed, the groom raising the alarm, and a yelling mob in pursuit. They drove as far as Vauxhall, where they were overtaken, when they pacified the groom with a liberal fee. Sheridan, it was remarked, could never bear to be reminded of this frolic.

More amusing was the following pleasant trick: He had asked Fox, Tickell, and Richardson to dine with him down at Putney, and the two latter were to go in a chaise. Muffling himself and Fox in huge coats, they rode down, and, the night being dark, amused themselves all the way by riding close to

And died so poor, too! He whose trade
Such profit cleared by draught and deed,
Though pigeons called him murmuring Brooks,
And dipped their bills in him at need.
At length his last conveyance see,
Each witness mournful as a brother,
To think that this world's mortgagee
Must suffer judgment in another!
Where no appeals to Courts can rest,
Reversing a supreme decree;
But each decision stands confessed
A final precedent *in re.*'

the carriage and seriously alarming its occupants, who took them for highwaymen.

Yet another of the humorous freaks of his time was a proposal to rob Lord J. Townshend, who had won a good deal at Brooks's. This scheme was, of course, only in jest. Sheridan and General Fitzpatrick stopped the chaise ; but they were resisted by the Irish chairman, who declared he knew Mr. Sheridan well, and 'had the greatest regard for him, but could not let him rob his lordship.'

When, in 1780, the Westminster Committee passed some resolutions as to reform, Fox signed as chairman, and the report of the sub-committee was drawn up by Sheridan—evidence that he was already in a position of some importance. The old Utopian schemes of annual Parliaments and universal suffrage are here recommended for adoption. So Radical a programme adopted by the young manager of a great theatre, whose whole system of rule was based on the strictest despotism, might excite astonishment.

It was now that he was busily working to secure a seat in Parliament, and made trial of various boroughs ; but the prospect was not promising. He first turned his attention to Honiton, where his friend Reynolds interested himself for him.* The following curious letters contain the history of this attempt, as given by Dr. Watkins :

* Why Mr. Moore should doubt this story, with these letters before him, is not clear.

'My dear Sir,

'Upon my soul, I believe you were wrong about Honiton, as I have been close to it; but, though courted, was obliged to go to another place. Therefore, now do two things : first, write a letter to Honiton (by express better), and tell them that before the election yet a good man and true may offer, and pay them too, and that they should act accordingly.   Secondly, send me a letter to the Post Office, Bridgewater, which will notify that I am the person, and puff me too.   All this is in case, on my return from where I am going, if unsuccessful, I should want to try Honiton, having an offer of a very strong support.   Do these two things.

'Yours, in real haste,

'R. B. Sheridan.'

In compliance with the request, his friend accordingly wrote the following letter to a leading person in the borough :

'Dear Sir,

'I know not how to apologize for presuming to address you on the subject of an election, whose natural disposition is probably averse to such concerns ; but a gentleman, a very particular friend of mine, has signified a wish to become a candidate, if there is any probability of his succeeding.   I think it would be prudent, if there are any voters unengaged, to keep themselves so till I can send them

something more satisfactory. This gentleman is
Mr. Sheridan, a particular friend of Mr. Charles Fox,
Mr. Fitzpatrick, and all the first and most considerable characters in this kingdom ; himself of the most
shining talents and independent principles.

'Either Ministry or Opposition would be happy
to engage him ; but he will be independent.

'If you should choose to interest yourself, and
should have any of your voters unengaged, you
could never bestow them on one who has more
ability to be generally useful, or who can be more
particularly serviceable to the inhabitants of Honiton,
as he is beloved and almost adored by all parties.

'September 3rd, 1780.'

It seems, however, that he was anticipated by a
more wealthy candidate, in conjunction with the late
Sir George Yonge :

'My dear Sir,

'I am very much obliged to you for the
trouble you have taken, and for your letter. I
assure you I am the farthest in the world from
being indifferent in this matter, for something has
happened since I saw you, to make me think still
more of it. Do you think it would be impolitic if I
were to talk a little with our friend Crispin ? If you
were to send him to me, I could do it without letting
him conceive that I was the person in question.
They are damned fellows, if they think to mend

themselves by choosing a Scotchman, and a Mac too!
But let me see: you will be at Honiton on Wednesday, and I may have a letter from you on Friday;
and I assure you I shall be most seriously obliged
to you if you will get the best intelligence you can
immediately. My reason for wishing to be so quick
in it is, that if there appears a tolerable probability,
I would get Sir George Yonge applied to immediately not to engage his interest, if he has not
done it.

'I have been looking at the account of the voters
of Honiton, and I find that Sir George Yonge had
them almost all for him; and it must be bad if he
supports this Scot.

'Yours faithfully,

'R. B. SHERIDAN.'

At last, the Dissolution which took place in the
autumn of the year 1780 brought him the opportunity he was longing for, and he succeeded in finding
a seat at Stafford, through the interest of Mr.
Monckton, brother of Lady Cork. His pleasant
manners, we are told, helped him in his exertions.
A gentleman was found to lend him the cash to
purchase the voters, who was well repaid by a share
in the Opera House; and indeed many of the voters
were said to have been purchased by promises of
places in the Drury Lane Theatre.

He made his first speech on November 20th.

From the report we see that his *début* was rather a failure. He chose an occasion when his own particular interest was concerned, which was not a subject for inspiration. He complained of the petition presented against him, and suggested that some reform was called for in the system by which constituencies were left to lie under the stigma of corruption for a year and more. Mr. Rigby was merry on this subject, and pitied 'poor Stafford;' adding sarcastically, 'Poor Stafford must endure suspicion and even imputation for a time.' Fox came to the rescue of his friend, and rebuked this tone, indignantly declaring that 'gentlemen who robbed and plundered their constituencies might despise them, but there were others of a different sort. It was no doubt more acceptable to pay them than to rob them.'

That most celebrated of reporters, Mr. Woodfall, was present on this occasion, and used to describe the beginner coming up to him in the gallery and asking his opinion of this first attempt. 'I am sorry to say,' was the answer, 'I do not think that this is your line—you had much better have stuck to your former pursuits.' On hearing which, Sheridan rested his head upon his hand for a few minutes, and then vehemently exclaimed, 'It is in me, however, and, by G—d, it shall come out!'*

* This intelligent man had so trained his faculties to acquire the habit of recording the essence of all he listened to in both

After this failure, it seems difficult to account for his extraordinary progress and rapid advance to the

Houses, it being forbidden, under severe pains and penalties, to take notes. Hence his name of 'Memory Woodfall.' He was also careful, by other methods, to supplement his record.

'A few days since,' says a writer in the *Pall Mall Gazette,* ' I stumbled upon the following reference to those patriarchs of the reporting world, Woodfall and Perry, in some notes by a very plain-spoken old doorkeeper of the Commons : " Reporters are a set of people who frequent the gallery for the purpose of reporting the speeches of the members in the newspapers the next morning, several of which, being too lazy to come soon enough to get in on great days, are continually boring me in the lobby. Why don't they come in time, like Woodfall ? Let the doors be opened ever so early, one is sure to see him in the gallery in his old place, with his chin rested on his gold-headed cane, ready for the debate ; and it is well for the members that he and others who are clever at it attend for that purpose, for I always think the speeches are a cursed deal better to read than to hear. Friend Perry tells me the great art is to know what to forget and not what should be remembered, as two-thirds at least of what is said would, if put down, utterly spoil the debate and bring the papers into contempt. Friend Perry says the National Assembly have short-hand writers to take down the debate ; but I'll be damned if their short-hand writers give the speeches like our reporters. They are a very useful people, and there are none that I so much like to have about me ; not, God knows, that I get anything by them. Little Shiells, who is a mercenary dog, knuckles them just as he pleases, and never yet had the good manners to ask me to take a glass of the wine they treated him with. None of the reporters, too, ever praised me in the papers ; but Woodfall may speak well of me when I die. We have always been good friends." '

Another antiquated rule of the House of Commons was the exclusion of ladies from its precincts, of which a relic survives in the well-*grilléd* ' Ladies' Gallery.' This was strictly enforced, though some singular forms of evasion were tolerated, and we rank of a first-class debater. But Lord Brougham, who knew him, tells us that ' by constant practice in small matters and before private committees, by diligent attendance on all debates, by habitual intercourse with all dealers in political wares, from the chiefs of parties to the providers of daily discussion for the public, he trained himself to a facility of speaking, and an acquaintance with the science of politics.'

With happy discrimination the same experienced judge goes on to analyze what those gifts were which made Sheridan famous : ' He had a warm imagination, though more prone to repeat with variations the combinations of others, or to combine anew their creations, than to bring forth original productions ; a fierce, dauntless spirit of attack ; a familiarity (acquired from his dramatic productions) with the feelings of the heart ; a facility of epigram and point (the more direct gift of the same theatrical apprenticeship) ; an excellent manner, not unconnected with that experience ; and a depth of voice which suited the tone of his declamation.' He then speaks of his wit, which occasionally descended to farce. ' But the wit was not the inspiration of argument.'

But how account for the existence of these sober, laborious efforts at learning the rules of politics, amid

find Sir Gilbert Elliot writing to his wife that he had seen Mrs. Sheridan brought in, disguised in men's clothes, which he reports without astonishment.

the drudgery of committees, along with the practical
jokes, the midnight *séances* at the drinking club, and
the disorderly administration of the theatre ? For
in these earlier exhibitions in Parliament, we often
have to admire the sobriety, good sense, and tact
he displayed. Just as when Fox uttered the rather
revolutionary threat, 'That should the House become so lost to all sense of public duty, so sunk
in corruption as to abandon the rights of the
people, and to become the passive instrument of
the Crown, *then it may be justifiable to revert to the
original principles of the Constitution, and to resume
the direction of their own affairs, so that the popular
weight may be preserved in the scale of Government.*
The present Administration is the first since the
Revolution which has dared to deny this right.'
Sheridan here interposed to explain, showing that
even if Fox should become Minister, he was not
likely to be the man to carry such doctrines into
practice as the present Government had done.
' No,' he said ; ' were my friend in office and place,
and should he ever forfeit the confidence of Parliament, he would fly to the people, not to Parliament
or to the Throne, for support. *He* would not cling
with the convulsive grasp of despair to the helm
which he could no longer conduct. *He* would instantly retire—not, indeed, probably, to another
assembly, but to a situation more honourable in the
hearts of the people.' A happy and spontaneous
turn !

It may be imagined that when so many rough and rude retorts were given, the telling one of Sheridan's profession (his was the first and only instance of a manager of a theatre finding his way into the House) was not likely to be neglected. Like Burke, he laboured under the serious disadvantage of being an adventurer—an Irish adventurer also—and came to politics unfortified by any of those connections of birth and Parliamentary life which favoured the course of Pitt, Fox, Windham, and others. As Wraxall tells us : 'Many persons thought, perhaps very illiberally, that a Member of the Legislature should not be the conductor of a public theatre. At this vulnerable part, malevolence or satire directed its blows, before Sheridan was scarcely seated in the House. I remember an instance of it which took place during the debate of the 26th of February, when Pitt first presented himself to public notice. Now Courtenay's wit seemed more adapted to a tavern, or to a convivial board, than to the grave deliberations of such an assembly as the House of Commons. Sheridan reprehended him for thus introducing a style of debate altogether unbecoming the gravity of a legislative body. No sooner had he sat down, than Courtenay, who was not easily disconcerted, rising in his place, observed that " the honourable gentleman seemed to be inimical to mirth and to wit *in any house except his own.*" This allusion, which did not admit of being misunderstood, would probably have provoked some reply, perhaps a severe or acrimonious retort, if the Speaker, apprehensive of the consequence, had not interposed his authority, and interdicted the further prosecution of such personalities.'

The enmity of the two Irishmen seemed to grow, just as by-and-by there was to be no one he was so much inflamed against as Burke. Later, when Courtenay had ridiculed the Opposition for their perpetual cries of ' O my country !' adding that ' all the while the patriot eye had *a wistful squint at the Minister,'* Sheridan asked was there not a lack of decency in thus turning everything into ridicule ? As to the insinuation that they were envious of those ' who basked in the sunshine' of power, he reminded him that there was also a heat that *tainted and infected.* He had spoken of the drag-chain of opposition ; but was not that always applied *when the machine was going downhill ?*

The opening of Sheridan's political life thus seemed to offer extraordinary promise, and we can gather from the allusions to him in the lives of Fox and other works, that he conducted himself with due seriousness and much sagacity. This happy state of things only lasted till the days of the first Regency question, when the fatal attraction of an 'illustrious personage' overcame him. Thus Walpole, in his diary, takes note of his behaviour—how, on the second reading of Burke's Civil List Bill,

'the young men in Opposition made a considerable
figure, particularly John Townshend, and Sheridan
(manager of the theatre), both intimate friends of
Charles Fox.' He was presently exhibiting a happy
pleasantry of retort that was relished by the House,
and contrasted favourably with his later carefully
prepared and *inserted* fragments of wit. Thus
during an attack on a well-known official, when
Mr. Rigby was defending himself, uttering the
highest encomiums on his friend the Lord Advocate,
whose speech of that day he pronounced the finest he
had ever heard—a proof of which, he said, was that
it was the speech which had most galled the Opposition—Sheridan replied wittily, that if those speeches
were the best which gave most offence, Rigby himself was the Demosthenes of the House. It was
very true—nobody was so apt to provoke by indiscreet violence. 'Charles,' wrote General Burgoyne,
'in his very first form, and Sheridan much above
anything he has yet done in the House. I think I
never heard more wit than part of his speech against
the Advocate.'

Another instance of Sheridan's early sagacity
occurred in June, 1782, when a treaty with France
was being set on foot, through the agency of Mr.
Grenville, with Franklin at Paris. It was suspected
that Lord Shelburne kept an emissary of his own at
Paris, to counteract the agent of his fellow-Ministers,
and Sheridan seems to have been the first to write

'a letter of suspicion' to Mr. Grenville. This is shown in a letter written by that Minister to him on June 8, which begins with a pleasant stroke at Sheridan's habits.

'DEAR SHERIDAN,—After all the doubts I had expressed of ever hearing from you, it was not very natural that you should find in me the same idleness which I reproached you with by anticipation ; nor can I myself account for it, except that my surprise was so great as to require some time to persuade myself that I had actually and *bonâ fide* received two letters from you. I am, however, at length convinced of it, for certainly your hand is not easily counterfeited.'

In connection with this matter, we find in the Buckingham papers some letters of Sheridan's written to Mr. Grenville at Paris, of so thoughtful and sober a character as to show clearly that he was on the road to responsible statesmanship.

'St. James's, May 26, 1782.

'MY DEAR GRENVILLE,—Charles not being well, I write to you at his desire, that you may not be surprised at having no private letter from him with the despatch which Mr. Oswald brings you. There is not room, I believe, for much communication of any very private nature on the subject of your instructions and situation, as his public letter, you will see, is very sincerely to the purpose. If anything in it admits of modification, or is not to be very literally taken, I should conceive it to be the recommendation of explicitness with Oswald ; on which subject I own I have suggested doubts ; and Charles wishes you to have a caution for your own discretion to make use of.

' I perceive uniformly (from our intercepted information) that all these *city* negotiators—Mr. Wentworths, Bourdeaux, etc.—insinuate themselves into these sort of affairs merely for private advantages, and make their trust principally subservient to stock-jobbing views, on which subject there appears to be a surprising communication with Paris. Mr. Oswald's officiousness in bringing over your despatch, and other things I have been told since by those who know him, lead me to form this kind of opinion of him ; but you will judge where this will apply to any confidence that should be placed in him.

' Surely, whatever the preliminaries of a treaty for peace with France may be, it would be our interest, if we could, to drop even mentioning the Americans in them ; at least the seeming to grant anything to them as at the requisition of France. France now denies our ceding Independence to America to be anything given to them, and declines to allow anything for it. In my opinion it would be wiser in them to insist ostentatiously (and even to make a point of allowing something for it) on the Indepen-

dence of America being as the first article of their
treating ; and this would for ever furnish them with
a claim on the friendship and confidence of the
Americans after the peace.   But since they do not
do this, surely it would not be bad policy, even if we
gave up more to France in other respects, to prevent
her appearing in the treaty as in any respect the
champion of America, or as having made any claims
for her ; we giving her up everything she wants
equally, and her future confidence and alliance being
such an object to us.   Were I the Minister, I would
give France an island or two to choose, if it would
expose her selfishness, sooner than let her gain the
esteem of the Americans by claiming anything essential for them in apparent preference to her own
interest and ambition.   All people, of all descriptions,
in America will read the treaty of peace, whenever
it comes, which France shall make with this country ;
and if they should see there that she has claimed
and got a good deal for herself, but has not appeared
to have thought of them, however they may have
profited in fact, it would certainly give us a great
advantage in those sort of arguments and competi-
tions which will arise after a peace ; whereas if it
appears as a stipulated demand on the part of France
that America should be independent, it will for ever
be a most handy record and argument for the French
party in that country to work with ; and this, as
things stand now, and as far as my poor judgment

goes, appears not to be a very difficult thing to have either way. And so these are my politics on that subject for you.

'There is nothing odd or new to tell you, but that here is a most untimely strange sort of an influenza which every creature catches. You must not mind the badness of my scrawl : and let me hear from you. Does Lafayette join your consultation dinners with Franklin, as some of our Roupell intelligence sets forth ? I take it for granted the French Ministers will think it a point of spirit to seem rather less desirous of peace since your defeat in the West ? What mere politics I write to you ! One might as well be a newspaper editor at once, I believe, as anything that politics can make one : but all other pursuits are as idle and unsatisfactory, and that's a comfort.

' Yours ever,

' R. B. SHERIDAN.'

The political changes of this time have been so often told and re-told, that it would be tedious to rehearse once more the familiar tale of how Lord North at last fell, overborne by the disgrace of the catastrophe in America ; and how the Liberals and ' Radicals ' at last ' came in ' to enjoy a short snatch of power. The Marquis of Rockingham being now Prime Minister, all of the party were duly provided for, Sheridan obtaining office and becoming Under-

18—2

Secretary of State. Such promotion is difficult to conceive at the present time. The truth was that, though ostensibly manager of a theatre, he hardly exercised the duties seriously, or altogether neglected them. And his situation rather answers to that of Sir E. Bulwer when engaged in writing some of those dramas which made him famous.

We find him heartily supporting a motion for Irish independence, though the matter was not then pressed. But this patriotic ardour soon abated. Mr. Moore, either unconsciously or from some artistic sense, in dealing with his hero's character, always appears to take a cynical view of his political attitude, and supplies some rather gratuitous explanation of his course. In the same spirit he dealt with his Radical views. Noticing his silence on a pressing Irish question, he suggests that it may be accounted for from his reluctance to share the unpopularity attached by his countrymen to those high notions of the supremacy of England, which, on the great question of the independence of the Irish Parliament, both Mr. Fox and Mr. Burke were known to entertain.

Here we now again meet with Charles Sheridan, the comparatively obscure brother, who, being possessed of a less mercurial temper, and having a better regard to his personal interests, was to enjoy a more orderly and respectable career. He was so fortunate as to enter diplomacy, obtaining at the early age of twenty the post of Secretary to the British Embassy in Sweden, where he cleverly seized the opportunity to write an account of the Revolution, being assisted with materials furnished by the Ambassador there.*

Why he resigned this promising office is not known, but we find him about the year 1779 established in Dublin, and following the profession of the Bar.   When his brother came into office, he applied to him to ' do something for him.'   He was 'member for Belturbet,' in Ireland, and in a sort of jaunty, lively style, which is not uncommon among his countrymen, preferred his request :

'Dublin, March 27, 1782.

' DEAR DICK,—I am much obliged to you for your early intelligence concerning the fate of the Ministry,

---

* Johnson's extravagant appreciation of this work will be recollected.   Before a dinner-party, where were Miss Seward and others, 'he seized,' says Boswell, 'upon Mr. Charles Sheridan's " Account of the late Revolution in Sweden," and seemed to read it ravenously, as if he devoured it, which was to all appearance his method of studying.   " He knows how to read better than any-one," said Mrs. Knowles ; " he gets at the substance of a book directly ; he tears out the heart of it."   He kept it wrapt up in the tablecloth during the time of dinner, from an avidity to have one entertainment in readiness when he should have finished another : resembling (if I may use so coarse a simile) a dog who holds a bone in his paws in reserve, while he eats something else which has been thrown to him.'

He was also author of a letter to Blackstone on the question of Irish Constitutional Rights, which excited the admiration of Dugald Stewart.

and give you joy on the occasion, notwithstanding your sorrow for the departure of the good Opposition! I understand very well what you mean by this sorrow; but as you may be now in a situation in which *you may obtain some substantial advantage* for yourself, for God's sake improve the opportunity to the utmost, and don't let dreams of empty fame (of which you have had enough, in conscience) carry you away from your solid interests.

' I return you many thanks for Fox's letter—*I mean, for your intention to make him write one;* for as your good intentions always satisfy your conscience, so that you seem to think the carrying them into execution to be a mere trifling ceremony, as well omitted as not, your friends must always take the *will* for the *deed.* I wish the present people may continue here, because I certainly have claims upon them ; and considering the footing that Lord C—— and Charles Fox are on, a recommendation from the latter would now have every weight— it would be drawing a bill upon Government here, payable at sight, which they dare not protest. So, dear Dick, I shall rely upon you that will *really* be done ; and, to confess the truth, unless it be done, and that speedily, *I shall be completely ruined;* for this damned annuity, payable to my uncle, plays the devil with me. If there is any intention of recalling the people here, I beg you will let me know it as soon as possible, that I may take my measures

accordingly ; and I think I may rely upon you also
that, whoever comes over here as Lord L——-t, I
shall not be forgot among the number of those who
shall be recommended to them.'

This rather cynical bit of special pleading is
amusing.

Sheridan accordingly took care of his brother,
who was appointed Secretary for Ireland. After the
rout of the Coalitionists on the India Bill, we find
this rather pliable politician still holding his office,
which excited the remonstrances of his brother, who
declared that in Ireland they were all ' so void of
principle' as to be unable to enter into *their* situation
in England. This drew from the placemen an
ingenious vindication worthy of his brother's ' Joseph.'
He laboriously tried to prove that so different were
' the system, circumstances, and manners of the two
countries, that nothing could be more absurd than to
extend the English party distinctions to Ireland.'

Here was his argument : ' You will admit that to
a party in England no friends on this side of the
water would be worth having who did not possess
connections or talents ; and if they did possess these,
they must, of course, force themselves into station,
let the government of this country be in whose
hands it may, and that upon a much more permanent
footing than if they were connected with a party in
England. What, therefore, could they gain by such

a connection ? *Nothing but the virtue of self-denial,
in continuing out of office as long as their friends
were so ;* the chance of coming in when their friends
attained power, and only the chance, for there are
interests in this country which must not be offended ;
and the certainty of going out whenever their friends
in England should be dismissed. So that they would
exchange the certainty of station upon a permanent
footing acquired by their own efforts, connections,
or talents, for the chance of station upon a most
precarious footing, *in which they would be placed in
the insignificant predicament of doing nothing for
themselves,* and resting their hopes and ambition
upon the labours of others.'

When the Rockingham Ministry fell to pieces
after four months, and was succeeded by Lord Shelburne, Fox and his friends resigned. During his
short rule, Burke had shown his zeal by his well-
known Bill for reducing sinecure places and pensions.
Admirable patriot as he was, he had, strange to say,
the very weakness his Bill was intended to destroy
or cure—viz., an insatiate hunger for place. Mr.
Moore had heard of a letter found among Walpole's
papers, to the effect that as the Ministry was breaking up, he had asked a place for his son. Lord
Russell, in his ' Memoirs of Fox,' actually furnishes
this and other letters—one from young Burke, in
which he said : ' My father always intended to get
this for me ; therefore he omitted the Clerk of Pells

from the list of places to be reduced! *You won't mention this.'* ' In 1782, when Lord J. Cavendish had resigned, only forty-eight hours before his leaving his office Burke came to Walpole and requested him to apply to his brother. Sir Edward (who was a stranger to Burke, and a warm enemy of his politics), to resign his place of Clerk of the Pells, in consideration of the full yearly value being secured to him by Mr. Burke, and of the disposal of a small place then in the younger Burke's possession. Walpole convinced him that the proposal (which he terms " frantic ") was quite inadmissible ; and, though Walpole did not refuse to convey it to Sir Edward, Burke gave it up.' This seems a questionable transaction, in all its aspects.

Again, in Lord Russell's ' Memoirs' are given two papers written by Burke, advising an extraordinary, even crafty course, with a view to ' keeping place,' Fox being in office with Lord Shelburne. His *finale* is thus happily described by Sir N Wraxall : ' So great an accession of moral strength to administration was justly appreciated by the Sovereign and by the Minister. Two pensions, amounting together to £3,600 a year, were bestowed on him, *each for three lives*, as his remuneration. I believe he obtained for them by sale near £36,000. Honours and distinctions followed. George III. accompanied him from one end to the other of Windsor Terrace, covering with attentions and expressions of regard the champion of order, monarchy, and good government.' *

When the Coalition Ministry was formed, on the fall of Lord Shelburne's Government, Sheridan again found himself in office as Secretary to the Treasury, with Burke's brother Richard as coadjutor. Bishop O'Beirne told Mr. Moore that 'he had some expectation of being made Chancellor of the Exchequer, and accordingly shut himself up for three weeks to study figures, which he made himself thorough master of, though perfectly ignorant of the subject before. This accounts for his taking the *financial line* afterwards in his opposition to Pitt.' This is certainly the case, as it often seemed puzzling to account for Sheridan's frequent performances in finance debates.

The famous Coalition has been stigmatized as immoral, and, by the impartial, little can be urged in its favour. † It will be amusing to contrast the

* Even at this opening of his political life, it is curious to find Sheridan charged with a breach of faith in quoting a declaration of the Duke of Richmond, made at a society meeting, and using it against the Duke's colleagues. There was a conflict of assertion, the Duke declaring that he had desired his words not to be repeated, Sheridan saying that he had not. But certainly an ordinary instinct of delicacy and confidence would prompt one to refrain from thus using unrestrained speech as a means of setting one colleague against the other.

† Fox's extraordinary declaration, made early in 1782, is sufficient to condemn it. 'I mean not,' he said, 'to enter into any connection with Ministers. From the instant when I so act, or come to terms with one of them, I will rest satisfied to be deemed

official estimate of Sheridan's behaviour given by his biographer with the true view of later times, helped as we are by authority.

Mr. Moore shows us the wise, prudent, just, and talented Sheridan, who did all he could to dissuade his friends from so fatal a step. 'With that sagacity which in general directed his political views, Mr. Sheridan foresaw all the consequences of such a defiance of public opinion, and exerted, it is said, the whole power of his persuasion and reasoning to turn aside his sanguine and uncalculating friend from a measure so likely to embarrass his future career. Unfortunately, however, the advice was not taken ; and a person who witnessed the close of a conversation, in which Sheridan had been making a last effort to convince Mr. Fox of the imprudence of the step he was about to take, heard the latter, at parting, express his final resolution in the following decisive words : " It is as fixed as the Hanover succession." '

Sheridan himself always declared that he had disapproved of and opposed this immoral Coalition. So he assured Lord Holland and others. But Lord

---

infamous. I cannot for a moment contemplate a coalition with men, who, as Ministers, in every transaction, public or private, have proved themselves devoid of honour or honesty. *In the hands of such men, I would not entrust my own honour for a single minute.*' Within a few months he had joined them in the Government !

John Townshend, one of the actual contrivers of the Coalition, who was alive in 1830, positively and indignantly contradicted the story. 'Sheridan,' he says, 'was then beginning to acquire some of that influence he afterwards more fully possessed over your uncle (C. Fox), and which, not many years after that, he entirely lost—*you know how*. Well, Sheridan, do you know, instead of being adverse to the Coalition, as I dare say *you have often heard the vapouring rogue declare*, was, on the contrary, I assure you, one of the most eager and clamorous for it. His hatred of Pitt, and his anxiety to get into office, were motives sufficient. It is true he had no hand in carrying the measure into effect, for nobody had any sort of trust or confidence in him. Think of his impudence afterwards, in boasting that he had always deprecated the Coalition, and foretold its disastrous consequences !'

'Upon my acknowledging,' says Lord Holland, 'that Sheridan had cajoled me into a belief that he had strenuously deprecated the Coalition, Lord John sent me the following :

' " I have laughed heartily at your account of Sheridan's having duped you into a belief of his noble sacrifice of judgment and opinions to the wishes of others, by his acquiescence in the Coalition and handsome support of a measure he originally disapproved. In his great wisdom it seems he foresaw (foretell he certainly did not) all the ill consequences of the imprudent step. These secret thoughts, however, he kept carefully locked up in his own breast, never uttering a syllable of disapprobation of the measure, in the course of it, to Mr. Fox, to Fitzpatrick, or myself, or to any one of his intimate friends, till more than a twelvemonth afterwards ; when, I allow, he was one of the loudest in his lamentations and condemnations, though I don't think he had the impudence, *even then*, to say that he had been prepared for the events that followed." '*

Allowance may be made here for that dislike which Fox and his party gradually came to have for Sheridan ; but the fact may be accepted, and indeed it might be guessed beforehand, that he was not likely to take the heroic view of what Lord Russell calls the ' much-calumniated Coalition.'

It was in February, 1783, that he made his first really important speech, on the war and the conduct of Ministers in conducting it, one of a series of reviews of facts and policy in which he indulged. It was on this occasion that Pitt, in default of rational arguments, unhandsomely taunted him with his professional avocations, ironically commending his wit and dramatic sallies, which he declared were entitled to the applause of *the audience in their proper place.* Sheridan knew how to turn such an attack to the best advantage, and pointed out that ' the propriety, the taste, the gentlemanly point of these allusions,

* Lord John Russell's 'Correspondence of C. J. Fox.'

must have been obvious to the House.   But let me
assure him,' he went on, 'that I do now, and will at
any time he chooses to repeat this sort of allusion,
meet it with the most sincere good-humour.   Nay,
I will say more—flattered and encouraged by the
right honourable gentleman's panegyric on my talents,
if ever I again engage in the composition he alludes
to, I may be tempted to an act of presumption—to
attempt an improvement on one of Ben Jonson's
best characters, the character of the Angry Boy in
" The Alchemist." '

Here was the actual beginning of an animosity
which, within a year or two, became so inflamed that
we find the young member using this heated language : ' How shuffling,' said he, ' is this conduct in
a young Minister, unhackneyed in the ways of men !
This is an instance of duplicity scarce to be paral-
leled by the most hoary hypocrite that ever guided
the councils of a great nation.   If, in the very
outset, this young Minister thus tramples on the
constitution, what may you not expect or apprehend
from the audacity of his riper years ?'

The well-known India Bill, presently introduced by
the Coalition, must be pronounced, when viewed in
connection with the aims and situation of its authors,
a daring attempt at seizing on power.   It proposed
to hand over the whole control of India to seven
Commissioners—with powers to appoint as well as to
displace *every* official—with an assistant board of

eight, subject to *their* control. These were to rule
for five years. When we think that Fox, Burke,
Sheridan, Fitzpatrick, and most of their friends were
needy, impoverished men, gamblers, turfites, etc.,
and many men of pleasure, it may be conceived how
welcome would be such spoils. Further, with this
power and patronage they would virtually control
Parliament, and the electors become demoralized.
It may be conceived that with such a prize to win and
such a scheme to defeat, great bitterness and ardour
were infused into the debates, while it really furnished the finest opportunity for Sheridan's pleasant
wit and repartee. Wraxall declared that his memory
was baffled, so many were the lively allusions and
exercises of fancy : ' The "Apocalypse" of St. John
furnished images, which, by a slight effort of imagination, or by an immaterial deviation from the
original text, were made to typify Fox, under the
form of the " Beast that rose up out of the sea,
having *seven* heads." Their application to the *seven*
Commissioners could not be mistaken. The words
which were made to designate the Secretary of State
himself, seemed almost to identify him : " And there
was given to him *a mouth speaking great things.*" '

This ingenuity may cause a smile, but it furnished
a device, always a favourite one with Sheridan.
He ran out and procured some leaves of the Book
of Revelation, and supplied *other* ingenious applications, but in Fox's favour. ' Citing, with the most

happy ease,' says the report, ' passages, almost the same pages, from the Bill, he quoted three more verses from the Revelation, by which he metamorphosed the Beast with the seven heads and the crowns on their heads, " into seven angels clothed *in purest white linen."* ' The House was extremely entertained with the turns he gave. Burke, stimulated by the hope of wealth and place, seems to have been wild and frantic with excitement in this case. A member having said that his restoring two corrupt and incriminated officials was a gross and daring act, he flew to his feet, choking with passion, and was beginning in a fury, ' It is a gross and daring——' when Sheridan, fearful he would commit himself, seized him by his coat-tails and dragged him down into his seat. Indeed, a fit of madness appeared often to seize on this great man.

The general shipwreck of the Coalition on the India Bill, and the loss of the expected plunder, with the spirited taking of office by Pitt, a young man of four-and-twenty, are familiar incidents. This defeat consigned Sheridan and his friends to a barren opposition for some twenty-three years. For Sheridan this was to be the first of a series of early disappointments. Henceforth he was ever to be on the eve of grasping power, to find it snatched from him at the moment of victory, or at most was allowed but a few months of the sweets of place.

Now dismissed to retirement, he was free from

official cares, having held the post little over eight
months, during which he is said to have paid so very
little attention to the duties of the office, that a
pasquinade was placed upon the door of the Treasury
to the effect that ' no applications were received on
Sundays, nor any business done there the rest of
the week.' This might seem one of the regular
Sheridan jests always in circulation, but for the
fact of a remarkable declaration made by Burke
in one of his speeches, when much irritated by
some of Sheridan's attacks. He declared that so
neglectful had Sheridan been of his duties, that
many a time he had been on the point of throwing
up his own office in despair! How inconvenient
was this neglect will be understood from the close
relation between the duties of Paymaster and the
Secretary to the Treasury.

In the general rout of the Liberals which took
place on the dissolution of 1784, Sheridan was fortunate in being re-elected for Stafford. This was
secured, as Mr. Moore shows us, by the purchase of
248 burgesses at £5 apiece, amounting to a sum of
about £1,300.* It was while canvassing at Stafford,

---

* How costly this election must have been to Sheridan will be
seen from what Lord Campbell, who stood for the same place
before the Reform Bill, tells us : ' I had represented Stafford in two
Parliaments, and had complied with the well-known custom, which
had prevailed in the borough at least ever since Sheridan first
represented it, of paying them "head-money." This could not
properly be called *bribery*, for the voter received the same sum on

probably for the election, that Sheridan and his wife
were invited by Mrs. Crewe to her country seat.
There was found Windham, who went to help
Sheridan at Stafford, and also Tickell. The mercurial pair naturally played some of their favourite
pranks for the general entertainment. Sheridan
had been asked to invite his friend Richardson, of
whose talent there was a high opinion; but he had
received a letter stating that Mr. Richardson was
unable to come. He kept up the expectation of the
house-party, and having seen a good-looking man
about, a visitor to the servants, he procured a suit
of clothes, had the man dressed in them, availed
himself of the sound of an approaching carriage, and
formally introduced him to the host as Mr. Richardson. Sheridan had previously tutored the man not
to speak, but to bow when any remark was addressed
to him. The guests were struck with the rustic
manner of the supposed Mr. Richardson, but thought
that his conversation would amply compensate for
any awkwardness in his deportment. The host
was particularly attentive to the new arrival; but,

---

whichever side he voted, but it might be treated as bribery in a
court of law.'

It seemed fitting that this exceptional custom should have been
associated with the profuse Sheridan. Lord Cochrane, it may be
remembered, once paid all his supporters, after he had been
defeated, inviting them by public proclamation to come to him,
with the result that he was returned triumphantly on the next
occasion.

after many vain attempts to draw answers from
him, went to Sheridan, and observed that if Mr.
Richardson had not had so high a reputation, one
would have thought he was a very stupid fellow, and
had never been used to good company. Sheridan
said, ' *Wait till you see him at supper, when the wine
has warmed him.*' All present expressed astonishment that so discerning a judge as Mr. Sheridan
should be such a bigot to friendship. At length
supper was announced, and Sheridan, thinking the
joke had gone far enough, and having contrived to
get the countryman away, revealed his whimsical
imposition.

One day when Mrs. Crewe was driving out,
accompanied by Sheridan and Tickell on horseback,
the two gentlemen rode on in advance. Their
hostess was presently horrified at seeing Tickell
stretched on the road, as if lifeless, the two horses
standing near, while Sheridan, in a melodramatic
attitude of despair, was bending over his friend.
There is a slight flavour of buffoonery about these
jests.

Being in Opposition, Sheridan could interest himself much in Irish affairs, and delivered a long and
serious oration on the ' Irish propositions.' He also
turned his attention to the dockyards, and criticized
finance. But all these topics were now to be over-
shadowed by one of absorbing interest, in which
the Opposition were to find a grand opportunity

19—2

for repairing their fortunes, concentrating public attention on themselves, and perhaps destroying the Ministry. This was the famous Hastings *cause célèbre*, which dragged on for so many weary years— even beyond the intentions of the promoters—and which was to raise Sheridan to the highest pitch of celebrity.

WE have now arrived at one of the most dramatic episodes of modern English history—the impeachment of Hastings, accused of having oppressed millions. At this distance of time the whole arraignment of iniquities, made by Burke and his friends with almost frantic oratory, seems exaggerated. This fury of Burke's being the motive-power of the whole, his followers were eagerly inclined to second him, and gleefully accepted such showy parts as he allotted them in the trial. The accused, remote and unfriended, far from all that could justify him, without eloquence or eloquent friends, was branded and described as a species of wild beast whom it was lawful to kill. There was something piteous in the spectacle of his isolation and helplessness.*

* One of the most successful and picturesque essays of Lord Macaulay has made this exciting episode familiar to the world, and few productions have been more admired for its rich and even gaudily descriptive scenes. It was of the essence of those contrasts which the writer found essential for his style, that the principal personages should be made to stand out in violent colouring as conspicuous figures of depravity.

The proceedings were commenced in March, 1786, and in May Hastings was at the bar of the House. But almost at the outset a curious and suspicious incident occurred, which seemed to give a doubtful aspect to the motives of the prosecutors. Major Scott, Wraxall tells us, assured the House that during Fox's India Bill, Hastings had 'received a message or intimation from persons in office, holding out security against the threatened impeachment, provided his friends would engage to remain neuter. Fox instantly rose to repel the accusation, and solemnly denied that any proposal had ever been made for an accommodation with Mr. Hastings, either with *his* knowledge or concurrence. The same positive denial he repeated on the part of all his colleagues. Scott, nevertheless, maintained the accuracy of his assertion ; but as the gentleman from whom the overture came was not then present in his place, either to confirm or to contradict it, all further explanations were by mutual consent postponed till he should appear.'

There was much speculation as to 'the gentleman from whom the overture came ;' but presently it was found that the individual in question was no other than Sheridan, whose fate it seemed to be, whenever there was a political difficulty, either to volunteer or to be persuaded to undertake the most compromising offices. A day or two later he came forward to 'explain,' and this he did in the following in-

genious and characteristic fashion. He admitted
that he *had* sent 'a confidential person' to Scott to
consult him as to bringing back Hastings to England. 'For I thought there remained only two lines
of conduct to be pursued : one, to recall him instantly
by the strong arm of Parliament, and to inflict on
him exemplary punishment ; the other, to bring in
an East India Bill, which on the ground of expediency, and from regard to the difference of opinion
respecting the Governor-General's public merits,
should banish all retrospect. These being my
opinions, and *the latter measure appearing to me most
expedient to be adopted*, I therefore commissioned a
mutual friend to put the question above stated to
the Major. *In the course of their conversation
the East India Bill was mentioned; but not with
the most remote idea of bartering impunity to
Mr. Hastings in return for his support of that
Bill.'* Thus early Sheridan's ingenuity began to
disclose itself.

The Major, in reply, admitted that his informant
agreed that Sheridan's view might *now* be the correct one ; but he urged 'that though he was *now*,
therefore, bound so to think, he had understood the
reverse *at the time, and had remained ever since
under that impression*. Here, therefore, the matter

* This was, in fact, almost an anticipation of the ingenious
denial of the so-called 'Kilmainham contract,' which, a hundred
years later, exercised all Mr. Gladstone's powers of casuistry.

ended, and Fox expressed great gratification at its being so satisfactorily (!) explained.'

'No man,' adds Wraxall,. 'could doubt, after Sheridan's own confession made in the House of Commons, scarcely four weeks earlier, that *he* would willingly have extended impunity and oblivion to Hastings. In lending all the charms of his persuasive eloquence, as he did, to prove Hastings's criminality before his judges in Westminster Hall, Sheridan only acted from a spirit of party, sustained by attachment to Fox.'

During all the stages and proceedings of this exciting struggle Burke seemed to rage and foam. The language he used was of the most extraordinary kind.*

One of the most glorious traditions of Parliament is Sheridan's speech on the Begum charge. This is admitted by all hearers to have been one of the most effective, animated, and vigorous displays of oratory ever heard. This performance was given

---

* 'This,' he said, 'was the golden cup of abominations; this was the enchanted chalice of the fornications of usury and rapine, which was tendered to Ministers by the Eastern harlot! But do Ministers suppose that no reckoning is to follow this lewd defaulter?' Benfield he described as 'a criminal, who ought long since *to have fattened with his offal the region of kites.*'

Much of his grotesque vituperation excites laughter, if not disgust; such as, 'He lay down in his sty of infamy, wallowing in the filth of disgrace, and fattening upon the offal and excrements of dishonour.'

on February 7, 1787, and lasted for more than five hours—not an extravagant duration for so famous a speech. Moore declares, ' Its effect upon its hearers has no parallel in ancient or modern times.' There can be no doubt that it was extraordinarily success-ful and brilliant, delighting or surprising all who listened.* That interesting and amiable man, Sir Gilbert Elliot, gives this vivid and natural account of how *he* was affected. ' Sheridan,' he says, ' spoke five hours and a half with such fluency and rapidity that I think his speech could not be read in double that time. He surpassed all I ever imagined possible in eloquence and ability. The bone rose in my throat and tears in my eyes. His whole powers were employed to their utmost stretch, and indeed his own feelings were wound to their utmost pitch. He worked the House into such a paroxysm

---

* Wraxall, who was present, declared it to be the most splendid display which had been exhibited during the reign. Those who compared with it his second performance in Westminster Hall, are curiously divided in their estimate ; Mill, the historian of India, pronouncing that the latter was ' grander.' Mr. Rogers thought the House of Commons speech ' superior,' that in Westminster Hall ' contemptible.' Macaulay pronounces that the first was without doubt ' the most elaborately brilliant of all the productions of his ingenious mind.' Even the impression on severe and ex-perienced critics was no less strong. ' D. Stewart heard Sheridan's speech in Westminster Hall ; thought some parts particularly fine ; but said the transitions from the prepared declaration to the laxity of his business statements were sudden and ill-managed.' Mr. Windham, twenty years later, said that it deserved all its fame.

of passionate enthusiasm on the subject, and of admiration for him, that the moment he sat down *there was a universal shout*, nay, even clapping, for half a second ; every man was on the floor.'*

After Sheridan's oration an adjournment was demanded, which was resisted by Fox and supported by Pitt, who declared that a more able speech had never been pronounced, and that the House must have time to recover from its effect. The behaviour of the Minister in the whole transaction was extraordinary. It was expected that he would oppose the impeachment. Sir J. Bland Burgess tells us that he had been urging him to reply, and to take notes. But after the adjournment he announced, to the surprise of many, that he would support the motion. He thus, no doubt to his own later regret, set in motion the tremendous engine that for so many years was to encumber the ground, to the annoyance of all concerned. This has often been a device with statesmen in office. This is

* Unhappily, of this brilliant effort there is no record. Sheridan was pressed to give a corrected version, and was offered £1,000 by Debrett for so doing, but was too inert to comply ; yet, for one of his great speeches on the war he took down a reporter with him to the country, and devoted himself for days to drudgery. It is often thus with mercurial natures which work in 'spurts.' They can go on with unabated spirit longer than other men; but then the exertion is spent ; to take up the subject again is odious. He was pressed in the same way as to 'The School for Scandal,' and said he had been trying to satisfy himself for years as to that production, but could not do so.

further proved by a piece of indisputable evidence. Later on, Dundas, when asked for ministerial aid by one of the managers, who said, 'You cannot be indifferent to our success,' replied in his uncouth dialect: 'Troth am I. Ye hae done what we wanted. I shall gie myself nae trouble aboot what comes of ye.' 'Will ye say so to anyone else?' 'Troth shall I.' On which Lord Maitland called up Fitzpatrick and Sheridan, to whom Dundas repeated it.*

The second act of the drama which took place in the theatre of Westminster Hall was not less exciting. We owe to Miss Burney's vivaciousness an effective picture of the scene, but not so gorgeous as that of Lord Macaulay. On this brilliant stage Sheridan was to make his second appearance, and it was the fortunate chance of this gay *dégagé* genius to find everyone ready to furnish him with the most favourable opportunities for display. The case of the Princesses of Oude, whom Hastings was assumed to have cruelly despoiled, had been selected by Burke for his own special treatment; but he at once resigned it to Sheridan on his desire. Still it was found difficult to keep him up to the duty of

* See Sir J. Bland Burgess's 'Memoirs.' He was present. Lord Berkeley also heard the story. It is often supposed that Sheridan delivered but one speech in the House, that of Feb. 7; but he also spoke on the seventh charge on April 2. He obtained some reputation, too, for his fierce and vigorous cross-examination of witnesses.

necessary preparation, so much so that there seems to have been a 'coolness' or quarrel between them. Burke had to appeal to Mrs. Sheridan to use her influence, and to Sheridan himself Burke made this graceful *amende*: 'You have only to wish to be excused to succeed in your wishes ; for indeed, he must be a great enemy to himself who can consent, on account of a momentary ill-humour, to keep himself at a distance from you.' When he at last went to work, Sheridan, after his favourite fashion, laboured with all his might, while the faithful Mrs. Sheridan became a slave and scribe of all work.*

This famous day was June 3, 1788, and he spoke also on the 6th, 10th, and 13th, besides having a reply on May 14. As he had to deal with the Begum charges, it was actually proposed that he

---

* A large pamphlet copied by her, attests her share of that most trying form of drudgery. Some one calling, found the whole family, Tickell, etc., all engaged in copying, cutting out, pasting, etc., under directions from the extraordinary head of the house. He himself often frankly confessed that 'he knew nothing on any subject,' and had to 'get up' all his facts and figures for an occasion for which he was thus 'crammed.' 'Sheridan,' Tierney told Mr. Moore, 'worked very hard when he had to prepare himself for any great occasion. His habit was, on these emergencies, to rise at four in the morning (can this be true ?), to light up a prodigious quantity of candles around him, and eat toasted muffins while he worked.' He had always this fancy for the luxury of abundant wax-candles, flashing lights to his carriage, etc. Some time before, he had filled his carriage with all his notes, books, extracts, and other materials, and shut himself up in his country place, working day and night.

should re-deliver that oration.   Such was the expectancy and eagerness to hear Mr. Sheridan, that twenty guineas were offered for a ticket.   On the second of these performances there was quite a sensation.   A Mr. Bernard, who was present, wrote on June 10: 'I have been this morning at the trial it was Sheridan's third day.   It was near one o'clock before he began.   There was nothing very striking or brilliant in his oratory : he continued for about an hour and a quarter, and then retired.   Mr. Adam assisted him in the reading parts, and continued reading after he retired.   Presently he made a lame apology for him, saying that he had a very trifling affection, without specifying what, whether illness, agitation, or want of due preparation.   Mr. Fox soon afterwards made a more complete apology for him, and the Court adjourned.'   There was some disappointment at first, but he seemed to improve.   Many wept.*

* The Westminster Hall speech was thought to be lost, but a few months before Sheridan's death, the Duke of Norfolk told him that he had it.   Search was made among about two waggonloads of papers, and it was at last found in an old house at Dorking, in a sort of cupboard under the window-seat.   Sheridan, then in his last sickness, had passages read to him, and intended publishing it with others of his works.   The evidence was regularly printed during the trial, and filled nine folios.   Every sitting was attended by Gurney's shorthand writers, who took the speeches verbatim.   A set nearly complete in Lincoln's Inn Library was lately printed under Mr. John Bullen's editorship and under the direction of Sir G. Cornewall Lewis.   Mr. Fraser-Rae has compared many passages, vulgarly passing current, to show the superiority of the shorthand version.

The praises lavished on these efforts may have been not a little directed by the heat of party and the enthusiasm of friendship. Sir Gilbert Elliot made the same objection to the second performance as he had to the first, namely, the prepared and inserted passages. ' I object,' he wrote, ' to the style of these *fine parts* as bearing too evidently the marks of deliberate and cold-blood preparation just where the utmost degree of real passion and fire is to be represented. The previous and *considerate* study, and present animation and fire, are both before you at once, and are confounding and counteracting each other. One is disposed to call out, like the countryman at a conjurer's, " I see how that's done." ' It was probably the vast number of such passages that dazzled and surprised the audience. Wraxall, who with a view to his diary had practised his mind in this form of observation, again tells us that ' Sheridan, accustomed to study theatrical effect at Drury Lane, did not neglect to observe its principles or to practise its rules. In fact, the majesty of the tribunal was half swallowed up in the contemplation of the surrounding assemblage ; among which *females* formed, if not the largest, at least the most attractive portion. To *them*, indeed, the orator did not neglect indirectly to address much of his discourse.'

Boaden has also noted his theatrical device, ' the suiting the sentence exactly to the organ, and being

sure of the fancy and the judgment, taking care that
the rhythm should please as much almost as the
reason or the wit, and the ear anticipate the triumph
of the appeal to the understanding ; sentences written
to be *spoken.* The declamation of Mr. Sheridan
had always this pointed and musical character, and
when he quoted the rebuke to Mammon in Spenser,
during his famous speech in Westminster Hall, a
kind of audible surprise was felt that he should recite
poetry so finely.'*

Sir N. Wraxall also tells us that on the allusion to
'"the pure sentiments of morality with which it
abounded," many persons found it difficult to resist
thinking of Joseph Surface, in Sheridan's own
"School for Scandal." Certainly, the life and practice
of the orator did not furnish the best commentary
on that text. "Instead of resolving ourselves,"
continued Burke, "into a committee of miserable
accounts, let us, like the Romans after Scipio's
victories, go and thank the gods for this day's
triumph in Westminster Hall!"' This generous
treatment and unselfish praise ought never to have

---

* '"They talk of avarice, lust, ambition, as great passions," he
one day said to Lord Holland. "Vanity is the great commanding
passion of all. It is this that produces the most grand and heroic
deeds, or impels to the most dreadful crimes. Save me from this
passion, and I can defy the others. They are mere urchins, but
this is a giant." Sheridan's strong wish to make his power felt in
politics grew still stronger in his latter days from vanity and disappointment.'

been forgotten, and it is an unpleasing spectacle to find Sheridan assailing his former friend with all the animosity of which he was capable.*

Burke had said of the second Begum speech, ' That is the true style, neither prose nor poetry, but better than either,' and was so enthusiastic that many believed he changed his own style in consequence.†
Fox declared it was trumpery. When only half of Sheridan's speech was delivered, Burke said, ' Every member has been struck dumb with astonishment and admiration at the wonderful eloquence of his friend, who had that day again surprised the thousands who hung with rapture on his accents, by such a display of talents as was unparalleled in the annals of oratory, and as did the highest honour to himself, to that House, and to his country. Of all species of oratory, of every kind of eloquence that had been heard either in ancient or in modern times —whatever the acuteness of the bar, the dignity of the senate, or the morality of the pulpit could furnish —had not been equal to what that House had heard

* Fox did not estimate Sheridan's oratory so highly as Burke did. He said of the florid parts of the speech, ' I don't like these things, except in Burke—they are natural to him.' He also added that Burke's admiration of the Begum speech ' first proved to him his want of true taste.'

† Mr. Rogers said, ' It was the opinion of Mr. Fox that Burke's style altered after he heard this speech ; that it spoiled him, and that to the taste he acquired from it we owe the extreme floridness of his writings afterwards—the passage about the Queen of France, etc. etc. Lord Holland told Moore the same thing.'

to-day in Westminster Hall. No holy religionist, no man of any distinction as a literary character, could have come up in the one instance to the pure sentiments of morality, or in the other to the variety of knowledge, force of imagination, propriety, and vivacity.'

Gibbon, who was present, records how he listened with emotion to an allusion to his great history, the orator declaring that nothing equal to Hastings' criminality was to be found 'in the correct periods of Tacitus, or the *luminous* pages of Gibbon.' It has been usually stated that the speaker turned this compliment into a jest, saying that he meant ' voluminous.' The true version is this : Mr. Dudley Long was complacently asked by Gibbon to tell him *exactly* what Sheridan had said : 'Oh !' said the other, 'something about your voluminous pages.' Such is the authentic form of the oft-told anecdote, as it was told to Lady Minto by Lord Russell, who had it from Dudley Long himself.

At the close of the brilliant and overpowering display, it was felt to be a sort of douche when a practical member entered on the question of the *expenses* of the trial, which he complained of as enormous, and moved should be restrained.* This gave Burke an opportunity for an outburst which

---

* The costs of this great cause were enormous. The prosecution amounted to £60,000 ; the defence to £70,000, which was discharged by the East India Company.

added to his friend's glory, and he ironically con-
gratulated the mover on the high level to which he
had raised the question.

On this triumph, which had raised her husband to
fame and honour, Mrs. Sheridan wrote, in a tumult
of joy, to her sister-in-law :

'It is impossible, my dear woman, to convey to
you the delight, the astonishment, the adoration he
has excited in the breasts of every class of people
Every party prejudice has been overcome by a display of genius, eloquence, and goodness which no
one with anything like a heart about them could
have listened to without being the wiser and the
better for the rest of their lives. What must *my*
feelings be !—you only can imagine. To tell you
the truth, it is with some difficulty that I can "let
down my mind," as Mr. Burke said afterwards, to
talk or think on any other subject. But pleasure,
too exquisite, becomes pain, and I am at this
moment suffering for the delightful anxieties of last
week.'

In Sheridan's flush of triumph, amidst the joyful
and affectionate congratulations of his family and
the pride of his enthusiastic wife, what an assured
future seemed to be opening before him ! Place,
fortune, honours were his and theirs to a certainty.
Could he have even dreamed at this moment of the
sad *finale* of debt, misery, disorder, and inebriety
awaiting him ? Or who would have thought that

his fall was to be as low and conspicuous as his rise had been brilliant! Now all was bright and promising. 'Not yet had excesses of wine,' says Wraxall, 'degraded his lineaments, covered him with disgusting eruptions, and obtained for him the dramatic nickname of "Bardolph." At sixty he reminded me of one of the companions of Ulysses, who—

> '"lost his upright shape,
> And downward fell into a grov'ling swine."

Those persons, and those only, who have frequently seen Sheridan at the two different periods to which I allude, can form an adequate conception of the metamorphosis produced in his appearance by repeated and habitual intoxication.'

DURING the two or three years that followed the glories of the Hastings speech, it might have been expected that the hero of that episode would have used this triumph to further his progress and put his success to profit. Instead, we now find him falling under the influence of Carlton House, and cementing an intimacy with the Prince of Wales that was to last all his life. This proved an unprofitable and disastrous connection, for the situation and character of the Prince were such as to exact serious sacrifices of principle in return for the honour of suppers *en partie fine*, and the familiarity of being styled ' Dick ' or ' Charles.' Even Fox, who was welcomed to the same cordial intimacy, soon found it necessary to adopt a reserve, and never forgot what he owed to his party and its interests ; afterwards breaking altogether with temptation. The impulsive Sheridan, easily tempted and dazzled, yielded himself up to this flattering fascination, and was soon to learn how frail and reed-like was the support on which he leant.

He, however, remained constant throughout. There is something, indeed, almost pathetic in the record of his attachment to the Prince, for whom, during a course of nearly thirty years, he may be said to have sunk everything—consistency, character, —all. For this potentate's pleasures and private interests, for his political service, for his defence at the most awkward moments—for any, as it is called, '*dirty work*,' this faithful henchman was found ready.

Again and again he had to stand forward and make some ingenious plea for the Prince's debts or other embarrassments. At times he would seem to bewail himself for having the misfortune not to be in favour with his Royal Highness, from opposing some whim or plan of the Prince's ; but he almost unwaveringly continued his adherence.

In the numerous debates that arose on the question of the Prince's debts we find Sheridan and Fox taking an active part. An awkward incident occurred in the month of April, 1787, when the former was called on to exhibit his devotion to his royal patron by the sacrifice of some of his own credit. This was on the first public allusion to the supposed, or illegal, marriage of the Prince with Mrs. Fitzherbert, which had been whispered about ; and Mr. Rolle, a sturdy county member, made it a condition that previous to dealing with the debts, satisfactory explanations should be given of this delicate matter.*

* Mr. Rolle, not witty himself, was the cause of much wit in others; giving rise to the humorous idea of a poem named after him, and written by the leading political *farceurs*. To this all Sheridan's humorous friends contributed, but he did not write a line in it himself. This has always seemed a phenomenon, as he was likely to have excelled in such a production, with so tempting a subject offered to him. It can only be accounted for in this way, that he never could set himself to an allotted work, which he was inclined to consider a task. There were some rhymes among his papers which might have been intended as a contribution, a series of strophes:

> 'Glenbervie, Glenbervie,
> The world's topsy-turvy;'

or,

> 'Vansittart, Vansittart,
> For little thou fit art.'

But these did not approach the wit of the 'Rolliad,' of the origin of which one of its writers gave this singular account: 'What gave rise to the "Rolliad" was a sort of "smoking and spitting party," made in the House of Commons to interrupt and annoy Burke, of which party Rolle was the chief promoter. Tickell (I think said Moore) began the poem.' Lord Braybrooke furnished to the useful *Notes and Queries* (vol. ii., 2nd series) some curious information as to the 'Rolliad.' He found a list of the contributors in a copy in the library at Sunnyhill Park, written, he believed, by Mr. George Ellis. This included Dr. Laurence, Tickell, Gen. Fitzpatrick, George Ellis, Richardson, Mr. Adair, Mr. Reid, Lord John Townshend, Rev. H. Bate Dudley, Brummell, Pearce, Boscawen, Bishop of Ossory (Hon. W. Beresford), Bishop of Meath (O'Beirne), and Canning, then a youth. The 'probationary odes,' supposed to be written by public men who imagine themselves inspired to write verse, are based on a truly whimsical idea. Thus Dundas:

George IV., on the appearance of Moore's 'Life,' had a long conversation with Mr. Croker with reference to this doubtful episode of his marriage, to which we have already alluded.*

> ' Hoot ! hoot awaw !
> Hoot ! hoot awaw !
> Ye lawland Bards' who' are ye aw ?
> What are your sangs ? what aw your lair too boot ?
> Vain ere your thowghts the prize to win,
> Sae dight your gobs, and stint your senseless din.'

This highly popular production, which passed through twenty-two editions in twenty-seven years, was the occasion of a scene in the House, which exhibited Sheridan in his most good-humoured aspect. Mr. Rolle, who suggested the image of a Devonshire rustic, accused Sheridan of going down into Lancashire and circulating seditious and inflammatory handbills. ' I will not say who did so; but if I could bring it home to the proper party,' said the irate member, ' I would have his head stuck on Temple Bar !' Sheridan denied all knowledge of the handbills, but added pleasantly : ' I can easily conjecture the reason of the soreness expressed in the article of publication. Compositions less prosaic, though more popular, have, I believe, produced that irritability.' Sheridan then assured Rolle, on his honour, that he never saw a line of the verses till they met his eye in a newspaper. It is remarkable that the widow of this gentleman, afterwards Lord Rolle, survived up to last year; her husband having been born over one hundred years ago !

* The King's account of this incident is in effect that when Fox mentioned the rumours, ' I contradicted them at once with " Pooh ! ridiculous ! nonsense !" which prompted Fox to make the statement in the House : " Mr. Moore states that I applied to Mr. Grey to set the matter right, and that when he refused, I said then we must bring Sheridan into play. There is not a word of truth in this. I had no kind of communication

Fox privately put the question to the Prince, and in plain terms ; and was told as plainly that ' there was no truth in the rumour.' Thus authorized, he boldly denied the charge in the House. The Liberal party was relieved and delighted, for all had had their suspicions. Friends, however, of Mrs. Fitzherbert took the matter up ; persons at Brooks's actually declared they had witnessed the marriage ; while the lady herself seems to have had ' a scene ' with her royal admirer. ' On her indignation and reproaches, he was ready to make all amends and remove the mischief, now that his case had been laid before the House of Commons and the public. He sent for Mr. Grey, and after much preamble, and pacing in a hurried manner about the room, exclaimed : " Charles certainly went too far last night. You, my dear Grey, shall explain it ;" and then, "as Grey," adds Lord Holland, " has, since the Prince's death, assured me, though with prodigious agitation,

---

with Mr. Grey on the subject, and Sheridan's interference was perfectly accidental."' The King's version unfortunately is contradicted by Lord Grey, who states that he was applied to by his Majesty. It will be seen, too, that his denial of the marriage is ambiguous. It is clear that he always spoke with casuistical ' reserve,' implying that the *illegality* of the ceremony was equivalent to its having never taken place. The clergyman is known ; the witnesses were men of rank and position ; and the papers proving it are now in the vaults of Messrs. Coutts. For this interesting question, see the author's 'Life of George IV.,' Mr. Langdale's 'Life of Mrs. Fitzherbert,' 'Lady Morgan's Memoirs,' and the recently published 'Life of Mary Frampton.'

owned that a ceremony had taken place."* Grey
observed that if there had been any mistake it could
easily be rectified by his Royal Highness speaking
to Mr. Fox himself, and setting him right. "No
other person can," he added, "be employed without
questioning Mr Fox's veracity, which nobody, I
presume, is prepared to do." A reply such as this
might be expected from a man of Mr. Grey's character. "It chagrined, disappointed, and agitated
the Prince exceedingly;" and, after some exclamations of annoyance, he threw himself on the sofa,
muttering, "*Well, Sheridan must say something!*"'

What a testimony to our hero! Fox broke off all
connection with the Prince for two years, and was
only reconciled to him by the necessity of harmony
during the crisis of the first regency. Mrs. Fitzherbert never spoke to Fox again; but Sheridan—
the less scrupulous Sheridan—remained faithful, and
performed the unpleasant function required of him.

As the Prince, some years after his accession,
told Mr. Croker, Sheridan went to Mrs. Fitzherbert
to soothe her. Her beauty and deep affliction
affected him. He was afraid, he told the Prince,

---

* The fact of 'a ceremony' having taken place has long been
fully established. The list of documents lodged in the bank of
Messrs. Coutts, by the Duke of Wellington and Sir William
Knighton, as executors of George IV., and the Earl of Albemarle
and Lord Stourton on behalf of Mrs. Fitzherbert, includes 'the
certificate of marriage,' dated 'December 21st, 1785.' See
'Memoirs of Mrs. Fitzherbert' (Bentley, 1856).

that her great power over him would be used to make a breach with Fox. So he assured her that Fox was misreported, and that he would set matters right in the House of Commons.

The King having consented to make an arrangement for paying the Prince's debts, Sheridan accordingly seized the opportunity to 'say something.' 'But, while the Prince's feelings had, no doubt, been considered on the occasion, he must take the liberty of saying, however some might think it a subordinate consideration, that there was another person entitled, in the judgment of every delicate and honourable mind, to the same attention ; one whom he would not venture otherwise to describe than by saying it was a name which malice or ignorance alone could attempt to injure, and whose conduct and character were entitled to the truest respect.'

As was said at the time, ' Mr. Fox had declared that a lady living with the Prince, to all exterior appearance, in the habits of matrimonial connection, had not the sanction of any canonical forms to support her ; whilst, on the other hand, Mr. Sheridan reversed the picture, by representing her as a paragon of chastity, the possessor of every virtue, and the ornament of her sex.'

A meeting was then fixed at Carlton House for general explanations, to which Mr. Pitt came, attended by his friend Dundas. He found the Prince waiting, *attended by Mr. Sheridan,* on which the Minister positively refused to enter on the business so long as one so opposed to the Government was present. The Prince then ordered both Dundas and Sheridan to withdraw, when all was satisfactorily arranged.

Such was the transaction in which Sheridan for the first time seemed to exhibit that preference for tortuous and shifty work, which he seemed to fancy, if not prefer, for the rest of his life. Was it that he had grown intoxicated by his recent triumph, and disdained the slow routine of Parliamentary work ; or that he was flattered by the affectionate attentions and preference of his august patron ; or had he a natural penchant for the shorter methods of intrigue, which *he* considered diplomacy ? The late display, after all, was barren enough in its fruits, and of a theatrical kind, and he had probably grown impatient, as the prospects of the party as regards office never seemed so gloomy. But a change was at hand.

We now come to the momentous crisis of the King's illness, which again offered the fairest and most promising issues for the party out of power, with highly favourable chances for their restoration, not only to office but to supremacy. It has been often told how almost at the very moment of success, the opportunity was lost, and office snatched from them when actually in their grasp. Seldom has there been recorded so mortifying a disappointment. All the offices had been filled—the most cheerful anticipations entertained—the Prince was to be virtually placed on the throne—when at the last moment the King recovered, and for seventeen years more the unlucky 'Liberals' were doomed to Opposition.

When the King was so unexpectedly seized with illness, the Liberal chief, Fox, was abroad. The Prince of Wales, suddenly called on to act, could find no better advisers at hand than Lord Loughborough, Sheridan, and 'Jack Payne,' the latter acting as the medium of communication between the Prince and the other two. The airs of importance, as well as the foolish incapacity exhibited for some weeks, must have shipwrecked the plans of the party but for the return of Fox. As is well known, one of Sheridan's plans was the foolish one of gaining over Thurlow, the Chancellor, an unprofitable intrigue, which presently broke down. Sheridan's active share in the business was indeed disastrous, and soon brought about divisions and open quarrels in the party, and we are not surprised to learn that the Duke of Portland had declared '*his determination not to act with Mr. Sheridan in committee,* who is just now Prime Minister at Carlton House. Charles Fox, besides ill-health, is plagued too all day long, dissatisfied with Mr. Sheridan's supremacy.'

On the first indications of the King's malady, this confidential relation between the Prince and Sheridan was shown by a sensible letter which the latter addressed to him, impressing the exercise of the strictest moderation, 'disclaiming all party views, and avowing the utmost readiness to acquiesce in any reasonable delay.' At the same time he admitted that this course would favour 'the arts,' so he called them, of the persons who wished to advance their own 'evil views.' In secret, however, his designs were truly ambitious, and so high were his expectations that he aspired to one of the most important posts in the future Government, and one for which he was utterly unfitted. 'He is on all hands understood,' Lord Auckland heard, 'to be the prime favourite, and to be so sensible of it as modestly to pretend to a Cabinet place, which is hitherto firmly resisted by the Duke of Portland, who says they cannot both be in the same Cabinet. Sheridan would willingly submit to be Chancellor of the Exchequer ; but it is thought things are not yet ripe enough for the manager of Drury Lane to be manager of the House of Commons.' This might seem incredible, but Sir G. Elliot heard the same story. With this view Sheridan spent weary hours of the night studying figures and finance generally, and it is said that his numerous later speeches on this topic were but the fruit of these studies. Yet at this moment the.intending Chancellor of the Exchequer and his wife had to find shelter at Mrs. Fitzherbert's, bailiffs being in possession of their house and furniture !

When the Regency Bill, with all its limitations and restrictions, was sent to the Prince by Mr. Pitt, a reply had to be settled. This document has been credited to Sir G. Elliot, but it was drawn up, he tells us, by Burke, and 'altered a little, but not improved, by Sheridan' and others; a 'strange performance,' as it appeared to the Duke of Leeds. When Pitt proposed allotting all the household patronage to the Queen, the proposal was vehemently assailed by Sheridan, who ridiculed it in his happiest style, drawing a picture of Pitt coming down to the House 'attended by his household.' No less than 250 places, it was calculated, would be thus lost to the party. Sheridan, giving up the idea of being at the Exchequer, had now fixed on his own place, which was to be the Treasuryship of the Navy. He had already received plans of his rooms at Somerset House. It must, however, be said that he had never been wholly sanguine, and even maintained that the King *would* recover.*

* Sheridan took a leading part in examining the doctors as to the King's death. Mr. Swinburne heard a good story of Dr. Willis's coolness. 'Sheridan, with a long string of questions, was ready to perplex him if possible. Willis said, "Pray, sir, before you begin, be so good as to snuff those candles, that we may see clear, for I always like to see the face of the man I am speaking to." Sheridan was so confounded at this speech of the basilisk doctor, that he could not get on in his examination.'—'Courts of Europe,' vol. ii., p. 75.

This physician he attacked in the House as an impostor.

The curious attitude of the Liberal party on this question, was not such as 'the party' ought to have adopted, being coloured by hostility to Pitt and his doctrines. Nowadays we should expect to find the Liberals supporting restrictions. Nothing was more natural or effective than Pitt's retort, that 'he would *un-Whig* Fox for life,' when the latter was so far carried away by partisanship as to contend that the Prince had '*a right*' to take on him the office without the sanction of Parliament; and it must have sounded oddly to hear Mr. Pitt declaring that this right 'was to be found in the voice and sense of the people.' Sheridan committed an even greater blunder, and actually seemed to threaten Pitt, reminding him *of the danger of provoking that claim to be asserted*, which, he observed, had not yet been preferred. Mr. Pitt turned this to account with all his usual mastery and haughtiness. 'He had now,' he said, 'an additional reason for asserting the authority of the House, and defining the boundaries of right, when the deliberative faculties of Parliament were invaded. Men who felt their native freedom would not submit to a threat, however high the authority from which it might come.'

This foolish outburst almost shipwrecked the party, and showed how unfitted Sheridan was to maintain the 'moderation' he had pressed on the Prince. As Mr. W. Grenville wrote in triumph: 'The day was closed by such a blunder of Sheridan's, as I never knew any man of the meanest talents guilty of before. During the whole time that I have sat in Parliament, in pretty warm times, I never remember such an uproar as was raised by his threatening us with *the danger of provoking the Prince to assert his right*, which were the exact words he used. You may conceive what advantage all this gives us.' This incident alone would show how impossible it is to take Sheridan *au sérieux* as a politician.

During this crisis, so inflamed were the passions of all, that Burke was led away into proposing a measure that was really treasonable. It was Sheridan who, long after at a City dinner at Merchant Tailors' Hall, indiscreetly revealed it to a party of Tories, among whom was Mr. Ward, who reports it. He said that 'at a meeting at Burlington House, Burke had proposed to keep the King from returning to power even if he had recovered his health. Strange to say, so treasonable a question, instead of being rejected by a common and instantaneous feeling, was allowed to be discussed ; and almost stranger still, Lord Loughborough was the only man at the meeting who sided with Burke in recommending it. Sheridan mentioned it to show that, with all his softness of demeanour, when wrong he could be most violently so.'* This revelation is

---

* Among Lord Loughborough's papers was found a pamphlet embodying this dangerous scheme. No wonder that when, in

curiously illustrative of Sheridan's character, for here his dislike to Burke overpowered his discretion.

The King, George IV., told Mr. Croker some characteristic anecdotes of Sheridan's behaviour at this period. On his Majesty's recovery, when Burke drew up for the Prince his lengthy paper, which was to be presented to the King, Sheridan read it over in private with the Prince, who described him as exclaiming 'Fine, very fine! mad, furious! admirable!' and saying that in future, 'instead of out-Heroded Herod, the phrase would be *out-Burked* Burke.' The paper, which the Prince's council thought quite too violent to be adopted, was then given into the charge of Jack Payne. Some time after Sheridan begged the Prince to let him see it; 'he could pick something valuable out of the paper.' He got leave to go to Jack Payne and read it over. 'He, however,' went on the King, 'with an *inaccuracy* not unusual to him, poor fellow! told Payne that he had my authority to take away the paper, which he did. Of course he never wrote anything, and I ordered him to return it. This he postponed and delayed year after year, and at last fairly confessed that he had either lost the paper, or that it was buried in what he called the chaos of his papers.'

_____

1806, there was a question of giving Sheridan a Cabinet office, it was opposed by the Duke of Bedford and vetoed, on the ground that Sheridan would 'blab.'

At last, early in February, it was known that the King was better; and though the Bill was all but passed, it was pronounced to be indecent to press the matter further.   And thus, after about ten weeks of the most exciting crisis, it was announced that all was at an end, and that the King was ready to take up his functions again.   It was only left to Sheridan, with affected cheerfulness, to give his Majesty's health at his own table.   Mr. Moore had from one of Sheridan's friends a description of this scene, which does credit to Sheridan's gaiety. 'He entered his own house' (to use the words of the relater of the anecdote) 'at dinner-time with the news.   There were present—besides Mrs. Sheridan and his sister —Tickell, who on the change of Administration was to have been immediately brought into Parliament; Joseph Richardson, who was to have had Tickell's place of Commissioner of the Stamp Office; Mr. Reid, and some others.   With his wonted equanimity he announced the sudden turn affairs had taken, and looking round him cheerfully, as he filled a large glass, said : "Let us all join in drinking his Majesty's speedy recovery."'

This exciting episode leaves the chief agent scarcely advanced in reputation.   There can be no doubt he suffered from the stories in circulation as to his unsuccessful intrigue and want of loyalty to his friends.   There can be no doubt that both Burke and the Duke of Portland were disgusted and offended ; but with happy audacity Sheridan took an early opportunity, in a debate on the Tobacco Laws, to strike one of those heroic attitudes which he fancied were enough to restore him. 'What he alluded to were whispers or reports of jealousies among some of his dearest friends, and of a certain opposition affirmed to have been made by a noble Duke against some views or expectations which he was said to have entertained. Now, concerning such whispers and reports, he could truly declare that there was not in them one grain of truth. The opinion which they ascribed to the noble Duke had never been entertained by him. On the contrary, Mr. Sheridan remarked that he would not venture to state the opinion which the noble Duke was pleased to entertain of him, lest he should be accused of vanity in publishing what he might deem highly flattering. All therefore that he would presume to assert on this occasion was, that if he had it in his power to make the man, whose good opinion he should most highly prize, think favourably of him, he would have that person think of him precisely as the noble Duke then did : and then his wish on that subject would be most amply gratified. He defied any man to charge him with a single act which could be tortured into a violation of any engagement founded in honour and integrity. If he could be charged, in truth, with anything dishonourable, mean, or unmanly, he should feel very differently indeed :

his mind, in that case, would sting him more than the most bitter reproaches of his most calumniating enemies.' But, alas! not many years later he was found sneering at the man of whose friendship he was once so proud, who, he said, 'was ready to take a place in *any* Cabinet; and no Minister could be distressed for want of aid while this obliging noble-man was to be found.' This unstableness of opinion marked every point of his career.

But soon we find this mistrust and suspicion leading to an open quarrel, and the incidents of one night in the year 1790 were to have a strange, im-portant significance, for they may be said to have 'broken up the Liberal party.' In those times poli-ticians were too honest and straightforward to 'gloze over' differences, by looking for a colourless formula which should reconcile them in appearance. This was the celebrated breach between Fox and Burke, which Sir G. Elliot said 'made more noise in London than any event I can recollect, and for which Sheridan was in part accountable. Fox had praised the conduct of the French Guards, who refused to obey the orders of the Court, on which Burke very temperately showed how dangerous the extolling of such principles might prove as an example to English soldiers. But he spoke in kindly terms of Fox. The latter, after defending himself, returned the compliment in language almost extravagant in its regard. He was so earnest indeed, and sincere, that

' he almost seemed to weep.' Burke, much softened, acknowledged this display in fresh terms of affection, though he warned his friend against giving ear to '*dangerous influences.*' When he sat down the incident might have seemed to be closed. But it was noticed that Sheridan had changed colour at this last allusion, and looked angry. Some malicious spirit prompted him to intervene, and, starting to his feet, he commenced a bitter attack on Burke—' a virulent personal invective,' as it was considered by those who listened —venomously reiterating the language of Fox, vindicating the National Assembly and the French Revolution, declaring it to be as justifiable as our own, and finally asking whether Burke ' had found his doctrines amidst the stones of the Bastile, or had collected them from the baggage of Marshal Broglie ?' This gross attack, which shocked everyone, at once renewed the original quarrel. Burke, in excited language, told Sheridan that in politics they were henceforth separated, and that he dismissed him from his friendship.' He added that ' he had expected that his honourable friend—*for so he had been in the habit of calling him*—would have treated him with some kindness, if from their long connection, or at least have represented his arguments fairly. Sheridan had cruelly and unexpectedly misrepresented his remarks, holding him out as a foe to freedom.' The sensation that this passage caused may be conceived, and Sheridan was universally condemned. Many reasons were suggested for the attack, and Sheridan himself, looking rather ashamed, offered some explanations, which, it was noted, were contradictory. He said he thought Burke was attacking *him*. But the true cause, no doubt, is that he had been glad that a breach had taken place between Fox and Burke, that he was annoyed at their reconciliation, and then artfully inflamed the sore which was on the point of being healed. Dr. Parr declared that the sole cause of the quarrel was ' Burke's jealousy of Sheridan, of his eloquence and popularity, and of his influence with Fox and with the Prince of Wales.' The jealousy is likely to have been on the other side. Efforts were promptly made to mend matters, and Mr. Dennis O'Bryan was despatched to Burke as mediator. It was settled that Sheridan should come to Burke's house in Gerrard Street, Soho, the next night, and be reconciled. He met Burke, who was returning home, at his own door. Burke greeted him, and proposed their going together to a party at the Duke of Portland's. On getting into the carriage the generous man shook hands warmly with his friend, and told him that ' nothing now remained but to make the matter up in a manner that would appear best to the public.' But now was to occur a characteristic yet natural incident. In the carriage it seemed to Burke that Sheridan, instead of excusing, was really justifying himself, and attempting to show that he had reason for the warmth of language he had used. This broke off the reconciliation, though at the Duke's every effort was made to cement it, up to an early hour of the morning.* Sir Gilbert Elliot furnishes this account. They were thenceforth hostile, and thus began a series of bitter, angry attacks and retorts which continued for many years. On this, too, followed the open breach between Fox and Burke, with the publication of the latter's work on the 'Revolution,' and the 'cleavage' in the Liberal party. ·

Everyone knows the famous scene between Fox and Burke, and the renunciation of Fox's friendship. He exclaimed, ' I quit the camp!' and suddenly crossed the House, and seated himself on the Ministerial benches. It was Sheridan who replied to Mr. Burke's attack, and concluded his speech with nearly these words : ' The honourable gentleman, to quote his own expression, has " quitted the camp;" he will recollect that he quitted it as a

---

* In a letter from that agreeable *viveur*, General Fitzpatrick (quoted in an early number of the *Westminster Review*), we have the view of this transaction held by one of Sheridan's intimate friends : ' I have very justly called it a near race over the Curragh, for no two Irish heads ever displayed their absurdity more completely. Everybody was struck with the absurdity of Burke, who chose to make a speech in answer to Charles, till Sheridan seemed to resolve to eclipse his countryman by an answer at least as ill-judged and as ill-timed as the attack.' . . . The Prince of Wales even gave a grand reconciliatory dinner to the combatants, but without effect.

deserter, and I sincerely hope he will never attempt
to return as a spy.   But I, for one, cannot sympathize
in the astonishment with which an act of apostasy
so flagrant has electrified the House ; for neither I
nor the honourable gentleman have forgotten whence
he obtained the weapons which he now uses against
us.'   These scenes and recriminations were truly
deplorable.*

This angry feeling towards Burke was now to be
shown in many rather unseemly wrangles between
the former friends.   Thus in February, 1793, on
Burke's falling foul of Fox, who was attempting to read passages from some former speeches,
and being stopped by the Speaker, Sheridan
defended his friend with much force and success,
declaring that Burke had excelled himself in his

---

* It is sad to have to contrast this hostile tone with his earlier
deference to the great orator and statesman, at whose feet he
seemed inclined to sit in his earlier days.   To him Sheridan wrote
in the year 1783 :

'MY DEAR SIR,—I protest to you nothing could mortify me
more than to think you can for a moment believe me such a coxcomb as to receive any advice or hint of any sort from you with
any other feeling than the most serious and grateful attention.   I
did not express what I meant last night, or you would not think
otherwise, which I am afraid by your note you do ; and I shall not
be set right in my own opinion until I find that you do not continue to judge so of me, by your again taking the trouble to give
me that advice and counsel which I must be an idiot not to know
the value of, and which I declare without a particle of complaint I
shall always feel the truest act of friendship and condescension
you can honour me with.'

display of bitterness and spleen 'towards the man he still professed to respect.' 'He did not seem,' he said, 'to take the interference of the Speaker kindly, though he ought to have been grateful for it; for never had man a greater interest in discouraging the practice of contrasting the past and present speeches, principles, and professions of any man. Let a set of his works be produced, and one member might read paragraph by paragraph his present doctrines, and another should refute every syllable of these out of the preceding ones.' This was telling enough, and true also. Later on he described Burke with much bitterness as 'a man talking of parties, who yet had long since stated he was unconnected with parties'; who had gone from the living Whigs to the dead, and whom he himself, having never deserted the camp, did not suspect of retiring as a spy.'

These scenes led on to the final division in the Liberal party, and to the secession of all the leading Whigs, and who actually accepted office under Pitt. Fox, whose conduct had caused the secessions, remained; and Sheridan also was left in this apparently Spartan isolation.* He was frank

---

* After this disagreement it was noted, Mr. Prior tells us, that Sheridan always sat silent in company when Burke was the subject of praise. Mr. Burke had frequently expressed his disgust at Sheridan's profane jests, his favourite subject being the Trinity. In fact, this indecorum so offended his friend and host, Lord Crewe, that he ceased to invite him to his house. Mr. Morley

enough to confess one at least of the reasons why he had not followed his friends' example and joined the Government. It is one that might be conjectured. He had *not* been asked to do so. 'I am not such a coxcomb,' he said in 1798, 'as to say that it is of much importance what part I may take ; or that it is essential that I should divide a little popularity, or some emolument, with the Ministers of the Crown ; nor am I so vain as to imagine that my services might be solicited. Certainly they have not. That might have arisen from want of importance in myself ; or from others, whom I have been in the general habit of opposing, conceiving that I was not likely either to give up my general sentiments, or my personal attachments. However that may be, certain it is they never have made any attempt to apply to me for my assistance.' This lack of invitation seems strange when we think of the members so invited—from Fox down to much more obscure persons. But Sheridan was now so disliked by his former friends that it was impossible to have him. This mortifying neglect certainly inflamed him, and lent a fresh bitterness to his tongue in the years of debate which we shall now proceed to follow.

By this time we find that Sheridan was in really desperate straits, and thus early had grown familiar

---

says justly that Burke's large and conscientious nature revolted at Sheridan's reckless lack of principle and assumption of whatever suited his purpose at the moment.

with bailiffs and civil processes for debt and difficulty.
A sketch by Miss Berry shows how little he was
affected by troubles of this kind, which he soon
acquired a practised skill in dealing with. ' Mrs.
Keppel,' she writes, ' has let her house at Isleworth
to Sheridan for £400 a year—an immense rate, and
yet far from a wise bargain. He has just been
forced out of his house in Bruton Street by his
landlord, who could get no rent from him ; almost
the night he came to Isleworth he gave a ball there,
which will not precipitate Mrs. K.'s receipts.'

CHAPTER XIV.

SHERIDAN'S oratorical reputation is mainly founded
on those 'set' and prepared speeches delivered on
stirring occasions, which are to be read in collections.
But these carefully studied efforts give little idea of
his general powers. It is only by going carefully
through the series of reports furnished so dramatic-
ally and accurately by 'Memory' Woodfall that we
see what a conspicuous figure he was in the ordinary
routine discussions of the House. Having carefully
followed him through some of these conspicuous
years, I find how industrious, versatile, and combative he showed himself. It was, in fact, as a
'*debater*' that he here exhibited those gifts, being
always ready with some brilliant, if not theatrical,
attack or reply to Pitt—or to Burke, when the latter
began to sit on the Treasury Benches.

Wraxall has left a really admirable picture of him,
with an acute analysis of the arts, gifts, and devices
by which he gained his influence over the House :

'Sheridan exposed an angry antagonist by sallies of wit, or attacked him with classic elegance of satire ; performing this arduous task in the face of a crowded assembly, without losing for an instant either his presence of mind, his facility of expression, or his good humour. He wounded deepest, indeed, when he smiled ; and convulsed his hearers with laughter, while the object of his ridicule or animadversion was twisting under the lash. Nor did he, while thus chastising his adversary, alter a muscle of his own countenance ; which, as well as his gestures, seemed to participate and display the unalterable serenity of his intellectual formation.'

It will be noted what a happy and subtle art of description is here shown by this observer, who goes on :

'Rarely did he elevate his voice, and never except in subservience to the dictates of his judgment, with the view to produce a corresponding effect on his audience. Yet he was always heard, generally listened to with eagerness, and could obtain a hearing at almost any hour. Burke, who wanted Sheridan's nice tact and his amenity of manner, was continually coughed down ; and on those occasions he lost his temper. Even Fox often tired the House by the repetitions which he introduced into his speeches. Sheridan never abused their patience.

'At this period of his life, when he was not more than thirty-three years of age, his countenance and features had in them something peculiarly pleasing; indicative at once of intellect, humour, and gaiety. All these characteristics played about his lips when speaking, and operated with inconceivable attraction; for they anticipated, as it were, to the eye, the effect produced by his oratory on the ear; thus opening for him a sure way to the heart or the understanding. Even the tones of his voice, which were singularly mellifluous, aided the general effect of his eloquence; nor was it accompanied by Burke's unpleasant Irish accent. Pitt's enunciation was unquestionably more imposing, dignified, and sonorous; Fox displayed more argument, as well as vehemence; Burke possessed more fancy and enthusiasm; but Sheridan won his way by a sort of fascination. At thirty-three it might be said of his aspect, as Milton does of the fallen angel's form,

> ' "His face had not yet lost
> All her original brightness." '

Lord Brougham, who had heard him speak, justly says: ' His worst efforts were those which he preferred himself, full of imagery often far fetched, oftener gorgeous and loaded with point that drew the attention of the hearer away from the thoughts to the words; and his best by far were those where he declaimed with his deep, clear voice, though somewhat thick utterance, with a fierce defiance of some adversary, or an unappeasable vengeance against some act ; or reasoned rapidly, in the like tone, upon some plain matter of fact, and exposed as plainly to homely ridicule some puerile sophism. In all this his admirable manner was aided by an eye singularly piercing ' (and he adds in a note that 'it had the singularity of never winking '), 'and a countenance which, though coarse and even in some features gross, was yet animated and expressive, and could easily assume the figure of both rage and menace and scorn.' With all his ingenious tropes and far-fetched similes (such as the picture of Napoleon having ' thrones for his watch-towers, and for the palisades of his castle sceptres tipped or stuck with crowns')—for he experimented in various forms of the image—there came some natural burst, like that on the liberty of the Press, when he pictured both Houses as venal and corrupt, Court and Prince bad : ' Give me but an unfettered Press, and I will defy them to encroach a hair's-breadth upon the liberties of England !' But it would take a volume to deal with the subject of this remarkable man's oratory.*

On the other hand, from perpetual exhibition, we find much that is artificial and mechanical in his various methods ; as, in contriving an apparently spontaneous reply to an adversary, if the latter used

---

* This could only be well illustrated by lengthy specimens, comparisons, and commentary on these specimens. But a sufficiently representative account will be given to enable the reader to form his own estimate.

a quotation, he would hurry out to consult the book, and discover something preceding or following the quoted passage which would give it a new turn. If a friend made a sally or used an original metaphor capable of political application, he would take it as his own on the first opportunity. He had also many pleasant thoughts carefully 'cut and dried,' as it is called, ready for application to certain characters. For some of his most telling replies his habit was to retire to a neighbouring coffee-house and write the most lively, stinging passages, which he would fit in here and there among more *level* portions. All this sort of 'workmanship' must have been soon found out, and no doubt impaired the weight and influence of his utterances. Latterly he must have been listened to with much the same feeling as have been certain licensed jesters and entertainers of the House in our own day.

In following him through those varied contests, we are struck by his airy pleasantry ; though he is not to be compared with Burke, who showed a higher sincerity and more classical versatility, and who was 'terribly in earnest' about principle, and utterly uncompromising in the smallest things. Sheridan, on the contrary, we find ready enough to make some light and airy retort, without much regard as to where he picked up the weapons ; and he varied the monotony of the contest by many a pleasant stroke, which must have been amusing to the House.

Another remarkable feature in most of his speeches was that he seemed to speak with effect only when making attacks on special objects of his enmity. One of these was almost invariably Mr. Pitt, to whom he showed the rancour that men of loose life often have against purists whose character and success are a rebuke. Another was Mr. Dundas—until he came to defend himself as roughly as he was attacked—an object of dislike whom Sheridan assailed with a genuine vigour and venom. Windham, too, he did not spare. Indeed, it came at last to this—that some of his most telling efforts were directed against his own former friends, with whom he had completely broken.

It will be entertaining to note, as in the case of Burke, the scenes, the disputes he so often had with Mr. Pitt, and which were continued through a long course of years. These were trifling, and certainly unworthy of both, the time of the House being taken up with their frivolous altercations. Thus, when Pitt had once taunted him with his theatrical pursuits, Sheridan retorted by a very unbecoming form of jest, which was then in the height of popularity—viz., sneering at his well-known regularity and strictness of life. These insinuations were taken from the satires of the 'Rolliad,' of which they were the regular stock-in-trade. As in a debate that arose in May, 1787, Sheridan bitterly inveighed against Pitt, who, he said, was the real culprit, dealing in professions, not acts. Pitt scornfully replied that he believed that he (Sheridan) was sincere in *this* case—*i.e.*, in making a charge against him ; and when it was thought what a field for ingenuity there was in spreading calumnies and reports against him, it was no wonder he seized on *this* matter as an excuse. ' I am glad he admits,' said Sheridan, ' that I generally speak with sincerity.' ' No,' said Mr. Pitt, across the table ; ' not so ; but merely in what you have said to-day against me.' On which Sheridan went off into a rather rambling series of charges as to Pitt's inconsistency, his waste of public money, his bestowing titles and honours corruptly. ' On the whole,' he said, using the favourite sneer, ' Mr. Pitt had always professed *purity*, but had acted with self-attention and neglect of others.'

Again, in March, 1788, Pitt glanced at Sheridan, saying that ' in most of his speeches there was much fancy, in many shining wit, in others very ingenious argument, in all great eloquence, and *in some few truth and justice.*' Sheridan said he rejected such compliments with scorn. He insinuated that Pitt was fond of shiftiness. He was, he said, one of a dark, concealed, and secret band skulking behind the throne.

Next, on Pitt's announcing that he intended to reduce the duties on brandies, Sheridan taunted him with his old boastings ' that he would put down smuggling,' and said that all his measures had failed.

Pitt replied that he wondered which he ought to admire most — his display of confidence or his ignorance. The other retorted that he was now convinced he was right, from Pitt showing himself so very angry. His behaviour was not decent.

All through these squabbles we find Sheridan boldly criticizing Bank Acts, loans, bullion, and topics of the kind. In reference to which Mr. Tierney told Moore that 'Sheridan was generally wrong about financial matters. It was certainly a fine holiday-time for Mr. Pitt when he had no abler critic of his financial schemes than Sheridan. Pitt, however, had a very high idea of him, and thought him,' Tierney added, 'a far greater man than Mr. Fox.' In the same spirit his friend Windham said of him that 'he was ignorant of almost every subject he had to handle, and manfully confessed it.'

In May, 1794, there was another scene, when Sheridan declared that those seditious conspiracies had no existence save 'in the *foul imaginations* of Ministers.' On which Pitt answered scornfully, that this sort of abuse of him had been too often 'repeated to have any novelty with him, or to be entitled to any degree of importance either with him or his friends.' Pitt was called on to make an apology, which he did, 'where alone it is due—to you, sir, and to the House.' On which Sheridan angrily said this apology was disorderly, and a breach in itself of order, as it seemed to except *him.* Still, it was no matter ; for he had received his apology with *the same contempt* with which he had the provocation. As to the 'foul imaginations' of the Ministers, etc., he repeated the words, for the Speaker had not called him to order at the proper time. As to Pitt, he left the House to judge of the manliness of a person who sheltered himself in the shade of his situation, and who dealt in insinuations which, but for his situation, *he durst not make.* On such conduct he would utter no comment, because he knew there were expressions of scorn and disdain which the House would not permit him to use. He would now ask an apology from Pitt for the provocation given inside the House to all, and he was convinced 'no *provocation would be given outside.*' This was certainly blustering.

In January, 1794, there was yet another of these altercations on pensions, 'jobbing,' etc., in which Sheridan put himself forward to assail certain allowances—among others, some to his own friends. He declared, however, it was only the system, not individuals, he was aiming at. Burke indignantly commented on this distinction ' between the jobber and the jobbed ;' and after the matter had been shown to be wholly trivial, Mr. Pitt asked scornfully, ' Would he now persevere in saying that he was only influenced by goodwill to the persons he incriminated ? Or if he did, could he imagine that anyone in the House would credit him ?' Sheridan was eagerly rising, when Fox interfered, and said that, 'in his opinion, founded on experience, Sheridan had as much credit as Mr. Pitt.' Sheridan then said he was glad he had been prevented answering, as he might have said something unpalatable. As to the opinion of the House of his credit, he would not venture to say anything; *but it was only in the House* that Pitt would venture to tell him so.' On which Mr. Stanley protested against these personalities; and Mr. Yorke, with excellent good sense, said it was hard for members, sent up from the country to mind their constituents' business, 'to *have to listen to such nonsense.*' Sheridan, therefore, who, in the common Irish phrase, had ' blazed,' it was clear, was eager to provoke the Minister to combat, as we find from his taunts on two or three occasions.

This hostility, however, was alternated with exercises of an agreeable pleasantry. Thus, when Pitt gravely proposed to levy a tax of a guinea on every horse starting for a race, this recognition of sport was too tempting to be passed by. ' Lord Surrey,' says Wraxall, ' who possessed much racing knowledge, advised him to alter his tax, and to substitute in its place five pounds on the winning horse of any plate of fifty pounds' value. The Minister instantly adopted, with many acknowledgments, the Earl's suggestion. Sheridan, who sat close by Lord Surrey, then rising, after having paid

some compliments to the Chancellor of the Exchequer on his dexterity and *jockeyship*, observed
that whenever Lord Surrey should next visit New-
market, his sporting companions, who would be
sweated by this new tax of his fabrication, instead of
commending his ingenuity, would probably exclaim,

> ' " Jockey of Norfolk, be not so bold !' "

This convulsed the House ; and even Pitt, whose
features did not always relax on hearing Sheridan's
jests, however brilliant or apposite they might be,
joined in the laugh.'

This was a specimen of that spontaneous gaiety
which made him so welcome to the House.   He
was not always so happy.   One of his stock devices
was to make some farcical pleasantry on the names
of statesmen ; as on Mr. Bragge : ' Brag is a good
dog, but Holdfast is a better ;' or when pressed to
' name' some one to whom he was making allusion,
he said he could do it as soon as you could say ' Jack
Robinson.'   Or he would tell of one ' Paterson, who
kept a shop at Manchester, and, having a tilted cart
in use for his business, had the names of " Pitt and
Paterson" painted on the front of it.   This man, who
was known to have no partner in his trade, was asked
what he meant by the name of Pitt on his cart, as
he had no share in the business.   " Ah !" replied he,
" he has indeed no share in the business ; but a very
large share in the profits of it." '   This seems a poor

sort of wit. One who is ever looking out for some superficial allusion of this kind to win a laugh will rarely enjoy respect.

Mr. Moore has laid open for us Sheridan's private laboratory where he compounded his oratory—the images, metaphors, prepared bursts—the accurately marked places where '*Good God, sir!*' was to come in.* These 'fireworks' kept by him for use do not belong to oratory, whose legitimate imagery is inspired by the emotion of the moment, and belongs to the occasion. It is extraordinary the difference of feeling found when comparing his images with those of Burke, so genuine, so apropos, so forcible! ' Burke,' said Sir Gilbert Elliot, 'abounds with these fine passages ; but no man could ever perceive in him the least trace of preparation, and he never

* So with the oft-quoted illustration as to ' resorting to memory for jokes,' which he showed so exquisite an instinct in shaping and refining. ' " He employs his fancy in his narrative, and keeps his recollections for his wit," is an idea expanded into " When he makes his jokes you applaud the accuracy of his memory, and 'tis only when he states his facts that you admire the flights of his imagination." But the thought was too good to be thus wasted on the desert air of a commonplace-book. So forth it came at the expense of Michael Kelly, who, having been a composer of music, became a wine-merchant. " You will," said the *ready* wit, " import your music and compose your wine." Nor was this service exacted from the old idea thought sufficient. In the House of Commons, an easy and apparently off-hand parenthesis was thus filled with it at the expense of Mr. Dundas, " (who generally resorts to his memory for his jokes, and to his imagination for his facts)." '

appears more incontestably inspired by the moment, and transported with the fury of the god within him, than in those finished passages which it would cost even *Shakespeare* long study and labour to produce.'

On a superficial view, it is often customary to class Sheridan with the statesmen of his party : 'Fox, Burke, Sheridan,' etc., are named together, as though he had an equally important influence on the political events of his time. But the truth, as we have before observed, is that Sheridan cannot be counted '*a serious politician.*' It would almost seem that he had few convictions. In all the abundant political memoirs of the time, of which there are scores, we rarely find his name mentioned as being *of account* at any crisis ; though he figures largely in schemes, and in tortuous intrigues, or as the supposed adviser of 'an illustrious personage.' Mr. Croker truly says : 'How many, after all, are the events in the public history of England with which posterity will, in any manner whatever, connect the name of Sheridan ? In fact, the history of England might be written without a single introduction of his name, and in all probability hereafter it will be so written.' Industrious, indeed, he was as a debater, and took part in discussing all manner of subjects ; but having read all these efforts carefully, they seem generally conceived in a laboured petty spirit, merely for the embarrassment of some Minister ; or, that he had 'got up' his facts without having any particular interest in the question.

And in this estimate of Sheridan as a politician, we must not overlook the fact that in these times of strict party spirit we always find him somehow estranged from members of his party, following the guide of his own interest, and fighting for his own hand. The reason seems to be that unhappily he was ever pressed with debts and difficulties, now surmounting them, now overpowered by them; a struggle which is certain to lend a shifting tone to political views. It is difficult indeed for a man thus harassed to take up Spartan or heroic principles. This end, with so impulsive a character, seemed more likely to be gained by devotion to a person of such influence as was the Prince of Wales and Regent, than in barren service to the abstract principles of a party whose coming to power seemed hopeless; nor was it likely that a man pressed and straitened by debt, and notorious for the shifts and devices by which he strove to release himself from embarrassments, would be likely to be over-scrupulous in matters of party.

In reference to the two great questions of Reform and Catholic Emancipation, his biographer thus candidly expounds his hero's principles : ' It may be doubted whether Sheridan was, any more than Mr. Fox, a very sincere friend to the principle of reform ; and the manner in which he masked his *disinclination or indifference* to it was strongly characteristic both of his humour and his tact. Aware that the wild scheme of Cartwright and others, which these resolutions recommended, was wholly impracticable, he always took refuge in it when pressed upon the subject, and would laughingly advise his political friends to do the same: "Whenever anyone," he would say, "proposes to you a specific plan of reform, always answer that you are for nothing short of annual Parliaments and universal suffrage—*there you are safe.*" He also had evident delight, when talking on this question, in referring to a jest of Burke, who said that there had arisen a new party of reformers, still more orthodox than the rest, who thought annual Parliaments far from being sufficiently frequent, and who, founding themselves on the latter words of the statute of Edward III., that "a Parliament shall be holden every year once, and *more often if need be,*" were known by the denomination of the *Oftener-if-need-be's.* " For my part," he would add, in relating this, " I am an Oftener-if-need-be." Even when most serious on the subject (for, to the last, he professed himself a warm friend to reform) his arguments had the air of being ironical and insidious. Such were the arguments by which *he affected* to support his cause, and it is not difficult to detect the eyes of the snake glistening from under them.' Thus the candid Moore : ' It may be concluded that, though far more ready than his friend to inscribe Reform upon the banner of the party, he had even still less made up his mind as to the practicability or expediency of the measure. Looking upon it as a question, the agitation of which was useful to liberty, and at the same time counting upon the improbability of its objects being accomplished, he adopted at once the most speculative of all the plans that had been proposed, and flattered himself that he thus secured the benefit of the general principle, without risking the inconvenience of any of the practical details.'

There was another important question—the Catholic—on which again and again the great Whig patriots had suffered loss of office and exclusion from office, rather than compromise. This obligation should never be forgotten by the Catholic even of this time. But here again we find Sheridan fail. He started with the grandest declarations. As Mr. Croker points out : 'From the commencement of his public life, he professed himself to be the devoted friend of the Catholics ; and it is well known that in one of his very last speeches in Parliament, he used these words : " I will never give my vote to any administration that opposes the question of Catholic Emancipation ; in fine, I think the case of Ireland a *paramount consideration*." But still he joined the anti-Catholic administration of Lord Sidmouth ; or made, to use Mr. Moore's phraseology, " one of those convenient changes of opinion by which statesmen can accommodate themselves to the passing hue of the Treasury-bench, as naturally as the Eastern insect does to the colour of the leaf on which it feeds."' 'It must be owned, indeed, that, though far too sagacious and liberal not to be deeply impressed with the justice of the claims advanced by the Catholics, *he was not altogether disposed to go those generous lengths in their favour, of which Mr. Fox and a few others of their less calculating friends were capable.* It was his avowed opinion, that though the measure, whenever brought forward, should be supported and enforced by the whole weight of the party, they ought never so far to identify or *encumber themselves with it,* as to make its adoption a *sine quâ non.*'

This is not an exaggerated view of Sheridan's politics. It was little wonder that his friends and fellow-politicians fell away from him. All these give their opinion *seriatim* against him. Lord Lansdowne frankly confessed to Moore that his own opinion of Sheridan, which was very low indeed, *had been formed principally from what he had heard Mr. Fox say of him.* Sir J. Mackintosh declared that had he possessed discretion in conduct, he might have ruled his age. Lords Grey and Grenville held also the lowest opinion of him. Burke's, we have seen. Windham, Horner, Pitt, Wilberforce, all join in chorus. Moore himself, above all others, gives him the most insidious strokes, many of which, for their insinuations and reserves, are worthy of Mrs. Candour or Sir Benjamin.*

* Here are some specimens of this damaging kind: '*Without, in the least degree, questioning his sincerity in this change of tone,* it

In these debates we are further struck by some 'notes' which invariably distinguish him from his friends. He seems to come to every question with an air of wishing to find fault; there was a sort of wantonness and recklessness which is confined to him. Hence the contradictions and inconsistencies in his long course. He took up the case of the Scotch Boroughs—a subject which could have no interest for him, and which belonged to Scotch members—at the invitation certainly of the Scotch themselves, and at this laboured in and out of season. But the most indiscreet and unbecoming passage in his history was the line he took in defence of revolutionary doctrines, which, in his petulant ardour to oppose the Ministry, he pushed to lengths that were truly extravagant. It was notorious that sedition was rife in the country, that clubs were in communication with the French; and it is a fact that

may be remarked, that the most watchful observer of the tide of public opinion could not have taken it at the turn more seasonably or skilfully.'

An insinuation of treachery combined with insincerity : 'It was suspected indeed, *I know not with what justice,* that in advising Mr. Fox, as he is said to have done, to withdraw from public life altogether, he was actuated by a wish to succeed him at Westminster, and had already set on foot some private negotiations towards that object.'

'His friend Mr. Rogers has heard him on two different occasions declare he had written every word of "The Stranger," and *as his vanity could not be interested in such a claim,* it is *possible* that there was at least *some* valid foundation for it.'

Mr. Fox, when the Minister was sent to Russia, despatched an emissary of his own to watch all he did.

His reply to Lord Mornington's speech on moving the Address in January, 1794, has been considered one of his finest efforts ; but it was one of his 'set' speeches, when he could put aside his petty methods. In it he reiterated the stock arguments of his Radical friends, that the Revolution was in the main just and noble, and not accountable for the excesses of a few ; and that these were artfully used by Ministers to inflame the passions of the nation.

In his ardour to damage Ministers, he once fell into an amusing blunder, very significant of his mode of attacking. He had solemnly accused them of leaving the whole line of the Americas unprotected. When pressed for his facts, he produced a letter from a correspondent at Falmouth of whom he knew nothing. To this person he had written a grateful letter of thanks, saying he had mentioned it in the House, and found his intelligence 'confirmed in every particular. I shall be happy at all times to be favoured with any intelligence which you think may be *made use of* for the advantage of the country.' There was great merriment, and much contempt expressed, when it was discovered that the letter from Falmouth was a hoax. Sheridan's grateful acknowledgment was handed to a young midshipman of fifteen, who was naturally amazed at such a communication. Sheridan, however, brazened it out, as it is called, declaring that it was his own mistake, that he had addressed the wrong person from haste, etc. He then claimed credit for his warm patriotism ; a line that becomes an Old Bailey lawyer, but is not welcome to the House of Commons.

When voluntary subscriptions were invited for the war, it was urged that this was an unconstitutional measure ; and Sheridan opposed it with very fantastic arguments, one of which was that people might be led to subscribe for the abolition of Parliament ! They might even become so infatuated as to volunteer their personal services and property for the destruc- of their own liberties. It was fairly retorted that this came ill from those who were subscribing to seditious societies, which was so forcibly urged by Windham that Sheridan, as usual, falling back on personality, challenged him to come forth boldly and impeach those he suspected, instead of having re- course to skulking and invidious jeers. This had nearly led to a quarrel. There was to be another instance of his wantonness. When a vote of thanks was proposed to Lord Hood and others who had reduced Corsica, Sheridan vehemently opposed it, invidiously contrasting that admiral with Sir John Jervis and Lord Howe, saying he had done nothing to deserve it. An unguarded allusion to the Westminster election betrayed his reason for this animosity. . As a member said, ' he let the cat out of the bag.' He next proposed thanks to other officers, who it was ludicrously discovered had not taken any part in the business. On this being pointed out, he coolly remarked ' that he was only concerned there were not more mistakes in the business, as being more congenial to the proposition.'

In January, 1795, when plots and conspiracies and informers were rife, Sheridan, in moving the restoration of the Habeas Corpus Act, again condescended to the grossest charges against the Ministers. All these plots were their inventions, for the base purpose of misleading the people and rendering the Opposition hateful. Mr. Windham, now a Minister, replied warmly that 'the speech of Sheridan was a wretched coarse rhapsody, founded on vulgar topics of declamation, fitted only to make an impression upon the rabble.' ' Such calumnies are only to be resisted by the shield of character. I am truly sorry the honourable gentleman is not ashamed of such low traffic.' Other weak arguments he had no scruple to use. As, in the same year, when events were advancing rapidly, this dangerous spirit was rife, and the King had been attacked in the streets, we find him renewing the old excuses. ' These outrages,' he said, ' might probably be traced to some one of the army of spies, who, having been thrown out of employ in consequence of plots being discredited, might be desirous of reviving *the trade of alarm*, and might think, too, that this measure would be grateful to Ministers, by affording them a plausible pretext *to destroy the liberties of the country.* If Ministers should follow up the inquiry with respect to the authors, it might end by the execution of one of their own spies.' We find him also laying down the then new doctrine of *mandat impératif*, that members were only the agents of their constituents.

This spectacle of his former friends, some seated on the Treasury Bench, others opposing him, always seemed to inflame him to the utmost; and on June 21 we find him making an elaborate attack on the deserters, as he held them to be, inveighing against Ministers for giving them offices, and recapitulating their names—Lords Loughborough, Carlisle, Porchester, Hertford, Malmesbury, Yarmouth, Elliot, Douglas, etc.—saying, 'What a compliment to the Minister's own connections and attachments! Could he not find among them any fitted for offices of trust? No. It was from *this* side of the House alone the country could be served, or the favours of the Crown duly repaid! Can it be,' he asked, 'that *this* was the execrable faction of 1784, who were accused by the very man who then was and is Minister, of the most rooted malignity to the Constitution, of endeavouring to enslave the House of Lords, and making a captive of the King? Oh, if this be so, what a lesson it ought to be to those who listen to the venial libels and calumnies of a

Ministerial press! Can it be that people of high rank, and professing high principles—that *they* or *their families* should seek to thrive on the spoils of misery, and fatten on the meals wrested from industrious poverty? Can it be that this should be the case with the very persons who state the *unprecedented peril of the country* as the *sole* cause of their being found in the Ministerial ranks? Oh, shame! shame! is this a time for selfish intrigues, and the little dirty traffic for lucre and emolument? Does it suit the honour of a gentleman to ask at such a moment? Does it become the honesty of a Minister to grant? Is it intended to confirm the pernicious doctrine, so industriously propagated by many, that all public men are impostors, and that every politician has his price? Or even where there is no principle in the bosom, why does not prudence hint to the mercenary and the vain to abstain a while at least, and wait the fitting times? Improvident impatience! Nay, even from those who seem to have no direct object of office or profit, what is the language which their actions speak? The throne is in danger!—" we will support the throne; but let us share the smiles of royalty." The order of nobility is in danger!—" I will fight for nobility," says the viscount; " but my zeal would be much greater if I were made an earl." " Rouse all the marquis within me," exclaims the earl, " and the peerage never turned forth a more undaunted champion in its cause than I shall prove!" "Stain my green riband blue," cries out the illustrious knight, "and the fountain of honour will have a fast and faithful servant!" What are the people to think of our sincerity? What credit are they to give to our professions? Is this system to be persevered in? Is there nothing that whispers to that right honourable gentleman that the crisis is too big, that the times are too gigantic, to be ruled by the little hackneyed and everyday means of ordinary corruption?' This was really a fine burst, and no doubt directed at Burke or Windham, to whom the emoluments of office were an object.

This feeling against Burke, so often alluded to before, seemed to grow into positive hatred, when in April, 1794, a scene of unexampled bitterness and animosity occurred. A complaint had been made that two or three leading persons engrossed all the time, and left no opening for others. Fox deprecated referring to what he had done when in power, adding that he was sure Lord Rockingham would have done nothing but what was proper. Burke intervened, quoting, as to long speeches—

> 'Solid men of Boston, make no long potations,
> Solid men of Boston, make no long orations.
>   Bow! wow! wow!'

'This injunction he said he could the more readily comply with, as he had in fact very little to say on the subject. At the period alluded to, Mr. Fox must know that though he held an office supposed to be very high and advantageous, that of Paymaster-General, yet he was as completely ignorant of what was done in the Cabinet as any man in England.' Sheridan then proceeded to turn these allusions to the account of his animosity. He accused Burke of being ungrateful to the Marquis, and contrasted Fox's generous language with his. 'He supposed that the injunction against "long orations" was not the only moral precept in the system of ethics which served to regulate the practice of the right honourable gentleman. He would take the liberty to remind him of another passage in the same approved writer, in which he says:

'"He went to *Daddy* Jenky, by *Trimmer* Hal attended,
    In such company, good lack! how his morals must be mended.
                 Bow! wow! wow!"'

It is amusing to find that Sheridan had hurried out in the interval to search in this doggerel for some lines that would apply. But the sting of the whole was that Burke was commonly supposed to be disappointed at his not being handsomely remembered in the Marquis's will. Sheridan thus justified what one of his friends said of him, that when offended 'he would search his memory for the most malignant weapons.' He now charged Burke with inconsistency in abusing the place he had formerly held, and whose loss he had bewailed in such piteous terms, with all its 'enjoyments, in-

cluding the music of drums and fifes, which regularly
afforded him a morning's entertainment.' In a
passion Burke ironically thanked 'the philosopher'
for the *moral* lessons, which were enhanced by the
good example offered by the *preacher's own life.*
Without vanity, he hoped that he would rely on his
own character and reputation, which could receive
neither addition nor diminution from any testimony
Sheridan might give. As to his complaining of his
situation, he always openly said he liked office and
its emoluments, and 'condemned the ridiculous
jargon of those who affected the contrary.' Sheridan
replied that as to morality, he, Burke, might spare
some—he had it in such superabundance—to the right
honourable gentlemen seated round him. (Burke
was on the Treasury Bench.) Again Burke retorted that he seldom alluded to past debates, though
Sheridan always 'held out to him the *douceur* of
hearing the whole conduct of his life ripped up and
ransacked.' As to the situation he once held, when
Sheridan was Secretary to the Treasury, it had been
rendered so irksome to him by the *neglect of others,*
that he had nearly thrown it up. He concluded
with a censure of Sheridan for arraigning the morality
of a man of whom he *knew so little.* All which showed
a painful and exasperated state of hostility.

In April a proposal to employ the French *émigrés*
in the English armies was vehemently opposed by
Sheridan, who asked, if they were taken and put to

death, 'would we retaliate on the prisoners in our hands?' A loud 'Yes!' came from Burke. 'Good heavens!' cried Sheridan, 'consider that the lives of many millions depend on that single word "yes."' Burke replied in one of his heated diatribes against revolutionary doctrines, hoping that his monosyllable 'yes' contained no deleterious poison, concluding by saying 'he admired and feared Sheridan's talents.' In a further debate on April 17, Burke again excelled himself, lashing socialism and the professors of humanity, and then returned to his 'yes,' which he vindicated. Sheridan again replied to him with much force and argument.

Burke's extraordinary habit of taking everything *au sérieux* becomes amusing at times, as when on the report of the Select Committee advising the search for secret societies, Sheridan said any Minister who brought in such a measure deserved to lose his head. Burke said that here the broad axe was held towards them—that this menace was actually introducing the guillotine among them.

The connection of the Prince of Wales with the party was fraught with disastrous results, for in their support of him against Pitt and the King they were drawn into sacrificing some of their most cherished principles, and by-and-by the leaders found that the game was all to the advantage of one side only.

There were several questions which proved the

weakness of this alliance, such as that of the Prince's debts, his marriage, and the struggle for giving him the Regency, in all of which sad blunders were made ; for the public noted the inconsistency of declaiming against the sums lavished on the wars, etc., and demanding vast amounts to satisfy the extravagance of a spendthrift. But Sheridan made himself yet more the Prince's instrument, in spite of occasional quarrels or coolnesses, and stood by him, as the phrase runs, 'through thick and thin.'

By the year 1786 the Prince, for the second time, was so steeped in debt that his situation became one of almost painful inconvenience. He knew not where to turn to for money. In his desperation he accepted the offer of a large loan from the Duke of Orleans. When this transaction was discovered his friends were in great alarm, and the Duke of Portland wrote earnestly to Sheridan to interfere, and get rid of this 'odious engagement.' Sheridan seems to have done so with success, as we find the Duke thanking him for his interference. But it was often the fate of this impulsive man, for some sudden whim or feeling of sensitiveness, to sacrifice the labours that had gone before during a course of years. This indiscretion was curiously exhibited on the occasion of the Prince's marriage, when the latter claimed the promised payment for the sacrifice he had made of himself to wedlock. Sheridan was known as the *âme damnée* of the Prince—his

ardent advocate. The Prince, however, had supported the cause adopted by the Whig seceders in
the House of Lords ; and so inflamed with anger was
Sheridan against Burke, Windham, and others, that
he had even reflected on his Royal Highness. He
had fallen out of favour, and ceased to go to Carlton
House.

Nothing could be in worse taste than the exhibition he was now to make. It was found that in
spite of all promises of economy, the Prince's debts
had run up to £600,000. There was nothing to be
done but to devise some plan of payment, and
Ministers proposed a suitable income, subject to
yearly deduction, for paying off the debt. Fox
accepted this reasonable offer as favourable to the
Prince's interests ; but Sheridan opposed vehemently, declaring that the House ought not to be
deluded and deceived in that style. Parliament
would be thus virtually made responsible for those
debts which ought to be paid off at once, and he
added, in offensive language, that 'the Prince ought
not to be seen rolling about the streets in his state-
coach as an insolvent prodigal. But while he urged
a complete and instant release of the Prince from his
embarrassments, he contended that the public ought
not to be burthened with the pressure of a hair to
afford that relief. By coming to that House at all,
the Prince had been ill-advised ; and he sincerely
believed that the King *had not an honest Minister*

about him, or else such an application as this would never have been made to Parliament. If it was meant to keep monarchy respectable in the eyes of this country, and of the world, a different conduct ought to have been pursued. The sum of two or three hundred thousand pounds he reckoned trifling, when compared to the unbecoming situation of an heir-apparent to the Crown, without independence, and, what was worse, without character.' He objected to the debts being deducted from the income to be granted by the House, but announced that he would not vote at all! 'This,' he said, 'seemed to surprise some gentlemen opposite ; but that was natural with those who made up their minds before coming down to the House.' On which inconsequent speech Mr. Pitt commented sarcastically, as well as on Sheridan's not having made up his mind on a question in which he yet felt himself so interested.

Later another debate took place on the same subject, in which Sheridan made a still more singular exhibition. He began by objecting to the sale of the Duchy of Cornwall, 'as the Duke of York had contingent rights. Why not tell the King how he ought to act on this occasion. If there were anything base and incorrigible in the Prince, if he had so acted as to turn his father's heart from him in hatred, then the King would be justifiable——' Here there were loud cries of 'Order!' 'Then I say,' he went on, ' would his Majesty's *Ministers* have been justifiable in advising him not to inter- fere.' ' In an excited and impassioned tone,' adds Woodfall, ' he said that a much-execrated and most detestable band of Jacobins had wished to throw odium on the Prince, and shake the throne. They could not have done anything more mischievous than in preventing the King acting in the matter. " Yes, I give *you* " (pointing to Ministers) "credit for it all. Your interruption has made me lodge it on the proper shoulders." He would allow that the Prince had been prodigal and extravagant; but were his errors so new and extraordinary that they could find no excuse or lenity in the royal breast for one so justly dear to his subjects for his domestic virtues ? This was naturally thought to be ironical, so there were loud cries of " Order !" " I hear," went on the undaunted Sheridan, "gentlemen cheering me, as though I should transfer my praises to his Majesty's Ministers as well as my censure. No, no ; I can, with Lord Chatham, separate the personal character of the man from the vices of his Government, which arise from *wicked and corrupt Ministers.*" So ad- mirably ready was he in retort.' He then went on to say that ' as the House was favourably inclined to hear him, he would give them some curious in- formation about the debts of the Prince, though it might be unpleasant to have to hear it. They knew he had *formerly* been honoured by a considerable degree of the Prince's confidence, the Prince knowing that his regard was perfectly uninterested. The Prince knew he would accept of no favour. He was not indebted to him for a horse or a picture. He would assert there that he stood the most unobliged man by the Prince existing. Indeed, the Prince was indebted to *him*, " in the obligation of a true and faithful service." Whatever circumstances may have altered the Prince's society or political connection, he would say he did not deserve the unkind criticism passed on him.' He then explained the undertaking of 1787. ' It was Lord Thurlow who had advised the Prince to go into complete retirement, to turn the key on Carlton House, and put confidence in his own family, and abstain from all political connection whatever. Then came a great change in public affairs—happily,' he added maliciously, ' described in a printed paper signed, it appears, by Earl Fitzwilliam, most richly illustrative of the Duke of Portland's coalition, whose Ministry is strengthened (if it could admit of such increase) by an increased degradation of character. The Duke is here described as possessing half an office, half duties, whole salary, and no character.' The House must have listened with amusement to this attack, in which he hit out at his own former friends. He went on : ' " What, sir !" whispered Lord Loughborough, " give up your dignity, retire from the world." The heir-apparent ! That would

be too like Philip Egalité. Become a *citizen!*
Oh, there is too much reason to suspect whence
came *that* advice!' He then pointed out that the
King's purse was never so full as at present. So
let the debts be paid out of the useless sinecures.
On which extraordinary burst, Mr. Dundas replied
with some sneers at the singular 'impersonation' they
had received, which was all correct possibly. But
he begged that the personage on the throne should
not be spoken of in that strain. The observations,
he was sure, were not intended for *that place.*

In one of the later discussions, Mr. Fullerton
made a curious, grotesque attack on Sheridan,
saying he was like one of his own characters, the
'd——d good-natured friend.' He had informed
them that he had been the most confidential friend of
the Prince, who had treated him with extraordinary
marks of confidence, yet whose most secret counsels
he had revealed to them all. He lamented that so
much good counsel, with which he, *obliged* or *dis-
obliged*, had obliged the Prince, should have been
gratuitously expended; thus, like Sir Benjamin
Backbite, lodging his bullet in the thorax. He
would recommend statesmen not to hold communication with Sheridan in future, 'except as they would
with a herald at Charing Cross.'

One is inclined to suspect that some of Sheridan's
incoherencies were prompted by wine, in which
he had now begun to indulge to excess. Yet

there was also method in this incoherency, as he seemed to be bidding for a return of the Prince's favour. Here it is that we specially recall Lord Brougham's estimate of him: 'As a statesman he is without a place in any class or any rank : it would be incorrect and flattering to call him a bad, or a hurtful, or a short-sighted, or a middling statesman : *he was no statesman at all.*' For we find him at this moment assailing the Ministers, glancing indignantly at the Prince, and ridiculing the leaders of his own party. Who could depend on such a being ?

When it came to the year 1797, an unexpected phenomenon was to occur. The vehement denouncer of a tyrannous Ministry, this friend and apologist of the French, and patron of everything Radical, was to make a surprising *volte face*—to become a defender and supporter of government, an impassioned denouncer of Bonaparte and the French, and an ostentatiously loyal servant of his Majesty. The immediate occasion of this happy but mysterious change was the breaking out of the celebrated mutiny. He joined, indeed, in vituperating the Ministers, whose behaviour had, of course, led to the mutiny ; but with much vehemence, and much applause, he condemned the mutineers— they were traitors, betrayers of their country at a critical moment—and wound up with a nautical metaphor : 'When people tell them that the navy can be managed without subordination, they may as

well tell them a ship can be managed without a
rudder; they had better, indeed, pull down the
shrouds and the masts, and lay them on the deck,
than listen to such misrepresentation.'

On April 20, 1798, on the question of the Habeas
Corpus Act, Sheridan spoke in the same patriotic
vein, urging all to rally round the throne and muster
for defence, though he opposed the suspending the
Habeas Corpus.   He suggested humorously, among
other ideas, the enrolling for defence 'those sturdy,
hulking fellows we see behind counters, and those
employed in offices; also the young gentlemen of
high rank who are daily mounted on horses of high
blood.   They might be better employed than in
foraging in fruit-shops, in blockading Bond Street,
or in taking the field in Rotten Row.'   Here, no
doubt, he produced a laugh, which he seemed to
take notice of.   'It would ill become me to erect
myself into a rigid censor of amusement and dissipation.   That line of argument would not exactly
suit my own line of conduct; nor am I an enemy to
their amusements.'

Notwithstanding this ostentatious support, as
Wraxall says, 'Mr. Pitt did not receive his advances,
nor accept his magnanimous aid, with the liberality
of mind, or with the testimonies of goodwill and
respect, merited by such a conduct.   Dundas ventured, as I have been assured from good authority,
to reproach his friend, in the freedom of private

conversation at Wimbledon, for such a repulsive treatment of the man who, in a moment of general dismay, proffered his assistance to the Administration. It cannot admit of a doubt, that if Sheridan had brought his abilities into the market, and, like Dundas, had exclaimed, " Wha wants me ?" or if, like Eden, he had quitted his party, made his bargain, and gone over to Pitt, endowed as he was with such various talents, he must have gladly been received into the Ministerial ranks.'

We can well imagine the great and haughty Minister receiving such support with disdain. For Sheridan he scarcely seemed to take the trouble to conceal his contempt. No doubt he put it down to the worst motive of self-interest.

It was in this year (1801) that the first symptom of separation between Sheridan and his friend Fox was shown. Fox, ever true to consistency, still professed his faith in Bonaparte and the French ; while the other, full of his new-born patriotism, warmly supported the peace. He made apologies : ' From any opinion he may express, I never differ but with the greatest reluctance. For him my affection, my esteem, and my attachment are unbounded, and will only end with my life.' But, notwithstanding, here began coldness, and then came separation. Thus, one by one, was Sheridan parting from all his friends. He was now heard declaiming against the French and the Corsican ogre. They were

coming to seize our ships and destroy our commerce.
He offered to support Ministers, and proposed that,
sinking differences, all should join in this national
duty. Mr. Pitt paid him some cold compliments,
but it was plain received these offers with suspicion.
We shall see presently what manifestations of personal loyalty he was to display to the King.

It is difficult to settle accurately what were the
motives for this change. It might have arisen from
the sense of weariness arising from profitless opposition, to which there seemed no end ; or, more probably, it was the example of his late friends, gone over
to the enemy, and enjoying place and office, which
were destined not to come within his reach. There
was much sarcastic remark on this conduct, and
Sheridan felt these sneers so sorely that, as usual,
he felt bound to make an impassioned assertion of
his honour and disinterestedness.

In April, 1798, he thus vindicated his **conduct** :
‘ I am ashamed to say anything concerning myself.
although it should be a very few words. I am sorry,
also, that it is hardly possible for any man to speak
in this House and obtain credit for speaking from a
principle of public duty, that no man can expose
a Minister without being accused of faction, and
none who usually opposed can support a Minister
without being accused of doing so from interested
motives. I am not such a coxcomb as to say that it
is of much importance what part I may take ; nor

am I so vain as to imagine that my services might
be solicited—certainly they have not. That might
have arisen from want of importance in myself, or
from others that I have been in the general habit of
opposing, conceiving that it was not likely that I
should give up my general sentiments or my personal attachments.' He then declared his enmity
to Ministers; that his attachment to Fox was
unaltered and unalterable. ' Let the world think
of me as it pleases ; I am conscious of the integrity
of my principles.' No doubt he sincerely believed
in these solemnly expressed sentiments, which are
worth all his elaborately prepared exhibitions. It
will be seen, when we next take up his political
situation, that he had become a Ministerialist, and
was to be duly recompensed for his adhesion.

CHAPTER XV.

TURNING from these scenes of political struggle, we may now view Sheridan in his domestic aspect—in the society of his accomplished wife, and among his friends. Unfortunately, his growing love of pleasure had impaired his relish for the tranquil pleasures of home; and the amiable heroine of Bath had herself taken an eager part in the frivolities of the society about her, although this remarkable woman showed powers of serious application and of devotion to her duties. She was always, however, frail in health. Nor did Sheridan, as he was drawn into politics and dissipation, show himself worthy of so accomplished and elegant a creature. This is yet one more of the Sheridan legends which must be exploded. He began to neglect her for 'metal more attractive.' In one of the MS. books which came to Mrs. Canning on her death were written some pathetic verses of Mrs. Sheridan's, which reveal her situation:

> ' When first the cruel truth I found,
>   Nor thou thy love of change disowned,
> Fierce madness seized my brain;

> But happier now, a milder grief,
> A softer thought, can give relief ;
> I weep and can complain.'

Mr. Smyth, the tutor of his son, learned from this lady, who lived in the village near his place at Wanstead, that he 'would tease and irritate Mrs. Sheridan until she was ready to dash her head against the wall.' She has seen her burst into tears, and leave the room. Then the scene changed, and the wall seemed as likely to receive his head as hers. This folly was not 'once and away,' but, as Mrs. Canning said, too often repeated. This lady was the bosom friend, as it is called, of Mrs. Sheridan, in whom the poor, much-tried woman found true sympathy and affection. She declared that by repeated treatment of this kind, 'torturing her while he loved her all the while, and by worse and less lawful excesses and desertions, he at last destroyed her patience, and alienated her heart.' She then, out of pique and bitter resentment, began to listen to other admirers, only too ready to compensate for the neglect of her husband. 'I could easily comprehend,' Mr. Smyth goes on, 'all Mrs. Canning told me of the sufferings of Mrs. Sheridan, who was destined this moment to adore the man for his affection and brilliant talents, the next ready to fly from him, overpowered and indignant at his teasing unreasonableness and nervous, unintelligible folly.' Here is the self-tormenting Faulkland of his own play.

24—2

'To say,' says Moore, in a characteristic apology
for his hero, 'that, with all her beauty and talents,
she was not happy, nor escaped the censure of the
world, is but to assign to her that share of shadow,
without which nothing bright ever existed on this
earth.   Not that she was at any time unwatched by
Sheridan ; on the contrary, he followed her with a
lover's eyes throughout ; and it was believed of
both, by those who knew them best, that, even
when they seemed most attracted by other objects,
they would willingly, had they consulted the real
wishes of their hearts, have given up everyone in
the world for each other.   They had, immediately
after their marriage, as we have seen, passed some
time in a little cottage at East Burnham, and it was
a period, of course, long remembered by them both
for its happiness.   I have been told by a friend of
Sheridan, that he once overheard him exclaiming to
himself, after looking for some moments at his wife,
with a pang, no doubt, of self-reproach, "Could anything bring back those melancholy first feelings ?"
then adding, with a sigh, " Yes ; perhaps the cottage
at East Burnham might."'

Not many months before Mrs. Sheridan's death,
an incident occurred which was the foundation of a
later odd adventure. About the end of the year 1791
the well-known Madame de Genlis had come to town,
attended by her pupil, the Duke of Orleans' daughter,
and also by another young lady, whom Mr. Moore

M⁹ SHERIDAN.

decorously styles 'her adopted daughter,' the well-
known 'Pamela.' At the time of her visit there was
also in London the ill-fated Lord Edward Fitzgerald,
then intimate with the Sheridans, and with regard to
whom Mr. Moore makes this strange insinuation :
'Lord Edward was *the only one* among *the numerous
suitors* of Mrs. Sheridan to whom she was supposed
*to have listened with anything like a return of feel-
ing;* and that there should be mutual admiration
between *two such noble specimens of human nature* it
is easy, without injury to either of them, to believe.'
This is in the best style of the 'College' in
Sheridan's own comedy. In another passage he
seems to define this 'return of feeling,' if not to
excuse it. 'Mrs. Sheridan was united,' he says,
'not only by marriage, but by love, to a man who
was the object of universal admiration, and whose
vanity and passions too often *led him to yield to the
temptations by which he was surrounded.** It was
but natural that, in the consciousness of her own

---

* Mr. Ward of Drury Lane, who married one of the Linley
sisters, told Moore that 'once when Sheridan was routed from one
house to another, and his things, I believe, sold, a collection of
gages d'amour, locks of hair, etc., which vanity induced him to keep,
were sent for custody to a trusty person, and left there till, this
person dying, they came into the hands of a fellow who resolved
to extort money from Sheridan and the women concerned, on the
strength of them. Sheridan consulted Ward, and the plan they
adopted was to employ a Bow Street officer, make a forcible and
sudden entry with pistols into the man's house, and then, having
gained the treasure, defy him to bring his action.'

power to charm, she should be now and then piqued
into an appearance of retaliation, and seem to listen
with complacence to some of those numerous wor-
shippers who crowd around *such beautiful and
unguarded shrines.*'   There is much awkwardness
of statement in this, and it is impossible to read her
last letters, so full of practical devotion, without
seeing that there was little beyond a love of admiration and a wish, perhaps, to pique her husband's
regard.   ' On one occasion, when Lord Edward was
paying her a visit, Sheridan came in and described a
beautiful French girl he had lately seen, and added
that she put him strongly in mind of what his own wife
had been in the first bloom of her youth and beauty.
On his leaving the room, Mrs. Sheridan turned to
Lord Edward, and said with a melancholy smile, " I
should like you, when I am dead, to marry that girl."'

Her little descriptive touches about her erratic
husband's character are always in a pleasant vein of
comedy : as when she says of a letter that came to
' Dick' from her sister-in-law in one of Charles's
franks, ' Dick undertakes to write himself with it, but
I think it safest not to trust him.'   And again of an
address which Dick had got, but which was of no
use ; ' for anything in his hands is *irrecoverable.*'
Nothing was more true : letters, books, articles
lent, bank-notes lying *perdu*, and used to stop the
shaking of windows with—all were *irrecoverable.*

The election which took place in 1790 (and these

repeated contests were of course a fruitful source of his embarrassments) was to show in a singular way the useful devotion of his charming wife. Her affectionate sympathy for him to the last withstood all shocks. Some letters of hers, written during the contest, suggest the most engaging idea of her character—womanly, vivacious, spirited, affectionately zealous, capable, with a delightful inconsequent mixture of dissipation and business — a mingled yarn of character more interesting than more sober, regulated, and orderly natures. Sheridan had gone down to Stafford, and his prospects seemed scarcely promising. But his devoted wife was working hard for him in her own way, collecting encouraging news from influential friends, having also to soothe his unquiet and jealous temper :

'I received your note from Birmingham this morning, and am happy to find that you and my dear cub were well, so far on your journey. I sent you Cartwright yesterday, and to-day I pack you off Perry with the soldiers. I was obliged to give them four guineas for their expenses. I send you likewise, by Perry, the note from Mrs. Crewe, to enable you to speak of your qualification if you should be called upon. So I think I have executed all your commissions, sir ; and if you want any of these doubtful votes which I mentioned to you, you will have time enough to send for them, for I would not let them go till I hear they can be of any use.

'And now for my journal, sir, which I suppose you expect. Saturday, I was at home all day busy for you—kept Mrs. Reid to dinner—went to the opera—afterwards to Mrs. St. John's, *where I lost my money sadly, sir*—eat strawberries and cream for supper—sat between Lord Salisbury and Mr. Meynell (hope you approve of that, sir)—overheard Lord Salisbury advise Miss Boyle by no means to subscribe to Taylor's Opera, as O'Reilly's would certainly have the patent—confess I did not come home till past two. Sunday, called on Lady Julia—father and Mr. Reid to dinner—in the evening at Lady Hampden's—*lost my money again, sir*, and came home by one o'clock. 'Tis now near one o'clock—my father is established in my boudoir, and, when I have finished this, I am going with him to hear Abbé Vogler play on the Stafford organ. I have promised to dine with Mrs. Crewe, who is to have a female party only—no objection to that, I suppose, sir? Whatever the party do, I shall do of course. Adam is sick in bed, and there is nobody to do any good left in town.' She then adds :

' I am more than ever convinced we must look to other resources for wealth and independence, and consider politics merely as an amusement—and in that light 'tis best to be in Opposition, which I am afraid we are likely to be for some years again.' In which remark was excellent sense.

It is extraordinary how popular Mrs. Sheridan

seems to have been. We find her now on a visit at Hampton Court—now at a house, Deepdene, lent them by the Duke of Norfolk—now at General Burgoyne's in Bruton Street, where they were to stay 'till their house was ready.' His own relations were eager to have them over in Dublin. It was curious that Sheridan should never have set foot in his native country during the whole of his life since the day he quitted it, a little lad of eight years old. His wife makes a pretty graceful excuse for not paying the visit : ' I don't believe what you say of Charles's not being glad to have seen me in Dublin. You are very flattering in the reasons you give, but I rather think his vanity would have been more gratified by showing everybody how much prettier and younger his wife was than the Mrs. Sheridan in whose favour they have been prejudiced by your good-natured partiality. But my guardian sylph, vainer of my beauty perhaps than myself, would not suffer me to destroy the flattering illusion *you* have so often displayed to your Irish friends. No; I shall stay till I am past all pretensions, and then you may excuse your want of taste by saying, " Oh, if you had seen her when she was young !" ' This is worthy of Steele.

In 1787 Sir Gilbert Elliot used often to meet Mrs. Sheridan at supper at Mrs. Crewe's, and ' heard the sisters sing together like angels. Nothing can be more enchanting !' Mrs. Sheridan he still oftener met there at suppers *en partie fine.* At these latter meetings would be found Elliot, Mrs. Davenport, the hostess, and Windham, who thought her very entertaining, and in a plainer, more intelligible way than Mrs. Crewe, whom he found 'refined, and double refined.' Sheridan was rarely found in company with his attractive wife.

With all his defects, Sheridan had a singularly feeling and affectionate disposition, though his emotions were mere transient, passionate impulses, little supported by acts. His son's tutor, Mr. Smyth, who observed him closely, has shown that these displays were purely emotional. All emotion, unsupported by practical effort, tends to harden the heart, and to extinguish real benevolence; the self-indulgent lover of pleasure lays this unction to his soul, and the display of feeling finally takes the place of all active exertion and charity.

Sheridan appears to have shown filial piety and devotion to his father. When the latter began to fail we find Mrs. Sheridan concealing the news from her husband; ' I would not show your letter,' she writes to her sister-in-law, ' to Sheridan; he has lately been much harassed by business, and I could not bear to give him the pain I know your letter would have occasioned. Partial as your father always has been to Charles, I am confident he never has, nor ever will feel half the duty and affection that Dick has always expressed. I know how deeply he will be afflicted, if you confirm the melancholy account of his declining health ; but I trust your next will remove my apprehensions, and make it unnecessary for me to wound his affectionate heart.'

The worthy old actor was, however, on the eve of closing his weary career. Unfortunately the last of his series of industrious plans for the improvement of education were to bring him the usual disappointments. Mr. Orde, the Lord Lieutenant's secretary, was disposed to aid him ; and the idea was to suppress some of the free or royal schools, and use the funds thus obtained in founding a Lyceum at New Geneva, near Waterford. The old actor's spirits began to rise ; but unfortunately the sudden death of his chief patron, owing to a fall when out hunting, and the removal of Mr. Orde, shipwrecked the whole. This blow, 'combined with other vexations,' completely prostrated him, and his health quite gave way. ·He was ordered a voyage to Lisbon, and after being reconciled in London with his old friend Sam Whyte, set off for Margate, where he was to embark.

It is sad to find that this touchy or quarrelsome old elocutionist was now once more estranged from his son. His daughter-in-law declared that for the sake of his daughter Elizabeth, 'I assure you I would be very glad to have Dick and his father on good terms, without entering into any arguments on the subject; but I fear where one of the parties at least has a *tincture* of what they call in Latin *damnatum obstinatum mulio*, "a damned obstinate mule," the attempt will be difficult, and the success uncertain.' It was, in truth, difficult for them to be reconciled. We fancy from the self-justifying phrase, 'I assure you, I would be very glad,' that Mrs. Sheridan was supposed to be in the way, and may not have been acceptable to her father-in-law. His son saw him in London, and wished to take him down to Deepdene, a house in Surrey, which the Duke of Norfolk had lent to Sheridan. At Margate he was seized with his last illness, and died on August 14, 1788. His son posted down, travelling all night, and was with him for two days until he died. He removed his sister, Mrs. H. Le Fanu, to Deepdene, and then set off again for Margate, accompanied by his friends Richardson and Tickell, travelling night and day, for the funeral. The local practitioner, Mr. Jarvis, was particularly struck with the son's affectionate attentions. 'I was with Mr. Sheridan,' he says, 'when the son arrived, and witnessed an interview in which the father showed himself to be strongly impressed by his son's attention. At his request I remained at the father's bedside till relieved by the son, about three o'clock in the morning; he then insisted on taking my place. From this time he never quitted the house till his father's death.'

There is in Margate Church a memorial to the

old actor, with a suitable inscription. It is characteristic that this tribute should not have been set up by the sorrowing son. It was left to the worthy local practitioner, who, after waiting nearly twenty years to hear from him, erected it himself!

From the various announcements in the fashionable newspapers of the day, we get a good idea of the eager pursuit of pleasure and dissipation by Sheridan and his wife. They seemed to live in a round of *fêtes*, parties, and visits at country houses. Thus in July, 1791, we hear of a very elegant *fête champêtre* at Isleworth to 600 persons, 'the whole executed in superior style.' More celebrated was his *fête* to the Prince of Wales, where all the delicacies of the season were provided, 'under the skilful management of Mr. Gunter'—a name even then of reputation. Eighteen hundred persons were entertained on this occasion, and Kelly, the singer, with two Italians, sang a glee, composed for the occasion —the ridiculous words whereof ran :

'E viva, e viva,
Il principe *adorato !*'

There was also a cantata on French horns, and the Scotch pipers ; while at the head of the room was 'a beautiful picture of Mrs. Sheridan and her infant.' At his villa, in the following year, he gave a grand harvest-home, where 300 persons were entertained in a tent, while a select party were banqueted at the house, the whole being enlivened by the good-

humoured sallies of his son.   These festivities, no
doubt, shortened the term of Mrs. Sheridan's life, a
fate which seemed to be foreshadowed in the serious
tone of her letters, reflecting her grief for the loss of
many who were so dear to her.   ' My letter,' she
writes, ' was a dismal one ; perhaps you lost nothing
by not receiving it, for it was not much calculated to
amuse you.'   Her husband had been seized with a
fever in London.   ' You may suppose I was kept in
ignorance of his situation, or I should not have remained so quietly here.'   He came down, suffered a
relapse, but was restored by 'a jewel of a doctor.'
And she herself became ill also.

We have before seen what misfortunes seemed to
overwhelm this interesting and amiable family.   Her
sister Maria had died at Bath, in 1784, and Mrs.
Sheridan bewailed her loss in some touching lines :

VERSES TO THE MEMORY OF MY BELOVED SISTER,
MARIA LINLEY.

Twice* hath the sorrowing Muse her tribute paid,
And the sad call of mourning Love obey'd ;
Again in cypress wreaths she veils her lyre,
And milder grief her plaintive strains inspire.
    *   *   *   *   *   *

The fair ! the young Maria ! she whose song
Charm'd with mute rapture the admiring throng,
Whose smiling loveliness all hearts subdu'd,
Whose gentle accents fond attention woo'd.
    *   *   *   *   *   *

---

* ' Alluding to the untimely deaths of my dear brothers, Thomas
and Samuel.'

Such charms on sweet Maria were bestow'd,
There innocence and health, united, glow'd ;
So shone the soften'd lustre of her eyes,
Such were the dazzling beams of glad surprise.
Ye, too, whose gentler souls confess the power
Of heavenly harmony, HER loss deplore,
Whose notes enchanting struck with magic art
On all the soft vibrations of the heart.

    *   *   *   *   *

While thus my tears with these sad numbers flow,
Still fondly cherishing my pleasing woe ;
While thus my lov'd Maria's form I trace,
Her animated look, her native grace,
I soothe the grief I wish not to subdue,
And all her sweet perfections still renew.*

Her husband, as we have seen, soon married again. He, too, died early, on November 4, 1793. This event was attended by an unfortunate catastrophe. 'He had apartments in Hampton Court Palace, and it had frequently been his delight to sit and read on a parapet-wall, or kind of platform,

---

* One of her daughters, Miss E. Tickell, appears to have been very intimate with various members of the Royal Family, and to have enjoyed the friendship of Canning, Lawrence, and other distinguished persons. Messrs. Robson and Kerslake were lately in possession of a curious album, belonging to Mr. E. L. Burke Sheridan, to whom it descended from Miss Tickell. It contained a chalk drawing by Lawrence of Miss Tickell, a water-colour drawing of Mrs. Sheridan by Westall, and many spirited sea-pieces, the work of Richard Brinsley Tickell, R.N., who was killed at the battle of Trafalgar. More interesting still was a pencil-sketch by Gainsborough of Richard Brinsley, differing much from the familiar conventional portraits, representing him as fat and bloated. It may be added that his father, Dr. Linley, died November 19, 1795.

before his window, in one of the upper apartments
of the palace ; he much delighted in the situation,
which was constantly filled with flower-pots. About
twelve at noon, while his carriage was waiting to
convey himself and his family to town for the winter,
Mrs. T. left the room for a moment, and on her
return, not finding him there, she ran into an adjoin-
ing chamber which commanded a view of the garden
beneath, where she beheld her husband lying on the
ground ; but before she reached the fatal spot he
had expired. By what unhappy cause, or by what
means he fell, never can be known to a certainty.
Mrs. Tickell was in a state of distraction.'

The death of her beloved sister, Mrs. Tickell, was
a further shock to her sensitive, affectionate nature.
This interesting woman died in July, 1787, at
Bristol, and was buried in Wells. Overcome with
grief, herself ill, and struggling with difficulties,
Mrs. Sheridan at once took on herself the charge of
the three bereaved children. In some touching
letters, she explains her plans :

' By constant attention and strict regimen I am
once more got about again ; but I never go out of
my house after the sun is down, and on those terms
only can I enjoy tolerable health. I never knew
Dick better. My dear boy is now with me for his
holidays, and a charming creature he is, I assure
you, in every respect. My sweet little charge, too,
promises to reward me for all my care and anxiety.

The little ones come to me every day, though they do not at present live with me. We think of taking a house in the country this summer, as necessary for my health and convenient to S., who must be often in town. I shall then have *all* the children with me, as they now constitute a very great part of my happiness. The scenes of sorrow and sickness I have lately gone through have depressed my spirits, and made me incapable of finding pleasure in the amusements *which used to occupy me perhaps too much.*

'My greatest delight is in the reflection that I am acting according to the wishes of my ever dear and lamented sister, and that by fulfilling the sacred trust bequeathed me in her last moments, I ensure my own felicity in the grateful affection of the sweet creatures, whom, though I love for their own sakes, I idolize when I consider them as the dearest part of her who was the first and nearest friend of my heart!'

Some years later Sheridan's sister was staying with her. She supplies a charming sketch of the affectionate care Mrs. Sheridan bestowed on her adopted orphans :

' Dick is still in town, and we do not expect him for some time. Mrs. Sheridan seems now quite reconciled to these little absences, which she knows are unavoidable. I never saw anyone so constant in employing every moment of her time, and to that I attribute, in a great measure, the recovery of her health and spirits. The education of her niece, her music, books, and work, occupy every minute of the day. After dinner, the children, who call her " Mamma-aunt," spend some time with us, and her manner to them is truly delightful. The girl, you know, is the eldest. The eldest boy is about five years old, very like his father, but extremely gentle in his manners. The youngest is past three. The whole set then retire to the music-room. As yet I cannot enjoy their parties ; a song from Mrs. Sheridan affected me last night in a most painful manner. Mrs. S. blamed herself for putting me to the trial, and, after tea, got a book, which she read to us till supper. This, I find, is the general way of passing the evening.'

Among her other gifts this engaging woman had a taste for composition, and wrote verses full of feeling and grace. Those on her sister's death, and the lines on her brother's violin, are full of natural grace and poetic feeling.* Once, indeed, she wrote

---

* That this attractive being was a genuine poetess is plain from the graceful verses which, on the death of her beloved and gifted brother, Thomas, she addressed to his violin :

'Sweet instrument of him for whom I mourn,
  Tuneful companion of my Lycid's hours,
How liest thou now neglected and forlorn !
  What skilful hand shall now call forth thy powers?

a little entertainment for the stage, which she called
'The Haunted Village,' and gave to her husband to
add some touches. She never could get it from
him again! It might have been, as she said on
another occasion, that 'anything given to Dick is
irrevocable ;' but her own brother was inclined to
think that 'he suppressed it from jealousy.'*

She had caught a cold just at this time, which
clung to her for some months, and brought on all
those dreadful complaints with which she was
afflicted at Mrs. Crewe's ; and it required months of
care to restore her. No doubt, like many frail,
delicate persons, her wish for amusement was
proportioned to its unsuitability to her constitution ; indeed, it is often the consequence of that
insidious malady, consumption, with which she
was now menaced. In 1792 she was approaching her confinement, and it was hoped that

> 'Ah ! none like his can reach those liquid notes,
>   So soft, so sweet, so eloquently clear ;
> To live beyond the touch, and gently float
>   In dying modulations on the ear !
>
> 'Thus o'er my Lycid's lyre as I complain'd,
>   And kiss'd the strings where he was won't to play,
> While yet in pensive sadness I remain'd,
>   Methought it sigh'd, and sighing seemed to say :
>
> '"Ah me ! forlorn, forsaken, now no more
>   Shall fame and just applause around me wait ;
> No power my gentle master can restore,
>   And I, alas ! will share his hapless fate."'

* Moore's 'Diary.'

after this event her health would amend. She only grew worse, and was removed to Bristol to try the effect of the waters there. This was in the June of the year. But her case was pronounced hopeless by the physician, Dr. Bain,* then a young man, who was afterwards to attend Sheridan on his own death-bed. Some letters from Miss Le Fanu, who was with her at this time, to her mother in Dublin, recount the incidents of this melancholy crisis in a very natural and touching way :

' Our dear departed friend kept her bed only two days, and seemed to suffer less during that interval than for some time before. She was perfectly in her senses to the last moment, and talked with the greatest composure of her approaching dissolution ; assuring us all that she had the most perfect confidence in the mercies of an all-powerful and merciful Being, from whom alone she could have derived the inward comfort and support she felt at that awful moment ! She said she had no fear of death, and that all her concern arose from the thoughts of leaving so many dear and tender ties, and of what they would suffer from her loss. Her own family were at Bath, and had spent one day with her, when she was tolerably well. Your poor brother now thought it proper to

---

* This Dr. Bain, who showed such kindness to Sheridan and his family, was a practitioner at Bristol, and later came to London to practise. The sum which Sheridan presented to him for his attendance on Mrs. Sheridan was the handsome one of £100.

send for them, and to flatter them no longer. They immediately came: it was the morning before she died. They were introduced one at a time at her bedside, and were prepared as much as possible for this sad scene. The women bore it very well, but all our feelings were awakened for her poor father. The interview between him and the dear angel was affecting and heart-breaking to the greatest degree imaginable. I was afraid she would have sunk under the cruel agitation : she said it was indeed too much for her. She gave some kind injunction to each of them, and said everything she could to comfort them under this severe trial. They then parted, in the hope of seeing her again in the evening, but they never saw her more ! Mr. Sheridan and I sat up all that night with her; indeed he had done so for several nights before, and never left her one moment that could be avoided. About four o'clock in the morning we perceived an alarming change, and sent for her physician. She said to him, " If you can relieve me, do it quickly; if not, do not let me struggle, but give me some laudanum." His answer was, " Then I will give you some laudanum." She desired to see Tom and Betty Tickell before taking it, of whom she took a most affecting leave. Your brother behaved most wonderfully, though his heart was breaking ; and at times his feelings were so violent, that I feared he would have been quite ungovernable at the last. Yet he summoned up

courage to kneel by the bedside, till he felt the last
pulse of expiring excellence, and then withdrew. She
died at five o'clock in the morning, 28th of June.

' I fancy it will not be disagreeable to you to hear
all the particulars of an event so interesting, so
afflicting, to all who knew the beloved creature !
For my part, I never beheld such a scene—never
suffered such a conflict—much as I have suffered
on my own account. While I live, the remembrance
of it and the dear lost object can never be effaced
from my mind.

' We remained ten days after the event took place
at Bristol ; and on the 7th instant Mr. Sheridan
and Tom, accompanied by all her family (except
Mrs. Linley), Mr. and Mrs. Leigh, Betty Tickell
and myself, attended the dear remains to Wells,
where we saw her laid beside her beloved sister in
the cathedral. The choir attended ; and there was
such a concourse of people of all sorts assembled on
the occasion that we could hardly move along. Mr.
Leigh read the service in a most affecting manner.
Indeed the whole scene, as you may easily imagine,
was awful and affecting to a very great degree.

' The day after the sad scene was closed we
separated, your brother choosing to be left by himself with Tom for a day or two. He afterwards
joined us at Bath.

' Your brother talks of having his house here
immediately furnished and made ready for the

reception of his nursery. I understand he has taken
a house in Jermyn Street, where he may see company ; but he does not intend having any other
country-house but this. Isleworth he gives up, his
time being expired there. I believe he has got a
private tutor for Tom—somebody very much to his
mind. At one time he talked of sending him abroad
with this gentleman, but I know not at present what
his determinations are. He is too fond of Tom's
society to let him go from him for any time ; but I
think it would be more to his advantage if he would
consent to part with him for two or three years. It
is impossible for any man to be more devotedly
attached to his children than he is, and I hope they
will be a comfort and a blessing to him when the
world loses its charms. The last time I saw him,
which was for about five minutes, I thought he
looked remarkably well, and seemed tolerably cheerful ; but I have observed, in general, that this affliction has made a wonderful alteration in the expression
of his countenance and in his manners.* The Leighs
and my family spent a week with him at Isleworth
the beginning of August, where we were indeed
most affectionately and hospitably entertained. I
could hardly believe him to be the same man. In

---

* ' I have heard,' says Mr. Moore, 'a noble friend of Sheridan
say that, happening about this time to sleep in the room next to
his, he could plainly hear him sobbing throughout the greater part
of the night.'

fact, we never saw him do the honours of his house before ; *that*, you know, he always left to the dear, elegant creature, who never failed to please and charm everyone who came within the sphere of her notice. Nobody could have filled her place so well ; —he seemed to have pleasure in making much of those whom she loved, and who, he knew, sincerely loved her. We all thought he never appeared to such advantage. He was attentive to everybody and everything, though grave and thoughtful ; and his feelings, poor fellow, often ready to break forth in spite of his efforts to suppress them. He spent his evenings mostly by himself. He desired me, when I wrote, to let you know that she had by will made a little distribution of what she called "her own property," evidently precluding all her *fine friends* from this last mark of her esteem and approbation. She had, poor thing, with some justice, turned from them all in disgust, and, I observed, during her illness never mentioned any of them with regard or kindness.'*

This account is not over-coloured. Sheridan's son's tutor tells us 'he showed genuine grief and compunction. "Oh, not a word of that kind !" he would cry, when some one excused him. "She is an angel if ever there was one ! It is all my fault. It was I —I that was *the guilty fiend !*" Then he would sink

* These and the previous letters are taken from Mrs. Le Fanu's 'Life of Mrs. T. Sheridan.'

into a chair in a paroxysm. He was tender and unremitting; he carried her in his arms, and read the
Scriptures to her. No doubt his grief for his elegant
and interesting wife was sincere and poignant; but
this, in one of his mercurial temperament, and one
who required distraction and constant amusement,
was not likely to be very lasting.' 'I never beheld,'
says his friend Kelly, 'more poignant grief than
Mr. Sheridan felt for the loss of his beloved wife;
and although the world, which knew him only as a
public man, will perhaps scarcely credit the fact, I
have seen him, night after night, sit and cry like a
child, while I sang to him, at his desire, a pathetic
little song of my composition, "They bore her to
her grassy grave."'

'When the tutor he had secured for his son first
went down to Wanstead, he noticed a beautiful and
refined-looking child, to whom Sheridan always
brought a ribbon or toy of some kind. A nurse had
been hired for it "at an extraordinary salary." This
was Mrs. Sheridan's infant, born a little before her
death. But it was plainly waning. One night they
had a sort of ball at Wanstead, the tutor about to
lead off, when of a sudden Mrs. Canning rushed in.
"Oh, the child—the child is dying!" It was in con-
vulsions. A well-known doctor was brought down
in an incredibly short time, but it died.* Sheridan's

* 'Oct. 23rd, 1793.—Mr. Sheridan's infant daughter, of convulsive fits in cutting her teeth, eighteen months old.'

moans on this calamity were terrible to hear. His friend Richardson came down and succeeded in drawing him away to town to business, or rather *des affaires*, where his mercurial temper made him presently forget what had occurred.'

The charming creature whom he had carried off from Bath, fought for, with whom he had lived fifteen years, and over whose death-bed he had exhibited his passionate grief, was soon to be forgotten. Within a very few months, or indeed weeks, we find him forgetting his sorrows in the company of Madame de Genlis and her fascinating charge.* His attentions and devotion became, indeed, so marked as to attract public notice. 'Mr. Rogers had seen Sheridan in company with Pamela. She was lovely—quite radiant with beauty; and Sheridan either was, or pretended to be, violently in love with her. On one occasion he kept labouring the whole evening at a copy of verses in French, which he intended to present to her, every now and then writing down a word or two on a slip of paper with a pencil. However, he understood French very imperfectly.'

This rumour is confirmed by Mr. Swinburne · 'They say Sheridan is in love with and wants to marry Pamela; and whether *his red face* will charm her is, I think, doubtful.' Sir R. Heron also notes the rumour of the marriage.

* See an agreeable paper by my friend the Ulster King at Arms, in his 'Vicissitudes of Families.'

When the French lady and her charge were at last obliged to set out on their return to France, the following singular adventure occurred to them.

'We left London,' she says, 'on our return to France, the 20th of October, 1792, and a circumstance occurred to us so extraordinary that I ought not, I feel, to pass it over in silence. When we were about a quarter of a league from London, the French servant, who had never made the journey from Dover to London but once before, thought he perceived that we were not in the right road; and on his making the remark to me, I perceived it also. The postilions, on being questioned, said that they had only wished to avoid a small hill, and that they would soon return into the high-road again. After an interval of three-quarters of an hour, seeing that we still continued our way through a country that was entirely new to me . . . it appeared to us very strange that people should lose their way between London and Dover. At last, after nearly an hour had elapsed, seeing that we still were not arrived at the end of the stage, our uneasiness increased to a degree which amounted even to terror. It was with much difficulty that I made the postboys stop : in spite of my shouts they still went on, till at last the French servant compelled them to stop. Concealing my suspicions, I took a guide in the village, and declared that it was my wish to return to London, as I found I was now at a less distance from that city than from Dartford. The postboys made much resistance to my desire, and even behaved with an extreme degree of insolence ; but our French servant, backed by the guide, compelled them to obey.

'As we returned at a very slow pace, owing to the sulkiness of the postboys and the fatigue of the horses, we did not reach London before nightfall, when I immediately drove to Mr. Sheridan's house. He was extremely surprised to see me returned, and on my relating to him our adventure, agreed with us that it could not have been the result of mere chance. He then sent for a Justice of the Peace to examine the postboys, who were detained till his arrival under the pretence of calculating their account ; but in the meantime the hired footman disappeared, and never returned. The postboys being examined by the Justice according to the legal form, and in the presence of witnesses, gave their answers in a very confused way, but confessed that an unknown gentleman had come in the morning to their master's, and, carrying them from thence to a public-house, had, by giving them something to drink, persuaded them to take the road by which we had gone. The examination was continued for a long time, but no further confession could be drawn from them. Mr. Sheridan told me that there was sufficient proof on which to ground an action against these men, but that it would be a tedious process, and cost a great deal of money. The post-boys were therefore dismissed, and we did not pursue the inquiry any further. As Mr. Sheridan saw the terror I was in at the very idea of again venturing on the road to Dover, he promised to accompany us thither himself; but added that, having some indispensable business on his hands, he could not go for some days. He took us then to Isleworth, a country-house which he had near Richmond, on the banks of the Thames; and as he was not able to despatch his business so quickly as he expected, we remained a month in that hospitable retreat.'

This story, which is utterly un-English in all its details, as well as inconsistent, is surely the product of a disordered imagination built up on some trifling facts — the postilions probably mistaking the unintelligible directions of an alarmed, excitable Frenchwoman. The misconceptions and misinterpretations put by our French guests on all that they see in this country are notorious. Mr. Moore, however, traces in her adventure an elaborate practical joke of Sheridan's. But it was not four months since his wife had died, and it was unlikely that even the most heartless would be in the vein for practical joking. 'His motive,' adds Moore, 'was an excuse for detaining so agreeable a party, whose society he enjoyed.' A solution that is unmeaning; for if Sheridan had desired her company, Madame de

Genlis must have been as willing to reside at his house then as she was afterwards; when we have seen that she stayed with him a month.

The sequel was agreeable. 'Mr. Sheridan having finished his business, we set off together for Dover—himself, his son, and an English friend of his, Mr. Reid. It was now near the end of November, 1792. The wind being adverse detained us for five days at Dover, during all which time Mr. Sheridan remained with us. I resolved, however, to venture, and Mr. Sheridan attended us into the very packet-boat, where I received his farewell with a feeling of sadness which I cannot express. He would have crossed with us, but that some indispensable duty at that moment required his presence in England. He, however, left us Mr. Reid, who had the goodness to accompany us to Paris.'

In her later memoirs an interesting recollection occurred to her which she had omitted. 'Two days before we set out, Mr. Sheridan made in my presence his declaration of love to Pamela, who was affected by his agreeable manner and high character, and accepted the offer of his hand with pleasure. In consequence of this, it was settled that he was to marry her on our return from France, which was expected to take place in a fortnight.'

All which is extraordinary; for it came out that Pamela was married within a very few weeks to Lord Edward Fitzgerald—viz., on December 27th,

1792. It may have been that Madame de Genlis mixed up or confounded the two admirers.

The best and most intimate view of this extraordinary character at this period—presented, too, with a partiality which yet cannot struggle against a sense of equity—is that of the late Professor Smyth, afterwards Professor of Poetry at Oxford—a man of congenial temper, who saw much of him in their latter days. The Professor became tutor to his son Tom, which gave him many opportunities of seeing the father in all his varying moods, which he presents to us in a natural, easy way.* Here we have, according to the new-fangled phrase, 'the real Sheridan.'

Mr. Smyth's family having fallen into difficulties, he, then a young fellow at Oxford, had to look out for a tutorship. A friend, Morris, who had written a comedy and a farce, and had thus become connected with Sheridan, learned that he was seeking a

* This amiable 'reminiscent' thus explains in a quaint pleasing style how he was induced to set down his recollections. 'You may remember, Miss Cotton,' he addresses a lady of his acquaintance in 1840, 'that after one of our pleasant dinners at Madingley you asked me while we were sitting round our evening fire what particulars I could recollect of Mr. Sheridan, to whose son I told you I had been tutor. In the morning, at breakfast, you were pleased to say "that the company had been much obliged to me for the entertainment you had thus procured them." As I walked home to my college, it struck me that what appeared to have been entertaining to you might be so to others, and in this hope I drew up the memoir which I now venture to print.'

tutor for his son Tom, who 'had been brought away
from Dr. Parr, who could do nothing for him, and
that he was running wild at Sheridan's place at Isleworth—the poor mother dead, the father never
there.' The young tutor hesitated : Sheridan's
habits of payment were well known ; but he was
assured that, whatever might become of others, he
would pay *him*. A dinner was accordingly arranged,
where was to be also the congenial Richardson and
the eminent man himself; but two hours of waiting
passed away—he never came. At last a note of
apology arrived from the House of Commons, in which
he invited the party to meet him at supper that night.
His friend Richardson made a characteristic excuse,
to the effect that Sheridan was never punctual, no
matter what the engagement. In due time the party
repaired to the tavern appointed, and 'found there
was no Sheridan, no supper ordered, no message left.'
The candidate tutor was returning to the country in
high dudgeon, when next morning arrived a letter
profuse in apologies, and an invitation to dine at
Isleworth. A chaise was to be ordered at Sheridan's
house in Grosvenor Square to take him down. The
tutor, who could not afford to wait, was surly, but
was persuaded by his friends. The house, he said,
appeared forlorn and dirty; but the servant told
him that since Mrs. Sheridan's death her husband
could not bear to live in it, but always slept at
Nerot's Hotel. It thus appeared that he had one

house to dine in, another to call at, a third into
which he put his family, and yet had his home in
none of them! This was the luxury of grief. Soon
after they got to Isleworth Sheridan drove up in his
curricle, and was so insinuating and gracious as to
quite win over Mr. Smyth, whom he put at his ease,
and who found, on reflection, that he himself had all
the time been talking, and Sheridan listening. He
was particularly struck with his modest air and
manner. Madame de Genlis and Pamela had only
just left the house. Next day Mr. Sheridan did not
appear until noon—his custom invariably—and did
the honours of the place in a most captivating
manner. He then set off in his carriage for town.

The tutor was duly engaged, and repaired to Wanstead, where he found his charge, and noted further
curious traits in the great man. Once, kept awake
by the cocks and hens, he insisted that all their
heads should be cut off! He showed a total absence
of self-control; every nervous fancy, right or wrong,
must be gratified; he was in a fever till any annoyance was at once abated. Such was 'the miserable
state of servitude to which long habits of self-indul-
gence had reduced him.' There was a strange
characteristic scene. Sheridan had come down from
town to dine on a boiled chicken 'at seven, eight, or
nine o'clock, just as it happened;' he had scarcely
drunk his claret and got the room filled with wax
lights, without which he could not exist, when a

sudden panic about his son Tom and the ice (there was a hard frost at the time) seized him. Tom would skate—would be drowned! He implored the Professor to rush off and save him. The latter, after many remonstrances, succeeded in tranquillizing him. Then he set out for Drury Lane Theatre, where he must be that night; he said 'it was then eleven o'clock, and London five miles off.' Just as the Professor was going to bed he heard a violent ringing at the gate; he was wanted; the carriage had returned; 'and, sure enough, what should I see glaring through the bars and outshining the lamps of the carriage—what but the fine eyes of Sheridan!' He had come back; he could not rest nor think of anything until he had got a promise that there should be no more skating. It was no wonder Lord Grey said to him, ' Have a glass case constructed for your son at once '—a remark which the lad used to repeat with great delight. No one could call this real affection; it was no more than an unreasoning selfishness which could not bear a moment's uneasiness or to be disturbed about anything.

The tutor, now fairly domiciled, found his charge Tom a pleasant, gay, bright lad, with whom, however, he could do little in the way of instruction. The scenes and incidents that occurred during his time of office were truly extraordinary, and would be most mirthful were it not for the piteous feeling excited at witnessing a man of talent and ripe years,

when sense might be looked for, guilty of such
follies. Whenever he figured, it might be said it
was in some strange, grotesque shift or struggle.
We see him, like the Prince of Wales, always on the
road from Brighton in his carriage or curricle, with
flashing lamps, posting off to London or down to the
country. This entailed the *keeping*—of course, not
the paying for—many horses. He would lie in bed
and take breakfast, dress himself, always smartly
and neatly, then pass out through his hall really to
escape into the street. 'For anyone who did not
catch him then, there was an end of him for the rest
of the day—no one knew where to find him afterwards.' The tutor, once waiting for him in his
study, noted the vast quantity of unopened letters all
lying heaped up, many with coronets. His treasurer,
Westley, who was also in the room, then related
how he thus once found his own letter, which contained £10, lying in a similar heap! He had
received a letter from Sheridan in the country,
headed '*Money-bound*,' imploring him to send the
first £10 he could lay his hands on. Sheridan,
meanwhile, had procured the sum from another
source, and never thought of the treasurer. His
valet, Edwards, actually declared that one morning
he found the windows, which had rattled, stuffed
with papers, and among them some bank-notes.
Sheridan had come in drunk, emptied his pockets,
and, fumbling in the dark, had taken the notes for

this purpose, 'as he never knew what he had in his pockets or what he had not.' This last anecdote was told to Mr. Moore, but it was not used by him. He, no doubt, thought it too incredible.*

The incidents that led to his second improvident marriage are all of a piece. In the year 1795 he had left his son and tutor down in Bognor in lodgings, and, having so disposed of them *more suo*, dismissed them and the subject of their maintenance from his mind altogether. Weeks, months passed by; they were in debt, and without money. At last one morning the son received this despatch: 'My dear Tom,—Meet me at dinner at six o'clock on Monday next at Guildford; I forget the number. I want particularly to speak to you.' The much-relieved pair settled that this mysterious and unusual call referred either to a seat in Parliament for Tom, or to the choice of a wife for him (Sheridan had often bidden him 'Take a wife;' 'Whose, sir?' being the well-known answer). The pupil set off in delight, and after nearly a week had gone by, his tutor received a letter from Guildford. 'Here I am,' it ran, 'and have been, and am likely to be. My father I have never seen, and all I can learn of him is, that instead of dining with me on Wednesday at six, *he passed through Guildford on his way to*

---

* Sheridan's brother-in-law, Ogle, looking through his papers after his death, found numerous letters of his own unopened.

London, with four horses and lamps, about twelve. I have written to him letter after letter to beg he will send me his orders, for I have only a few shillings, having paid the turnpikes faithfully ; and I am so vexed and wearied out with waiting here, and seeing neither father nor money, nor anything but the stable and the street, that I begin to wish myself with you and the books again.—Your dutiful pupil.'

Some weeks then passed over. At last arrived this letter from Tom :

'It is not I that is to be married, nor *you.* Set your heart at rest—it is my father himself; the lady is Miss Ogle, who lives at Winchester—that is the history of the Guildford business. About my own age. Better me to marry her, you will say. I am not of that opinion. Then father talked to me two hours last night, and made out to me that it was the most sensible thing he could do. Was not this very clever of him? Well, my dear Mr. Smyth, you should have been tutor to him. You see I am incomparably the most rational of the two.'

A sprightly and just estimate indeed ! While this provident plan was being pushed forward, the poor tutor was quite forgotten, left at Bognor, a year's salary due, and no money forthcoming. The housekeeper could not get any from Sheridan either to pay the bills in the place, or any answer to her urgent appeals. More weeks went by ; the company

departed ; the season closed ; winter was drawing on.
A year's salary was due to the tutor, who was sorely
pressed. He applied and applied in vain. As he says
truly, it was impossible to give an idea of the rage
and fury of people whom Sheridan subjected to this
sort of treatment. A favourite mode with him was
of disappearing—as it were, ignoring them and their
letters. Promises of the most solemn kind, engagements fixed for a day and hour, all he put aside in the
most lawless way. At last, indignant at such treatment,
Mr. Smyth wrote him an exceedingly strong letter
bringing matters to a point, declining to go on further.
Of this not the least notice was taken, on which he
made his way to London and got to see Sheridan.
He found him penitent and full of plans, and was
soothed by him in his own admirable way. Sheridan
was delighted, he said, to see him, and wondered
why he had stayed away so long (!). Tom had been
doing nothing but run about the town and get into
mischief—he would send him off next day. 'He
lamented that I had not come up before. He had
been so pressed with business that he could not
write me a long letter as he intended, *not being
willing to write me a short one.*' This last trait is
Sheridan 'all over,' and, we may be sure, is accurately reported. The tutor was to take Tom to
Cambridge, which plan, it seems, was fixed upon
because Sheridan wanted his country place for the
honeymoon ! The tutor insisted that this would be

simply ruin for Tom, who would learn dissipation
and habits of expensive living, and positively declined to go. Sheridan pressed him in the most
complimentary and irresistible terms, assured him
he should have his money, and frankly owned that
his marriage 'might appear to be an act of folly, or
madness, if you like, but it would surely turn out for
the best.'

On leaving Sheridan, the tutor felt qualms about
his strong letter, in which he had used some sharp
language. He made excuses for his irritation.
' Never trouble yourself about that, my dear fellow,'
said the good-humoured wit. ' It's all dismissed
from my mind.' Presently he said, ' By the way,
you can have it now.' And he took it out of his
pocket—*unopened*. The tutor succeeded in extracting bills for the amount due to him, being advised
to this step by some ' knowing ones ;' these he
passed to inexorable ' holders for consideration.'
When they fell due, every entreaty was made to him
to hold over, but he pleaded that they had left his
control. The holders pressed, and they actually
were paid.

Sheridan was at this time, though once handsome,
quite unattractive ; his face blotched and inflamed
with constant dissipation ; his mouth and chin coarse
and drooping, always the result of drink. His
marriage was owing to a foolish rencontre. Miss
Ogle, a young girl of a good family—which counted

in its ranks Admirals, no less than *three* Sir
Chaloner Ogles—was daughter of the Dean of
Winchester, who kept up the old state in equipages,
and maintained the dignity of the Church handsomely. At a party at Devonshire House, where
Miss Ogle was seated at the table, Mr. Sheridan
came up close to her. It seems the young lady
piqued herself on saying smart things, or 'everything that came into her head.' She called out to
him, ' Keep away, you fright, you terrible creature !'
and this though she was not acquainted with him.

' By this woman,' says Mr. Smyth, ' this silly man
was piqued. He wished to show his power, so
after some contrivance he obtained a word or two
more from her ; at the next party, a little conversation. Then she gave out that, though ' such a
monster,' he was very clever. So it went on until
the young lady thought there would be much *éclat*
in the conquest of so celebrated a man. Her father
refused his consent unless the suitor should settle
£15,000 on her, which seemed a prohibitive condition. The lady had herself £5,000. But Sheridan
contrived it. In the words of Mr. Richardson : ' To
the amazement of his friends and the confusion of
the Dean, it was found and paid down, Sheridan
laughing loudly, and boasting that he had outwitted
them—though he had indeed only outwitted himself.' This sum, Moore says, was raised ' by the
sale of Drury Lane shares.' Unfortunately this

transaction was not so immaculate. Moore, consulting Miss Ogle's sister on the transaction, learned these particulars : ' I mentioned with respect to the settlement Sheridan had made upon her sister, that I rather believed it was by getting the Linleys out of Drury Lane, and taking possession of the private boxes, he raised that money. She said she had always understood that he had injured some persons in order to make the settlement good, but whether it was the Linleys, or what were the particulars of the transaction, she did not know.' In another place he mentions having been told by one of the Linleys that ' Sheridan had persuaded the Linleys to part with their shares in Drury Lane for annuities which were never paid. He thus got the disposal of everything, the sale of private boxes, etc., all into his hands.'*

But there is an allusion to this in an unpublished letter of his son's, which seems to point to some awkward transaction. ' My father,' he writes, ' dare not face the compromise which must be made with the creditors. The funds from which Mrs. Sheridan's jointure were drawn, whatever face they may bear, are ultimately to be traced, with much besides, which he is endeavouring to conceal, though in no way

---

* The elder Mathews said to Sir W. Scott, that ' Tommy Moore was very simple, to be wondering where Sheridan got the money to buy out the Linleys and others.' It was well known, he seemed to insinuate, that he never paid them !

discreditable to him, otherwise than by showing how distressed a man he was when he did not wish to be thought so.'* It seems that the Ogle family and their business man knew enough of Sheridan to require that the money should *be lodged* before the marriage, and this was actually done. Sheridan, however, thought that he should be left the power of purchasing an estate with it. By some artful management, which we can well understand, Sheridan proceeded to buy an estate, no doubt satisfying the trustees that the money was 'lying there' for the payment, and he selected Sir William Geary, the Admiral, who had an estate at Polesden, near Leathstead, as the victim. I find, however, in an autograph catalogue now before me, certain letters, suspiciously noted as bearing on 'Sir William Geary's claims,' together with law proceedings. In fact, the estate was bought on the credit of the trust-moneys, and not paid for—the money remaining with the trustees, where Sheridan was not likely to be too eager to disturb it. Mr. Charles Butler describes a conversation Sheridan had with the victim of his manœuvre: 'He had sold him an estate; and the English language had, said Mr. Butler, not an expression of abuse or opprobrium which Sir William did not apply to Sheridan. He then marched off in a passion, but had not walked ten paces before he met Mr. Sheridan. Mr. Butler

* MSS. British Museum.

expected a furious onset ; but nothing like this **took**
place. In ten minutes Sir William returned, exclaiming, " Mr. Sheridan is the finest fellow I ever
met with ; I will tease him no more for money."
A gift of this kind was surely an income in itself.
Finally, however, the matter was settled by a resale
of the estate, at a profit of £1,000, for either
Sheridan or the late owner.'

Miss Ogle,* whose charms a beautiful picture
attests, was to have a sad and troubled course before
her. The honeymoon was spent at Sheridan's villa at
Wanstead, and Mr. Moore declares in his romantic
style that this ' union with a young and accomplished
girl, ardently devoted to him, must have been like

---

* One night, when they were staying with the Dean, Miss Susan
Ogle was listening to the singing of an officer, and expressed her
applause with much vivacity. ' Look at Susan,' cried Sheridan ;
' she's quite in raptures.' And he produced the following :

> ' By heaven above ! our Sue's in love
>   And nothing can assuage her :
> She's formed a plan for that smart man,
>   I mean that gay fife-major.

> ' But hark again, that merry strain !
>   Now, I'll bet any wager
> The overture has made it sure—
>   I wish you joy, fife-major !'

' The father of Miss Ogle, who was, perhaps, somewhat dissatisfied
with the choice his elder daughter had made, replied to the verses
in another stanza, in which (much to the annoyance of Sheridan)
he hinted that the choice of one daughter was not much more imprudent than that of the other.'

a renewal of his own youth ; and it is said by those
who were in habits of intimacy with him at this
period, that they had seldom seen his spirits in a
state of more buoyant vivacity. He passed much
of his time at the house of his father-in-law near
Southampton ; and in sailing about with his lively
bride on the Southampton river (in a small cutter
called the *Phædria*, after the magic boat in the
" Fairy Queen "), forgot for a while his debts, his
theatre, and his politics.'*   Mrs. Sheridan later took
some part in the concerns of the theatre, as will be
seen from the following. Writing to a gentleman,
she says she ' would be much obliged to him, when
he is going to Margate, to observe a Miss Kent.
Her wish is to be engaged at Drury Lane on any
terms whatever, was it only thirty shillings a week.
I know nothing of her abilities myself, having never
seen her.'†

* ' Among other distinguished persons present at these excursions
were Mr. Joseph Richardson, Dr. Howley (now Bishop of London),
and Mrs. Wilmot (now Lady Dacre) ;' a lady whose various talents,
' like the group of the Graces, reflect beauty on each other,' adds
the gallant Moore.

† Dean Ogle died in January, 1804, aged seventy-eight, when
Mrs. Sheridan inherited some addition to her fortune, connected
with which is a pleasant story told by Creevy to Sydney Smith :
' When dining with Sheridan, after the ladies had departed, he
drew the chair to the fire, and confided to Creevy that they had
just had a fortune left them. " Mrs. Sheridan and I," said he,
" have made the solemn vow to each other to mention it to no
one, and nothing induces me now to confide it to you but the

These nuptial delights withdrew him for a time from the House of Commons; and in a debate, already alluded to, on the Prince's debts, Mr. Pitt affected not to know the reason of his absence, always a subject of good-humoured indulgence with the House, and rebuked him haughtily.* 'Had he attended,' he said, 'previous debates, or even attended earlier that evening, he would have heard sufficient to help him to a decision.' Sheridan instantly retorted with the usual rude allusions, to which Pitt was well accustomed. 'It was unnecessary to state the reason of his absence, which was well known, though it *would probably be unintelligible* to the right honourable gentleman'—a thrust received with boisterous laughter by Mr. Whitbread and others.

---

absolute conviction that Mrs. Sheridan is at this moment confiding it to Mrs. Creevy upstairs." Soon after this I went to visit him in the country with a large party; he had taken a villa. No expense was spared: a magnificent dinner, excellent wines, but not a candle to be had to go to bed by in the house; in the morning no butter appeared, or was to be procured for breakfast. He said it was not a butter country, he believed. But with Sheridan for host, and the charm of his wit and conversation, who cared for candles, butter, or anything else? In the evening there was a quarrel amongst the fiddlers, they absolutely refusing to play with a blind fiddler, who had unexpectedly arrived and insisted upon performing with them. He turned out at last to be Mathews; his acting was quite inimitable.'

* Lord Encombe, Lord Eldon's son, was married at a time when there was a 'call of the House'; when he was called and found absent, a good-humoured laugh went round, and no notice was taken of the delinquent.

But soon the bride was herself to find out that she had been beguiled by an accomplished deceiver. It is stated that one day when she was looking over his papers, she discovered his letters to her predecessor, and found that those to herself during their courtship were merely copies of the former! She was thrown into a fury by such a piece of duplicity, but probably by that time she had found him out. Presently he began to treat her to his capricious humours exactly as he had worried poor Elizabeth Linley, and, it would seem, gradually wore 'away such affection as she had had for him.' Moore had a conversation with her sister 'Sukey,' as he calls her (which, with many other curious things about Sheridan, is recorded in his 'Diary,' but suppressed in the 'Life'). That lady told him how curious it was to compare the letters of his two wives to him, both beginning in the same strain of love and worship, and both gradually alienated by his selfish and vainglorious infidelities and extravagances, till they ended in disliking him. She added, however, something in his praise. 'He was fond,' she said, 'of domestic parties, delighted in children, and was altogether, where his vanity or his passions did not interfere, amiable and attractive. They, however, used very often to wish him dead, for her sister's sake, as they thought she might recover her health if she was rid of him; his jealousy latterly incessant and teasing.' She had indeed embarked on a troubled, painful

course, and was to suffer sorrows, anxieties, and
even miseries. We find her writing to the treasurer
of the theatre, in alarm, words having arisen between Grubb and Sheridan, 'Be sure and watch
and let me know, as I am afraid of the consequences.'* One of her letters, for assistance, to the
unfortunate Peake, speaks volumes. She wrote,
telling him that Mr. Sheridan had assured her
about a month ago that a certain sum should be
remitted to her every month. ' I have received none
of it yet, and can't go on any longer without money.
Have the goodness to tell me whether I am to have
it or not, that I may take the means to raise
money. It may be sent by my maid.'† Poor lady !
who was to assist at the terrible scene of Sheridan's death, when the bailiffs were with difficulty
kept out, and hardly an old rag of carpet was left to
them !

* MSS., Sheridan, British Museum.
† MSS. British Museum.

APPENDIX A.

MRS. ALICIA LE FANU.

MRS. A. LE FANU, Sheridan's sister, was a woman of some mark, and an early friend and adviser of Sydney Owenson, afterwards Lady Morgan. Her letters have much interest and character. In 1817 she wrote to her friend on Dr. Watkins's life of her father, which had recently appeared, in this trenchant style : 'I am very ill, and hopeless of being better. My great anxiety about Joseph made me forget and neglect myself until severe pain forced me to resort to medical aid. A severe cold, caught on Christmas Day, and great uneasiness of mind, have put me in a state of continual suffering. I wish I was able to write any satisfactory account of my brother. Watkins's history of him and my family is a tissue of falsehood. What satisfaction could it be to him to write the life of a man whom he evidently hates and basely calumniates ? Of my family history he knows nothing.

'But Sam Whyte did worse ; for he fabricated letters from my mother, etc., that she could not have written. He was the natural son of an uncle of my mother, who left him five hundred pounds, with which, and my father's assistance, he set up a school ; but he never was acknowledged as our relation—we never were boarded with him or placed under his care, etc., etc.—all lies.

' My mother's sketch of a comedy, unfinished, was put into my brother Richard's hands by my father at Bath, when we were resident there ; but my father never even hinted that he had made any use of it in " The Rivals." Of my own knowledge I can say nothing, for I never read it.'

This attack on poor ' Sam Whyte ' has surely no foundation. That she and her brother were placed ' under his care ' is certain. After nearly sixty years' interval, it was not unlikely that she imperfectly recollected the events of her infancy.

Many years before, when a precocious girl eager to be placed in some family of distinction, the lively Sydney Owenson was very intimate with her ; she took an interest in her, and tried to forward her plan. In 1803 Mrs. Le Fanu addressed her the following, which is of a depressed cast :

' Illness has prevented my answering your letter ; an epidemic cold attended with fever has borne very hard upon my family. My eldest son has been very near death, and I have been myself confined to my bed, and am still obliged to keep the house, with the usual consolatory reflections

that I am no worse off than other people, etc.,
etc. *If the miseries of others were to render us
satisfied with our own lot, no one would have a right
to complain.* You remember La Fontaine says,
" Et le malheur des consolations sur croit d'afflic-
tions." In real illness and sorrow one has often
occasion to think of that.

'I shall be very glad to see you when you are in
Dublin. Two gentlemen of my acquaintance have
added to my wish to know you, and yet they certainly saw you in society unsuited to you, and which
I am sure chance alone could have thrown you into.
My daughter has been taught music and still continues to learn, but has not, I think, any decided
taste or talent for it—both my sons have ; the eldest
son is a student in Trinity College, plays the harp
finely, and is also an excellent performer on the
pianoforte ; for him I shall thank you for the Irish
air you mention. No music more than the Irish
bears the stamp of originality ; none speaks more to
the affections ; I think it possesses more variety
than the Scotch, and expresses more forcibly the
gay and the tender. Poor Charlotte Brooks, my
friend and my relation, assisted in making me in
love with the Irish bards. I am sure you know her
beautiful translations of some of them. Carolan's
monody on the death of his wife is truly pathetic.'

This letter is worth giving, if only for the wise
remark in italics. It will be noted what a cast of

melancholy was over her character, with which was blended a certain shrewdness of observation ; and this mixture was to be noted in many of her family. The following illustrates this :

‘ Your charming letter, of no date, found me last Saturday very much indisposed with a severe headache, attended with feverishness, to which I am subject. I leave this quiet spot, liberty and fresh air with regret. In town I am plagued with the bustle of the city without being able to join in its amusements. The theatre I have long ceased to attend : when there is any performance worth seeing I dare not encounter the crowd, and what is misnamed private society is become almost as formidable on a similar account ; and my own immediate little circle that I used to draw about me, time and the chances in life have committed such depredations upon, that, like Ossian, "I sit alone in my halls." Exclusive, I should say, of my own family, whose society becomes every day more pleasing to me, as "knowledge to their eyes her ample page rich with the spoils of time" gradually unrolls, I shall be happy to see you in town, and wish my house admitted of offering you an apartment in it ; but we are already crowded like bees in a hive and inconvenienced for want of room, in a way that would try the patience of a female Job. Mind, I do not tell you that I am one. But though I have no *bed* to give you, every other attention I can show I shall

be delighted to do it ; and the more I see of you
(without encroaching on your time and the claims of
other friends), the better I shall be pleased.

'I make no doubt that your work will succeed :
going yourself to London is certainly the best
security for justice being done you.   The Bishop of
Dromore's advice is the best you can possibly be
guided by, and his high literary reputation will give
every weight to his recommendations and approbation of you.

'Above twenty years' absence from London (to
which place I was never permitted to return) has
broken or relaxed every tie I had there.   To some
my place has been supplied, others have pretended
to suppose themselves neglected by me, to excuse
their own neglect of me.   And there are a few who,
with more apparent reason, have thought themselves
forgotten by me because I was not at liberty to
explain *why* I did not pay them all the attention I
wished.'

Another of the family, the Rev. Peter Le Fanu, a
fashionable preacher, also took much interest in the
young Miss Owenson. He was commissioned ' to find
a young lady who would act as something between a
governess and a *dame de compagnie* to two young ladies,
daughters of the Right Honourable Charles Sheridan,
Secretary-at-War for Ireland, and the husband of
that beautiful woman who, you may remember, put
out the fire of the curtain of her box at the theatre

last winter, when the whole house rose up to applaud. Well, the idea of this visit from Mr. Le Fanu frightened me beyond everything. However, I was dressed very nicely, and seated on the sofa all in good time, and I took up Locke, "to call up a look," as Lady Pentweasle says, when I heard his knock at the door. Molly announced him—"The Rev. Mr. Peter ——," but could get no further. She was in such a rage. Well, now, dear papa, who do you think he turned out to be? Why, the clergyman who preached the charity sermon at the Lying-in Hospital last Christmas, and that we all cried at hearing, and you said, "That man is a regular pickpocket, for I have given a crown and I did not mean to give half."'

'Glorvina' then describes the following scene, in which due allowance must be made for vivacity and some natural vanity: 'Well, he took my hand, and we sat down. He looked very earnestly, and said, "Are you Miss Owenson, my dear—daughter of my old friend Mr. Owenson of the Theatre Royal?"

'I was ready to burst into tears, and could only answer, "Yes, sir."

'"But you are very young, my dear; I should say you were fitter to go to school than to commence instructress."

'"Perhaps so, sir; but great misfortunes have come upon poor papa unexpectedly, and——"

'Here I was obliged to cover my face with my

handkerchief. I suppose to give me time to recover, he gently drew Locke out of my hand, and appeared to be looking through it.

'"Upon my word," said he, laughing, "this is a very grave study for so young a lady. Now," said he, "let me hear *your* definition of an 'innate idea.'"

'He looked so comical that I could not help laughing, too.

'"Oh, my dear, don't hurry yourself; it is a question that might puzzle a conjurer."

'"Well, sir," said I, "I had no idea of *you* until I saw and heard you preach your beautiful sermon for the poor women of the Lying-in Hospital; but having seen and heard you, I have an *idea* of you which can never be removed."

'He actually threw himself back in his chair, and took my hand, and—would you believe it, papa!—kissed it. He is of French descent, you know.

'"Well," said he, "you are the most flattering little logician I ever coped with." He then took a serious tone, and said, "My dear little girl, I respect your intentions; and from what Dr. Pellegrini tells me, your acquirements fit you for the situation you are seeking, but you have at present one great fault. Don't be frightened" (I suppose I looked so)—"it is one that will mend but too soon. The Misses Sheridan are, I should think, much about your own age; and the worst of it is, there are two rascally boys, Charles and Tom, who have the bad habit of running into their sisters' study when they come home for vacation, and making a terrible row there. However, I shall meet Mr. and Mrs. Sheridan at dinner to-day at my brother's, Mr. Joe Le Fanu's, who is married to their sister. We will talk over this, and you shall hear from me early to-morrow." '

Unfortunately nothing came of this, and she had to write to her father:

'DEAR PAPA,—The Sheridan scheme is all ended. The beautiful Mrs. Sheridan would not have me, and I am glad, as, on consideration, I see it would not do ; but I have got something to console me, I think.'

This was another opening contrived by the good-natured preacher, a place in the Bishop of Limerick's family. Nothing, however, came of *that* either.

Mrs. Le Fanu died at her son's house in the Phœnix Park in 1817. She too was an authoress, and is described as 'a lady of genius and literary attainments.' She wrote 'The Flowers, or the Sylphid Queen,' a fairy-tale that appeared in 1810, and also, to contribute to the dramatic prestige of her family, a comedy entitled 'The Sons of Erin, or Modern Sentiment.'

APPENDIX B.

REMOTE ANCESTORS OF THE SHERIDANS.

In the College of Arms at Dublin is a pedigree of the family, carried back to the days of princes and Irish chieftains. This document appears to be wanting in dates, and merely gives the order of descent :

Oscar O'Seridan, of Castle Togher, Co. Caven.	=	d. of O'Rourke, Prince of Co. Leittrim.
Antony.	=	d. of O'Neil, Prince of Tyrone.
Conor.	=	d. of O'Donnell, Prince of Dongal.
Antony.	=	d. of O'Farrell, Prince of Longford.
Conor.	=	d. of the O'Conor Don.
Antony.	=	d. of O'Reilly, Prince of Cavan.
Conor.	=	d. of O'Rourke, Prince of Leitrim.
Antony.	=	d. of O'Connor, Prince of Sligo.
Thaddeus.	=	d. of E. O'Reilly, of Cavan.
Audven (Owen ?)	=	d. of T. O'Brady, Ballyhase, in Co. Cavan.
Denis.	=	Jane, d. of An. Atkinson.

This Denis was probably cousin to the Rev. Denis Sheridan referred to in the text. The latter was a remarkable member of the family, the confidential friend and assistant of Bishop Bedell, who gave him a living in the diocese of Kilmore, and employed him, as he was well known as an Irish scholar, with Mr. King, in preparing the translation of the Bible into Irish. When the unfortunate prelate was driven from his see by the Irish, he found shelter at Sheridan's house, who, though a Protestant, was respected and tolerated by the natives on account of the influence of his family, which was purely Irish. Under that friendly roof he expired, having contracted an illness from the hardships he had undergone, or from a fever caused by the overcrowding of numerous refugees of the English party, who were there protected. It has been usually stated that he had been a native priest, induced to conform by Bedell; and I find that he was Catholic 'P.P.' of Kildrumferton. Bedell induced many of the clergy in his diocese thus to abandon the old faith. Burnet records the respect shown him by the natives ' by reason of his extraction; though he had forsaken their religion and had married an Englishwoman, he continued firm in his religion,' etc. One of his sons, Patrick, Bishop of Cloyne, married, in 1677, Anne Hill, whose uncle was married to one of Bedell's sons, thus connecting the family with that eminent prelate.

The Rev. Denis died at a great age, having lived to see his children enjoy high office and preferment.

Two became generals in the imperial service, two were bishops, while Thomas was a Fellow of Trinity College, Dublin, Collector at Cork, a Privy Councillor, and Secretary of State. Thus early did the members of this remarkable family distinguish themselves.

This Thomas Sheridan was certainly a person of distinguished ability and of marked character, so much so as to be mentioned with peculiar bitterness and dislike by Bishop Burnet. He, too, showed the versatility of his race, for he was a scholar, a barrister, a politician, a philosophical writer, and a speaker of some power. This was a striking combination. He attached himself to the fortunes of the Duke of York, and followed him to France, but was, in 1680, brought to the Bar of the House of Commons, where he vindicated himself in a spirited speech from charges of disloyalty.

'In clearing myself,' he said, 'of this aspersion, I must say something, which nought but necessity, that has none and breaks all laws, can excuse from vanity, in that I was born a gentleman of one of the ancientest families and related to many considerable in Ireland. In one county there is a castle and a large demesne; in another, a greater tract of land for several miles together, yet known by our name. I need not say who has the land as chief, —'tis too much, that my grandfather was the last that enjoyed our estate; and that my father, left an orphan at the beginning of King James' reign, soon found himself dispossessed and exposed to the world,—that whole county, with five others in Ulster, being entirely escheated to the Crown. My parents Protestants,—my mother a gentlewoman of England, of good fortune, a Foster, who for my father's sake quitted her country and relations,— both famous for honesty, for their loyalty and sufferings in the late rebellion, when my father escaped narrowly with his life, and at last was forced to fly for relieving and protecting very many English.

'From my birth I had a suitable education. I have some pretensions to letters. I am not altogether a stranger to the civil law, nor to the laws of England, the means intended for my livelihood. But, without my seeking, some friends procured for me the Collectorship of the Customs of Cork, and the management of most of the inland revenue of that county.

'After this excuse, if I have no visible estate, I hope no man can doubt but I may live independently, though I happen to be a younger brother. So far from that being a prejudice, it's possible to prove to my advantage, being designed heir to my two elder brothers, who have not, nor are likely to have, any children. I do declare that I neither have nor had any relation of service to the Duke or Duchess of York. For my religion, as I was born a Protestant so I was bred a member

of the Church of England.   I have taken the oaths
eleven times.'

His 'some pretensions to letters' is more than
supported by his treatise, published in 1677, 'A
Discourse on the Rise and Power of Parliaments,'
a work of much thought and ability, in which he
seems to have many modern political ideas.   In it
he deals with the origin of government, and of
laws ; with liberty, property and religion, taxes, etc.
But the most remarkable portion was his enforcing
toleration, particularly in Ireland, which he did,
not merely on the ground of policy, but on that of
the teachings of the Christian religion.   It is impossible to rise from its perusal without feeling that
it is the work of a man of no common ability.*   He
also left a MS. history of the events of his time,
now preserved in the Royal Library at Windsor,
which was used and highly commended by both
Sir J. Mackintosh and Lord Macaulay in their
respective histories.

The branch of the family from which R. B.
Sheridan descended, was that of Patrick Sheridan
of Togher, described in the pedigrees as 'a near
relative' of the Rev. Denis Sheridan.   His son,
Thomas Sheridan, Swift's friend, was sent to college
by the Bishop of Cloyne, Dr. Patrick Sheridan,
which shows close kinship.

* Some years ago it was reprinted and edited by Mr. Saxe
Bannister, late Attorney-General of New South Wales.

In further illustration of what is stated in the text as to the difficulties owners of houses found in recovering their property from Sheridan, a characteristic instance has come to light, the incidents of which have been lately published in the provincial papers.

At one time he was tenant to Sir Thomas Channing, who, it seems, could never obtain payment of his rent, and who at last, his patience being exhausted, determined to eject him. To encounter these proceedings, Sheridan seems to have exhausted all the arts and devices for which his countrymen in a similar position have obtained notoriety. His lease had still a year to run ; he would not pay the rent ; he declined, moreover, to give up possession ; and he would allow no one else to look at the house with a view to taking it. 'Sir Thomas, as a last resort, instructed his agent in town, Mr. Christopher Ebdon, to inform Sheridan that he had resolved on selling the house to Mr. Castell. Sheridan replied that he himself thought of purchasing it, there being an optional clause in his lease to that effect. On the 5th of May the agent writes: " Mr. Castell being desirous to have an answer about the house, wrote again to Mr. Sheridan for permission to look at that part of it which would not disturb the family, and the servant was desired to wait for an answer. When he took the letter he was told Mr. Sheridan would not be stirring for two hours, and was desired to call again. He called again in about an hour, and then he was informed Mr. Sheridan had gone out. I had before told Mr. Castell there would be no chance of getting an answer without the servant waited. Next day he went again about twelve, and waited till near three, and then sent up word he was afraid his master would be angry with him for waiting so long, and then he was promised an answer in half an hour : but after waiting more than that time, Mr. Sheridan sent word that he should send an answer at night, but never took any further notice of Mr. Castell's letter. I went on the 26th, at twelve, according to his own appointment, to meet Mr. Westley ; but after waiting till three, no Mr. Westley came, and I just got a sight of Mr. Sheridan on the stairs, who, after saying he did not know I had been waiting so long, desired me to call next day. I called on the 27th, and had nearly as long attendance with as little effect. I desired the servant to say to Mr. Sheridan I wished to speak to him, but would not detain him two minutes. Mr. Sheridan sent word down that if it was about the house he could not give an answer. I then desired the servant to inform him I did not wish to press him for an answer about it; all I desired at present was that he would give Mr. Castell permission to look at the lower part of the house. To this message Mr. Sheridan sent me word he would write to Mr. Castell in the evening. I saw Mr. Castell on Friday, and he told me Mr. Sheridan had not wrote."

' In another letter Ebdon says : " I am advised to go with a witness and demand, as your agent, possession of the house. If that is refused, double rent immediately commences, and by proceeding against him he must soon quit the house." Sheridan still " held the field." Six months later, on December 10, he writes to Sir Thomas : " I have called twice at Mr. Sheridan's since I wrote to you, but have not seen him, and am advised to call no more." Every means was tried to get rid of the tenant, but without avail ; and it was not until *the roof of his house was removed* that he finally capitulated.'

END OF VOL. I.